COMPREHENSIVE

ILLUSTRATED SERIES™

MICROSOFT® OFFICE 365™

POWERPOINT® 2016

BESKEEN

For Microsoft® Office updates, go to sam.cengage.com

CENGAGE
Learning·

Australia • Brazil • Mexico • Singapore • United Kingdom • United States

CENGAGE
Learning

Illustrated Microsoft® Office 365™ & PowerPoint® 2016—Comprehensive
David W. Beskeen

SVP, GM Skills & Global Product Management:
  Dawn Gerrain

Product Director: Kathleen McMahon

Senior Product Team Manager: Lauren Murphy

Product Team Manager: Andrea Topping

Associate Product Manager: Melissa Stehler

Senior Director, Development: Marah Bellegarde

Product Development Manager: Leigh Hefferon

Senior Content Developer: Christina Kling-Garrett

Developmental Editor: Rachel Biheller Bunin

Product Assistant: Erica Chapman

Marketing Director: Michele McTighe

Marketing Manager: Stephanie Albracht

Marketing Coordinator: Cassie Cloutier

Senior Production Director: Wendy Troeger

Production Director: Patty Stephan

Senior Content Project Manager: GEX Publishing
  Services

Art Director: Diana Graham

Text Designer: Joseph Lee, Black Fish Design

Cover Template Designer: Lisa Kuhn, Curio Press, LLC
www.curiopress.com

Composition: GEX Publishing Services

For product information and technology assistance, contact us at
Cengage Learning Customer & Sales Support, 1-800-354-9706

For permission to use material from this text or product, submit all requests online at **www.cengage.com/permissions**
Further permissions questions can be emailed to
permissionrequest@cengage.com

Mac users: If you're working through this product using a Mac, some of the steps may vary. Additional information for Mac users is included with the Data Files for this product.

Some of the product names and company names used in this book have been used for identification purposes only and may be trademarks or registered trademarks of their respective manufacturers and sellers.

Windows® is a registered trademark of Microsoft Corporation. © 2012 Microsoft. Microsoft and the Office logo are either registered trademarks or trademarks of Microsoft Corporation in the United States and/or other countries. Cengage Learning is an independent entity from Microsoft Corporation and not affiliated with Microsoft in any manner. Microsoft product screenshots used with permission from Microsoft Corporation. Unless otherwise noted, all clip art is courtesy of openclipart.org.

Disclaimer: Any fictional data related to persons or companies or URLs used throughout this text is intended for instructional purposes only. At the time this text was published, any such data was fictional and not belonging to any real persons or companies.

Disclaimer: The material in this text was written using Microsoft Windows 10 Professional and Office 365 Professional Plus and was Quality Assurance tested before the publication date. As Microsoft continually updates the Windows 10 operating system and Office 365, your software experience may vary slightly from what is presented in the printed text.

Library of Congress Control Number: 2016932210
Soft-cover Edition ISBN: 978-1-305-87818-1
Loose-leaf Edition ISBN: 978-1-337-25093-1

Cengage Learning
20 Channel Center Street
Boston, MA 02210
USA

Cengage Learning is a leading provider of customized learning solutions with employees residing in nearly 40 different countries and sales in more than 125 countries around the world. Find your local representative at **www.cengage.com**.

Cengage Learning products are represented in Canada by Nelson Education, Ltd.

For your course and learning solutions, visit **www.cengage.com**

Purchase any of our products at your local college store or at our preferred online store **www.cengagebrain.com**

Printed at CLDPC, USA, 11-16

Brief Contents

Contents

Productivity Apps for School and Work

Corinne Hoisington

Lochlan keeps track of his class notes, football plays, and internship meetings with OneNote.

Zoe is using the annotation features of Microsoft Edge to take and save web notes for her research paper.

Nori is creating a Sway site to highlight this year's activities for the Student Government Association.

Hunter is adding interactive videos and screen recordings to his PowerPoint resume.

© Rawpixel/Shutterstock.com

Being computer literate no longer means mastery of only Word, Excel, PowerPoint, Outlook, and Access. To become technology power users, Hunter, Nori, Zoe, and Lochlan are exploring Microsoft OneNote, Sway, Mix, and Edge in Office 2016 and Windows 10.

In this Module

Learn to use productivity apps!
Links to companion **Sways**, featuring **videos** with hands-on instructions, are located on www.cengagebrain.com.

Introduction to OneNote 2016

notebook | section tab | To Do tag | screen clipping | note | template | Microsoft OneNote Mobile app | sync | drawing canvas | inked handwriting | Ink to Text

Bottom Line
- OneNote is a note-taking app for your academic and professional life.
- Use OneNote to get organized by gathering your ideas, sketches, webpages, photos, videos, and notes in one place.

As you glance around any classroom, you invariably see paper notebooks and notepads on each desk. Because deciphering and sharing handwritten notes can be a challenge, Microsoft OneNote 2016 replaces physical notebooks, binders, and paper notes with a searchable, digital notebook. OneNote captures your ideas and schoolwork on any device so you can stay organized, share notes, and work with others on projects. Whether you are a student taking class notes as shown in **Figure 1** or an employee taking notes in company meetings, OneNote is the one place to keep notes for all of your projects.

Figure 1: OneNote 2016 notebook

Each **notebook** is divided into sections, also called **section tabs**, by subject or topic.

Use **To Do tags**, icons that help you keep track of your assignments and other tasks.

Type on a page to add a **note**, a small window that contains text or other types of information.

Personalize a page with a **template**, or stationery.

Write or draw directly on the page using drawing tools.

Pages can include pictures such as **screen clippings**, images from any part of a computer screen.

Attach files and enter equations so you have everything you need in one place.

Creating a OneNote Notebook

OneNote is divided into sections similar to those in a spiral-bound notebook. Each OneNote notebook contains sections, pages, and other notebooks. You can use OneNote for school, business, and personal projects. Store information for each type of project in different notebooks to keep your tasks separate, or use any other organization that suits you. OneNote is flexible enough to adapt to the way you want to work.

When you create a notebook, it contains a blank page with a plain white background by default, though you can use templates, or stationery, to apply designs in categories such as Academic, Business, Decorative, and Planners. Start typing or use the buttons on the Insert tab to insert notes, which are small resizable windows that can contain text, equations, tables, on-screen writing, images, audio and video recordings, to-do lists, file attachments, and file printouts. Add as many notes as you need to each page.

Learn to use OneNote!
Links to companion **Sways**, featuring **videos** with hands-on instructions, are located on www.cengagebrain.com.

Syncing a Notebook to the Cloud

OneNote saves your notes every time you make a change in a notebook. To make sure you can access your notebooks with a laptop, tablet, or smartphone wherever you are, OneNote uses cloud-based storage, such as OneDrive or SharePoint. **Microsoft OneNote Mobile app**, a lightweight version of OneNote 2016 shown in **Figure 2**, is available for free in the Windows Store, Google Play for Android devices, and the AppStore for iOS devices.

If you have a Microsoft account, OneNote saves your notes on OneDrive automatically for all your mobile devices and computers, which is called **syncing**. For example, you can use OneNote to take notes on your laptop during class, and then open OneNote on your phone to study later. To use a notebook stored on your computer with your OneNote Mobile app, move the notebook to OneDrive. You can quickly share notebook content with other people using OneDrive.

Figure 2: Microsoft OneNote Mobile app

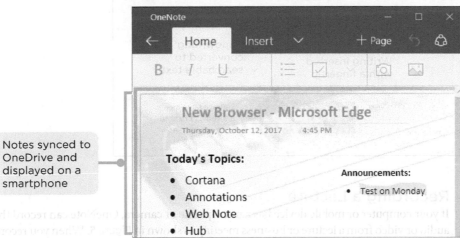

Notes synced to OneDrive and displayed on a smartphone

Taking Notes

Use OneNote pages to organize your notes by class and topic or lecture. Beyond simple typed notes, OneNote stores drawings, converts handwriting to searchable text and mathematical sketches to equations, and records audio and video.

OneNote includes drawing tools that let you sketch freehand drawings such as biological cell diagrams and financial supply-and-demand charts. As shown in **Figure 3**, the Draw tab on the ribbon provides these drawing tools along with shapes so you can insert diagrams and other illustrations to represent your ideas. When you draw on a page, OneNote creates a **drawing canvas**, which is a container for shapes and lines.

On the Job Now

OneNote is ideal for taking notes during meetings, whether you are recording minutes, documenting a discussion, sketching product diagrams, or listing follow-up items. Use a meeting template to add pages with content appropriate for meetings.

Figure 3: Tools on the Draw tab

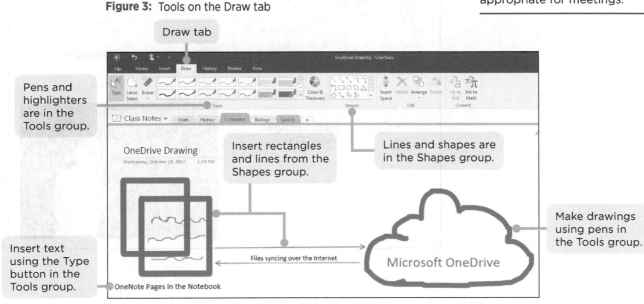

Draw tab

Pens and highlighters are in the Tools group.

Insert rectangles and lines from the Shapes group.

Lines and shapes are in the Shapes group.

Make drawings using pens in the Tools group.

Insert text using the Type button in the Tools group.

Files syncing over the Internet

Microsoft OneDrive

OneNote Pages in the Notebook

Converting Handwriting to Text

When you use a pen tool to write on a notebook page, the text you enter is called **inked handwriting**. OneNote can convert inked handwriting to typed text when you use the **Ink to Text** button in the Convert group on the Draw tab, as shown in **Figure 4**. After OneNote converts the handwriting to text, you can use the Search box to find terms in the converted text or any other note in your notebooks.

Figure 4: Converting handwriting to text

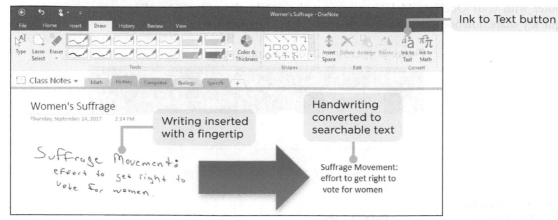

Ink to Text button

Women's Suffrage

Thursday, September 14, 2017   2:14 PM

Suffrage Movement: effort to get right to vote for women.

Writing inserted with a fingertip

Handwriting converted to searchable text

Suffrage Movement: effort to get right to vote for women

Recording a Lecture

If your computer or mobile device has a microphone or camera, OneNote can record the audio or video from a lecture or business meeting as shown in **Figure 5**. When you record a lecture (with your instructor's permission), you can follow along, take regular notes at your own pace, and review the video recording later. You can control the start, pause, and stop motions of the recording when you play back the recording of your notes.

Figure 5: Video inserted in a notebook

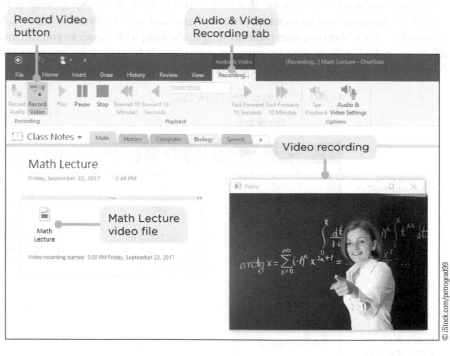

Record Video button

Audio & Video Recording tab

Video recording

Class Notes ▾   Math   History   Computer   Biology   Speech   +

Math Lecture

Friday, September 22, 2017   2:44 PM

Math Lecture

Math Lecture video file

Video recording started: 3:00 PM Friday, September 22, 2017

© iStock.com/petrograd99

Try This Now

1: Taking Notes for a Week

As a student, you can get organized by using OneNote to take detailed notes in your classes. Perform the following tasks:

    a. Create a new OneNote notebook on your Microsoft OneDrive account (the default location for new notebooks). Name the notebook with your first name followed by "Notes," as in **Caleb Notes**.

    b. Create four section tabs, each with a different class name.

    c. Take detailed notes in those classes for one week. Be sure to include notes, drawings, and other types of content.

    d. Sync your notes with your OneDrive. Submit your assignment in the format specified by your instructor.

2: Using OneNote to Organize a Research Paper

You have a research paper due on the topic of three habits of successful students. Use OneNote to organize your research. Perform the following tasks:

    a. Create a new OneNote notebook on your Microsoft OneDrive account. Name the notebook **Success Research**.

    b. Create three section tabs with the following names:

- **Take Detailed Notes**
- **Be Respectful in Class**
- **Come to Class Prepared**

    c. On the web, research the topics and find three sources for each section. Copy a sentence from each source and paste the sentence into the appropriate section. When you paste the sentence, OneNote inserts it in a note with a link to the source.

    d. Sync your notes with your OneDrive. Submit your assignment in the format specified by your instructor.

3: Planning Your Career

Note: This activity requires a webcam or built-in video camera on any type of device.

Consider an occupation that interests you. Using OneNote, examine the responsibilities, education requirements, potential salary, and employment outlook of a specific career. Perform the following tasks:

    a. Create a new OneNote notebook on your Microsoft OneDrive account. Name the notebook with your first name followed by a career title, such as **Kara - App Developer**.

    b. Create four section tabs with the names **Responsibilities, Education Requirements, Median Salary**, and **Employment Outlook**.

    c. Research the responsibilities of your career path. Using OneNote, record a short video (approximately 30 seconds) of yourself explaining the responsibilities of your career path. Place the video in the Responsibilities section.

    d. On the web, research the educational requirements for your career path and find two appropriate sources. Copy a paragraph from each source and paste them into the appropriate section. When you paste a paragraph, OneNote inserts it in a note with a link to the source.

    e. Research the median salary for a single year for this career. Create a mathematical equation in the Median Salary section that multiplies the amount of the median salary times 20 years to calculate how much you will possibly earn.

    f. For the Employment Outlook section, research the outlook for your career path. Take at least four notes about what you find when researching the topic.

    g. Sync your notes with your OneDrive. Submit your assignment in the format specified by your instructor.

Learn to use OneNote!

Links to companion **Sways**, featuring **videos** with hands-on instructions, are located on www.cengagebrain.com.

Introduction to Sway

Sway site | responsive design | Storyline | card | Creative Commons license | animation emphasis effects | Docs.com

Expressing your ideas in a presentation typically means creating PowerPoint slides or a Word document. Microsoft Sway gives you another way to engage an audience. Sway is a free Microsoft tool available at Sway.com or as an app in Office 365. Using Sway, you can combine text, images, videos, and social media in a website called a **Sway site** that you can share and display on any device. To get started, you create a digital story on a web-based canvas without borders, slides, cells, or page breaks. A Sway site organizes the text, images, and video into a **responsive design**, which means your content adapts perfectly to any screen size as shown in **Figure 6**. You store a Sway site in the cloud on OneDrive using a free Microsoft account.

Figure 6: Sway site with responsive design

You can display a Sway presentation in a web browser.

Sway uses responsive design to make sure pages fit perfectly on any device.

Creating a Sway Presentation

You can use Sway to build a digital flyer, a club newsletter, a vacation blog, an informational site, a digital art portfolio, or a new product rollout. After you select your topic and sign into Sway with your Microsoft account, a **Storyline** opens, providing tools and a work area for composing your digital story. See **Figure 7**. Each story can include text, images, and videos. You create a Sway by adding text and media content into a Storyline section, or **card**. To add pictures, videos, or documents, select a card in the left pane and then select the Insert Content button. The first card in a Sway presentation contains a title and background image.

Figure 7: Creating a Sway site

Design and create Sway presentations.

Share and play published Sway sites.

Arrange content in a Storyline, which contains all the text, pictures, videos, and other media in a Sway presentation.

Title your Sway

To add content, select a card, which is designed to hold a particular type of information.

After selecting a card, click the Insert Content button to add the content to the Sway presentation.

Adding Content to Build a Story

As you work, Sway searches the Internet to help you find relevant images, videos, tweets, and other content from online sources such as Bing, YouTube, Twitter, and Facebook. You can drag content from the search results right into the Storyline. In addition, you can upload your own images and videos directly in the presentation. For example, if you are creating a Sway presentation about the market for commercial drones, Sway suggests content to incorporate into the presentation by displaying it in the left pane as search results. The search results include drone images tagged with a **Creative Commons license** at online sources as shown in **Figure 8**. A Creative Commons license is a public copyright license that allows the free distribution of an otherwise copyrighted work. In addition, you can specify the source of the media. For example, you can add your own Facebook or OneNote pictures and videos in Sway without leaving the app.

On the Job Now

If you have a Microsoft Word document containing an outline of your business content, drag the outline into Sway to create a card for each topic.

Figure 8: Images in Sway search results

Select the source of media objects

Information about Creative Commons licenses

Storyline title

The Market for Commercial Drones

Drag an image to the picture placeholder box

Suggested images in the search results

On the Job Now

If your project team wants to collaborate on a Sway presentation, click the Authors button on the navigation bar to invite others to edit the presentation.

Designing a Sway

Sway professionally designs your Storyline content by resizing background images and fonts to fit your display, and by floating text, animating media, embedding video, and removing images as a page scrolls out of view. Sway also evaluates the images in your Storyline and suggests a color palette based on colors that appear in your photos. Use the Design button to display tools including color palettes, font choices, **animation emphasis effects**, and style templates to provide a personality for a Sway presentation. Instead of creating your own design, you can click the Remix button, which randomly selects unique designs for your Sway site.

Publishing a Sway

Use the Play button to display your finished Sway presentation as a website. The Address bar includes a unique web address where others can view your Sway site. As the author, you can edit a published Sway site by clicking the Edit button (pencil icon) on the Sway toolbar.

Sharing a Sway

When you are ready to share your Sway website, you have several options as shown in **Figure 9**. Use the Share slider button to share the Sway site publically or keep it private. If you add the Sway site to the Microsoft **Docs.com** public gallery, anyone worldwide can use Bing, Google, or other search engines to find, view, and share your Sway site. You can also share your Sway site using Facebook, Twitter, Google+, Yammer, and other social media sites. Link your presentation to any webpage or email the link to your audience. Sway can also generate a code for embedding the link within another webpage.

Figure 9: Sharing a Sway site

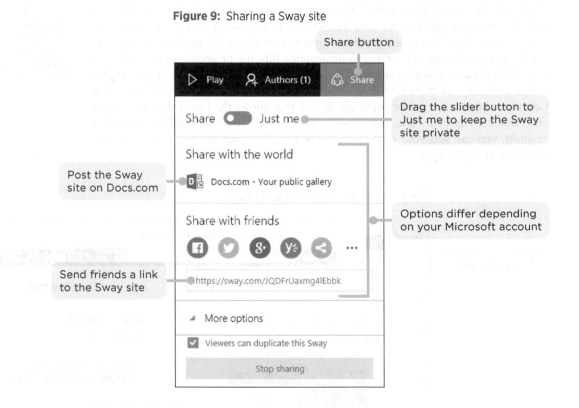

Try This Now

1: Creating a Sway Resume

Sway is a digital storytelling app. Create a Sway resume to share the skills, job experiences, and achievements you have that match the requirements of a future job interest. Perform the following tasks:

    a. Create a new presentation in Sway to use as a digital resume. Title the Sway Storyline with your full name and then select a background image.

    b. Create three separate sections titled **Academic Background, Work Experience**, and **Skills**, and insert text, a picture, and a paragraph or bulleted points in each section. Be sure to include your own picture.

    c. Add a fourth section that includes a video about your school that you find online.

    d. Customize the design of your presentation.

    e. Submit your assignment link in the format specified by your instructor.

2: Creating an Online Sway Newsletter

Newsletters are designed to capture the attention of their target audience. Using Sway, create a newsletter for a club, organization, or your favorite music group. Perform the following tasks:

    a. Create a new presentation in Sway to use as a digital newsletter for a club, organization, or your favorite music group. Provide a title for the Sway Storyline and select an appropriate background image.

    b. Select three separate sections with appropriate titles, such as Upcoming Events. In each section, insert text, a picture, and a paragraph or bulleted points.

    c. Add a fourth section that includes a video about your selected topic.

    d. Customize the design of your presentation.

    e. Submit your assignment link in the format specified by your instructor.

3: Creating and Sharing a Technology Presentation

To place a Sway presentation in the hands of your entire audience, you can share a link to the Sway presentation. Create a Sway presentation on a new technology and share it with your class. Perform the following tasks:

    a. Create a new presentation in Sway about a cutting-edge technology topic. Provide a title for the Sway Storyline and select a background image.

    b. Create four separate sections about your topic, and include text, a picture, and a paragraph in each section.

    c. Add a fifth section that includes a video about your topic.

    d. Customize the design of your presentation.

    e. Share the link to your Sway with your classmates and submit your assignment link in the format specified by your instructor.

Learn to use Sway!
Links to companion **Sways**, featuring **videos** with hands-on instructions, are located on www.cengagebrain.com.

Introduction to Office Mix

add-in | clip | slide recording | Slide Notes | screen recording | free-response quiz

To enliven business meetings and lectures, Microsoft adds a new dimension to presentations with a powerful toolset called Office Mix, a free add-in for PowerPoint. (An **add-in** is software that works with an installed app to extend its features.) Using Office Mix, you can record yourself on video, capture still and moving images on your desktop, and insert interactive elements such as quizzes and live webpages directly into PowerPoint slides. When you post the finished presentation to OneDrive, Office Mix provides a link you can share with friends and colleagues. Anyone with an Internet connection and a web browser can watch a published Office Mix presentation, such as the one in **Figure 10**, on a computer or mobile device.

Figure 10: Office Mix presentation

Adding Office Mix to PowerPoint

To get started, you create an Office Mix account at the website mix.office.com using an email address or a Facebook or Google account. Next, you download and install the Office Mix add-in (see **Figure 11**). Office Mix appears as a new tab named Mix on the PowerPoint ribbon in versions of Office 2013 and Office 2016 running on personal computers (PCs).

Figure 11: Getting started with Office Mix

Capturing Video Clips

A **clip** is a short segment of audio, such as music, or video. After finishing the content on a PowerPoint slide, you can use Office Mix to add a video clip to animate or illustrate the content. Office Mix creates video clips in two ways: by recording live action on a webcam and by capturing screen images and movements. If your computer has a webcam, you can record yourself and annotate the slide to create a **slide recording** as shown in **Figure 12**.

Figure 12: Making a slide recording

Record your voice; also record video if your computer has a camera.

Use the Slide Notes button to display notes for your narration.

For best results, look directly at your webcam while recording video.

Choose a video and audio device to record images and sound.

Use inking tools to write and draw on the slide as you record.

When you are making a slide recording, you can record your spoken narration at the same time. The **Slide Notes** feature works like a teleprompter to help you focus on your presentation content instead of memorizing your narration. Use the Inking tools to make annotations or add highlighting using different pen types and colors. After finishing a recording, edit the video in PowerPoint to trim the length or set playback options.

The second way to create a video is to capture on-screen images and actions with or without a voiceover. This method is ideal if you want to show how to use your favorite website or demonstrate an app such as OneNote. To share your screen with an audience, select the part of the screen you want to show in the video. Office Mix captures everything that happens in that area to create a **screen recording**, as shown in **Figure 13**. Office Mix inserts the screen recording as a video in the slide.

Figure 13: Making a screen recording

Record the action on the screen within the red dashed outline.

Record audio while capturing your on-screen actions.

Select Area button

Inserting Quizzes, Live Webpages, and Apps

To enhance and assess audience understanding, make your slides interactive by adding quizzes, live webpages, and apps. Quizzes give immediate feedback to the user as shown in **Figure 14**. Office Mix supports several quiz formats, including a **free-response quiz** similar to a short answer quiz, and true/false, multiple-choice, and multiple-response formats.

Figure 14: Creating an interactive quiz

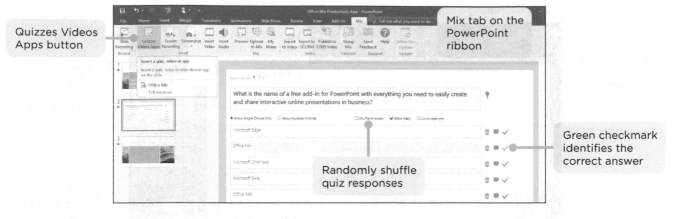

Sharing an Office Mix Presentation

When you complete your work with Office Mix, upload the presentation to your personal Office Mix dashboard as shown in **Figure 15**. Users of PCs, Macs, iOS devices, and Android devices can access and play Office Mix presentations. The Office Mix dashboard displays built-in analytics that include the quiz results and how much time viewers spent on each slide. You can play completed Office Mix presentations online or download them as movies.

Figure 15: Sharing an Office Mix presentation

Try This Now

1: Creating an Office Mix Tutorial for OneNote

Note: This activity requires a microphone on your computer.

Office Mix makes it easy to record screens and their contents. Create PowerPoint slides with an Office Mix screen recording to show OneNote 2016 features. Perform the following tasks:

    a. Create a PowerPoint presentation with the Ion Boardroom template. Create an opening slide with the title **My Favorite OneNote Features** and enter your name in the subtitle.

    b. Create three additional slides, each titled with a new feature of OneNote. Open OneNote and use the Mix tab in PowerPoint to capture three separate screen recordings that teach your favorite features.

    c. Add a fifth slide that quizzes the user with a multiple-choice question about OneNote and includes four responses. Be sure to insert a checkmark indicating the correct response.

    d. Upload the completed presentation to your Office Mix dashboard and share the link with your instructor.

    e. Submit your assignment link in the format specified by your instructor.

2: Teaching Augmented Reality with Office Mix

Note: This activity requires a webcam or built-in video camera on your computer.

A local elementary school has asked you to teach augmented reality to its students using Office Mix. Perform the following tasks:

    a. Research augmented reality using your favorite online search tools.

    b. Create a PowerPoint presentation with the Frame template. Create an opening slide with the title **Augmented Reality** and enter your name in the subtitle.

    c. Create a slide with four bullets summarizing your research of augmented reality. Create a 20-second slide recording of yourself providing a quick overview of augmented reality.

    d. Create another slide with a 30-second screen recording of a video about augmented reality from a site such as YouTube or another video-sharing site.

    e. Add a final slide that quizzes the user with a true/false question about augmented reality. Be sure to insert a checkmark indicating the correct response.

    f. Upload the completed presentation to your Office Mix dashboard and share the link with your instructor.

    g. Submit your assignment link in the format specified by your instructor.

3: Marketing a Travel Destination with Office Mix

Note: This activity requires a webcam or built-in video camera on your computer.

To convince your audience to travel to a particular city, create a slide presentation marketing any city in the world using a slide recording, screen recording, and a quiz. Perform the following tasks:

    a. Create a PowerPoint presentation with any template. Create an opening slide with the title of the city you are marketing as a travel destination and your name in the subtitle.

    b. Create a slide with four bullets about the featured city. Create a 30-second slide recording of yourself explaining why this city is the perfect vacation destination.

    c. Create another slide with a 20-second screen recording of a travel video about the city from a site such as YouTube or another video-sharing site.

    d. Add a final slide that quizzes the user with a multiple-choice question about the featured city with five responses. Be sure to include a checkmark indicating the correct response.

    e. Upload the completed presentation to your Office Mix dashboard and share your link with your instructor.

    f. Submit your assignment link in the format specified by your instructor.

Introduction to Microsoft Edge

Reading view | Hub | Cortana | Web Note | Inking | sandbox

Bottom Line
- Microsoft Edge is the name of the new web browser built into Windows 10.
- Microsoft Edge allows you to search the web faster, take web notes, read webpages without distractions, and get instant assistance from Cortana.

Microsoft Edge is the default web browser developed for the Windows 10 operating system as a replacement for Internet Explorer. Unlike its predecessor, Edge lets you write on webpages, read webpages without advertisements and other distractions, and search for information using a virtual personal assistant. The Edge interface is clean and basic, as shown in **Figure 16**, meaning you can pay more attention to the webpage content.

Figure 16: Microsoft Edge tools

Forward button | New tab button | Web address in the Address bar | Add to favorites or reading list button

Back button | Reading view button | More button

Refresh (F5) button | Hub (Favorites, reading list, history, and downloads) button | Share Web Note button | Make a Web Note button

Learn to use Edge!
Links to companion **Sways**, featuring **videos** with hands-on instructions, are located on www.cengagebrain.com.

Browsing the Web with Microsoft Edge

One of the fastest browsers available, Edge allows you to type search text directly in the Address bar. As you view the resulting webpage, you can switch to **Reading view**, which is available for most news and research sites, to eliminate distracting advertisements. For example, if you are catching up on technology news online, the webpage might be difficult to read due to a busy layout cluttered with ads. Switch to Reading view to refresh the page and remove the original page formatting, ads, and menu sidebars to read the article distraction-free.

Consider the **Hub** in Microsoft Edge as providing one-stop access to all the things you collect on the web, such as your favorite websites, reading list, surfing history, and downloaded files.

Locating Information with Cortana

Cortana, the Windows 10 virtual assistant, plays an important role in Microsoft Edge. After you turn on Cortana, it appears as an animated circle in the Address bar when you might need assistance, as shown in the restaurant website in **Figure 17**. When you click the Cortana icon, a pane slides in from the right of the browser window to display detailed information about the restaurant, including maps and reviews. Cortana can also assist you in defining words, finding the weather, suggesting coupons for shopping, updating stock market information, and calculating math.

On the Job Now

Businesses started adopting Internet Explorer more than 20 years ago simply to view webpages. Today, Microsoft Edge has a different purpose: to promote interaction with the web and share its contents with colleagues.

Figure 17: Cortana providing restaurant information

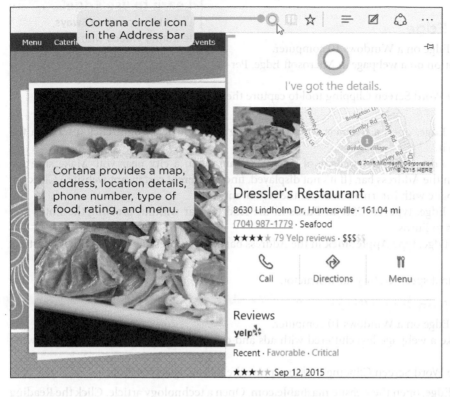

Annotating Webpages

One of the most impressive Microsoft Edge features are the **Web Note** tools, which you use to write on a webpage or to highlight text. When you click the Make a Web Note button, an **Inking** toolbar appears, as shown in **Figure 18**, that provides writing and drawing tools. These tools include an eraser, a pen, and a highlighter with different colors. You can also insert a typed note and copy a screen image (called a screen clipping). You can draw with a pointing device, fingertip, or stylus using different pen colors. Whether you add notes to a recipe, annotate sources for a research paper, or select a product while shopping online, the Web Note tools can enhance your productivity. After you complete your notes, click the Save button to save the annotations to OneNote, your Favorites list, or your Reading list. You can share the inked page with others using the Share Web Note button.

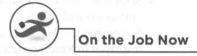

On the Job Now

To enhance security, Microsoft Edge runs in a partial sandbox, an arrangement that prevents attackers from gaining control of your computer. Browsing within the **sandbox** protects computer resources and information from hackers.

Figure 18: Web Note tools in Microsoft Edge

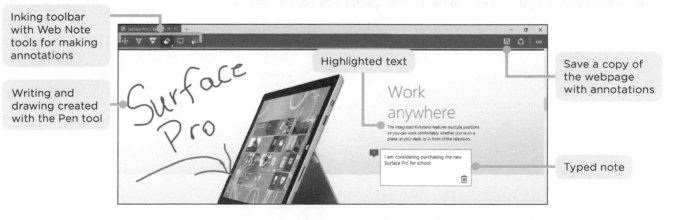

Try This Now

1: Using Cortana in Microsoft Edge

Note: This activity requires using Microsoft Edge on a Windows 10 computer.

Cortana can assist you in finding information on a webpage in Microsoft Edge. Perform the following tasks:

a. Create a Word document using the Word Screen Clipping tool to capture the following screenshots.

- Screenshot A—Using Microsoft Edge, open a webpage with a technology news article. Right-click a term in the article and ask Cortana to define it.
- Screenshot B—Using Microsoft Edge, open the website of a fancy restaurant in a city near you. Make sure the Cortana circle icon is displayed in the Address bar. (If it's not displayed, find a different restaurant website.) Click the Cortana circle icon to display a pane with information about the restaurant.
- Screenshot C—Using Microsoft Edge, type **10 USD to Euros** in the Address bar without pressing the Enter key. Cortana converts the U.S. dollars to Euros.
- Screenshot D—Using Microsoft Edge, type **Apple stock** in the Address bar without pressing the Enter key. Cortana displays the current stock quote.

b. Submit your assignment in the format specified by your instructor.

2: Viewing Online News with Reading View

Note: This activity requires using Microsoft Edge on a Windows 10 computer.

Reading view in Microsoft Edge can make a webpage less cluttered with ads and other distractions. Perform the following tasks:

a. Create a Word document using the Word Screen Clipping tool to capture the following screenshots.

- Screenshot A—Using Microsoft Edge, open the website **mashable.com**. Open a technology article. Click the Reading view button to display an ad-free page that uses only basic text formatting.
- Screenshot B—Using Microsoft Edge, open the website **bbc.com**. Open any news article. Click the Reading view button to display an ad-free page that uses only basic text formatting.
- Screenshot C—Make three types of annotations (Pen, Highlighter, and Add a typed note) on the BBC article page displayed in Reading view.

b. Submit your assignment in the format specified by your instructor.

3: Inking with Microsoft Edge

Note: This activity requires using Microsoft Edge on a Windows 10 computer.

Microsoft Edge provides many annotation options to record your ideas. Perform the following tasks:

a. Open the website **wolframalpha.com** in the Microsoft Edge browser. Wolfram Alpha is a well-respected academic search engine. Type **US$100 1965 dollars in 2015** in the Wolfram Alpha search text box and press the Enter key.

b. Click the Make a Web Note button to display the Web Note tools. Using the Pen tool, draw a circle around the result on the webpage. Save the page to OneNote.

c. In the Wolfram Alpha search text box, type the name of the city closest to where you live and press the Enter key. Using the Highlighter tool, highlight at least three interesting results. Add a note and then type a sentence about what you learned about this city. Save the page to OneNote. Share your OneNote notebook with your instructor.

d. Submit your assignment link in the format specified by your instructor.

Getting Started with
Microsoft Office 2016

CASE ▶ This module introduces you to the most frequently used programs in Office, as well as common features they all share.

Module Objectives

After completing this module, you will be able to:

- Understand the Office 2016 suite
- Start an Office app
- Identify Office 2016 screen elements
- Create and save a file

- Open a file and save it with a new name
- View and print your work
- Get Help, close a file, and exit an app

Files You Will Need

OF 1-1.xlsx

Understand the Office 2016 Suite

Microsoft Office 2016 is a group of programs—which are also called applications or apps—designed to help you create documents, collaborate with coworkers, and track and analyze information. You use different Office programs to accomplish specific tasks, such as writing a letter or producing a presentation, yet all the programs have a similar look and feel. Microsoft Office 2016 apps feature a common, context-sensitive user interface, so you can get up to speed faster and use advanced features with greater ease. The Office apps are bundled together in a group called a **suite**. The Office suite is available in several configurations, but all include Word, Excel, PowerPoint, and OneNote. Some configurations include Access, Outlook, Publisher, Skype, and OneDrive. **CASE** *As part of your job, you need to understand how each Office app is best used to complete specific tasks.*

DETAILS

The Office apps covered in this book include:

- **Microsoft Word 2016**

  When you need to create any kind of text-based document, such as a memo, newsletter, or multipage report, Word is the program to use. You can easily make your documents look great by using formatting tools and inserting eye-catching graphics. The Word document shown in **FIGURE 1-1** contains a company logo and simple formatting.

- **Microsoft Excel 2016**

  Excel is the perfect solution when you need to work with numeric values and make calculations. It puts the power of formulas, functions, charts, and other analytical tools into the hands of every user, so you can analyze sales projections, calculate loan payments, and present your findings in a professional manner. The Excel worksheet shown in **FIGURE 1-1** tracks checkbook transactions. Because Excel automatically recalculates results whenever a value changes, the information is always up to date. A chart illustrates how the monthly expenses are broken down.

- **Microsoft PowerPoint 2016**

  Using PowerPoint, it's easy to create powerful presentations complete with graphics, transitions, and even a soundtrack. Using professionally designed themes and clip art, you can quickly and easily create dynamic slide shows such as the one shown in **FIGURE 1-1**.

- **Microsoft Access 2016**

  Access is a relational database program that helps you keep track of large amounts of quantitative data, such as product inventories or employee records. The form shown in **FIGURE 1-1** can be used to generate reports on customer invoices and tours.

Microsoft Office has benefits beyond the power of each program, including:

- **Note-taking made simple; available on all devices**

  Use OneNote to take notes (organized in tabbed pages) on information that can be accessed on your computer, tablet, or phone. Share the editable results with others. Contents can include text, web page clips (using OneNote Clipper), email contents (directly inserted into a default section), photos (using Office Lens), and web pages.

- **Common user interface: Improving business processes**

  Because the Office suite apps have a similar **interface**, your experience using one app's tools makes it easy to learn those in the other apps. Office documents are **compatible** with one another, so you can easily **integrate**, or combine, elements—for example, you can add an Excel chart to a PowerPoint slide, or an Access table to a Word document.

  Most Office programs include the capability to incorporate feedback—called **online collaboration**—across the Internet or a company network.

FIGURE 1-1: Microsoft Office 2016 documents

Letter created in Word

Checkbook register created in Excel

Tourism presentation created in PowerPoint

Photos courtesy of Elizabeth Eisner Reding

Form created in Access

What is Office 365?

Until recently, most consumers purchased Microsoft Office in a traditional way: by buying a retail package from a store or downloading it from Microsoft.com. You can still purchase Microsoft Office 2016 in this traditional way—but you can also now purchase it as a subscription service called Microsoft Office 365, which is available in a wide variety of configurations.

Depending on which configuration you purchase, you will always have access to the most up-to-date versions of the apps in your package and, in many cases, can install these apps on multiple computers, tablets, and phones. And if you change computers or devices, you can easily uninstall the apps from an old device and install them on a new one.

Start an Office App

To get started using Microsoft Office, you need to start, or **launch**, the Office app you want to use. An easy way to start the app you want is to press the Windows key, type the first few characters of the app name you want to search for, then click the app name In the Best match list. You will discover that there are many ways to accomplish just about any Windows task; for example, you can also see a list of all the apps on your computer by pressing the Windows key, then clicking All Apps. When you see the app you want, click its name. **CASE** *You decide to familiarize yourself with Office by starting Microsoft Word.*

STEPS

1. **Click the Start button ⊞ on the Windows taskbar**

   The Start menu opens, listing the most used apps on your computer. You can locate the app you want to open by clicking the app name if you see it, or you can type the app name to search for it.

2. **Type word**

   Your screen now displays "Word 2016" under "Best match", along with any other app that has "word" as part of its name (such as WordPad). See **FIGURE 1-2**.

3. **Click Word 2016**

   Word 2016 launches, and the Word **start screen** appears, as shown in **FIGURE 1-3**. The start screen is a landing page that appears when you first start an Office app. The left side of this screen displays recent files you have opened. (If you have never opened any files, then there will be no files listed under Recent.) The right side displays images depicting different templates you can use to create different types of documents. A **template** is a file containing professionally designed content and formatting that you can easily customize for your own needs. You can also start from scratch using the Blank Document template, which contains only minimal formatting settings.

Enabling touch mode

If you are using a touch screen with any of the Office 2016 apps, you can enable the touch mode to give the user interface a more spacious look, making it easier to navigate with your fingertips. Enable touch mode by clicking the Quick Access toolbar list arrow, then clicking Touch/Mouse Mode to select it. Then you'll see the Touch Mode button 🖐 in the Quick Access toolbar. Click 🖐, and you'll see the interface spread out.

Using shortcut keys to move between Office programs

You can switch between open apps using a keyboard shortcut. The [Alt][Tab] keyboard combination lets you either switch quickly to the next open program or file or choose one from a gallery. To switch immediately to the next open program or file, press [Alt][Tab]. To choose from all open programs and files, press and hold [Alt], then press and release [Tab] without releasing [Alt]. A gallery opens on screen, displaying the filename and a thumbnail image of each open program and file, as well as of the desktop. Each time you press [Tab] while holding [Alt], the selection cycles to the next open file or location. Release [Alt] when the program, file, or location you want to activate is selected.

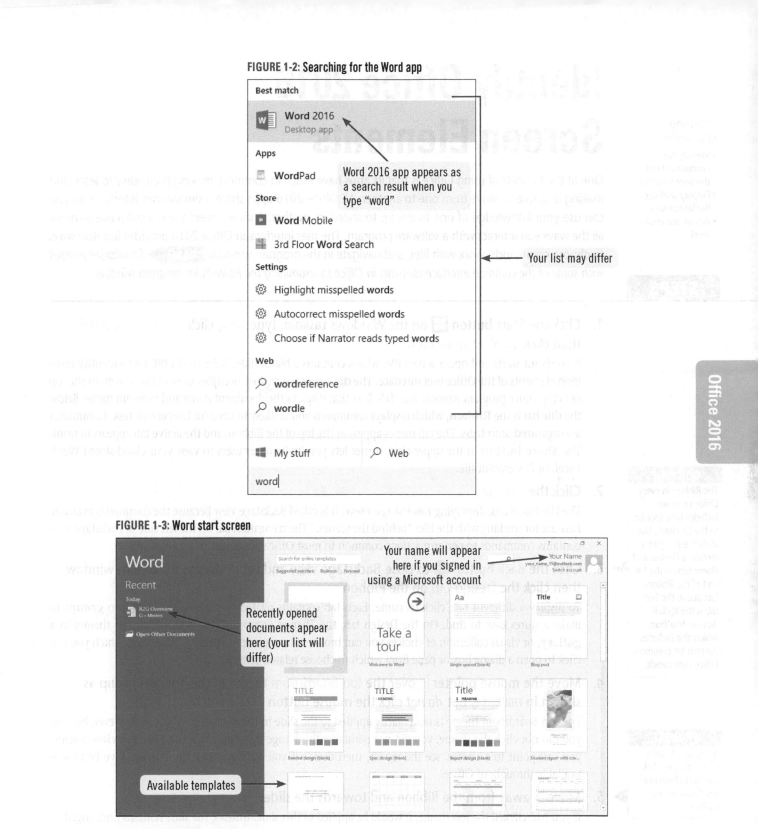

FIGURE 1-2: Searching for the Word app

Word 2016 app appears as a search result when you type "word"

Your list may differ

FIGURE 1-3: Word start screen

Your name will appear here if you signed in using a Microsoft account

Recently opened documents appear here (your list will differ)

Available templates

Using the Office Clipboard

You can use the Office Clipboard to cut and copy items from one Office program and paste them into others. The Office Clipboard can store a maximum of 24 items. To access it, open the Office Clipboard task pane by clicking the dialog box launcher 🔳 in the Clipboard group on the Home tab. Each time you copy a selection, it is saved in the Office Clipboard. Each entry in the

Office Clipboard includes an icon that tells you the program it was created in. To paste an entry, click in the document where you want it to appear, then click the item in the Office Clipboard. To delete an item from the Office Clipboard, right-click the item, then click Delete.

Office 2016

Identify Office 2016 Screen Elements

Learning Outcomes
• Identify basic components of the user interface
• Display and use Backstage view
• Adjust the zoom level

One of the benefits of using Office is that its apps have much in common, making them easy to learn and making it simple to move from one to another. All Office 2016 apps share a similar user interface, so you can use your knowledge of one to get up to speed in another. A **user interface** is a collective term for all the ways you interact with a software program. The user interface in Office 2016 provides intuitive ways to choose commands, work with files, and navigate in the program window. **CASE** *Familiarize yourself with some of the common interface elements in Office by examining the PowerPoint program window.*

STEPS

1. **Click the Start button ⊞ on the Windows taskbar, type** pow, **click** PowerPoint 2016, **then click** Blank Presentation

    PowerPoint starts and opens a new file, which contains a blank slide. Refer to **FIGURE 1-4** to identify common elements of the Office user interface. The **document window** occupies most of the screen. At the top of every Office program window is a **title bar** that displays the document name and program name. Below the title bar is the **Ribbon**, which displays commands you're likely to need for the current task. Commands are organized onto **tabs**. The tab names appear at the top of the Ribbon, and the active tab appears in front. The **Share button** in the upper-right corner lets you invite other users to view your cloud-stored Word, Excel, or Powerpoint file.

QUICK TIP
The Ribbon in every Office program includes tabs specific to the program, but all Office programs include a File tab and Home tab on the left end of the Ribbon. Just above the File tab is the **Quick Access toolbar**, which also includes buttons for common Office commands.

2. **Click the** File tab

    The File tab opens, displaying **Backstage view**. It is called Backstage view because the commands available here are for working with the files "behind the scenes." The navigation bar on the left side of Backstage view contains commands to perform actions common to most Office programs.

3. **Click the** Back button ⊛ **to close Backstage view and return to the document window, then click the** Design tab **on the Ribbon**

    To display a different tab, click its name. Each tab contains related commands arranged into **groups** to make features easy to find. On the Design tab, the Themes group displays available design themes in a **gallery**, or visual collection of choices you can browse. Many groups contain a **launcher**, which you can click to open a dialog box or pane from which to choose related commands.

4. **Move the mouse pointer ⍨ over the** Ion Boardroom theme **in the Themes group as shown in FIGURE 1-5, but** *do not click* **the mouse button**

    The Ion Boardroom theme is temporarily applied to the slide in the document window. However, because you did not click the theme, you did not permanently change the slide. With the **Live Preview** feature, you can point to a choice, see the results, then decide if you want to make the change. Live Preview is available throughout Office.

TROUBLE
If you accidentally click a theme, click the Undo button on the Quick Access toolbar.

5. **Move ⍨ away from the Ribbon and towards the slide**

    If you had clicked the Ion theme, it would be applied to this slide. Instead, the slide remains unchanged.

QUICK TIP
You can also use the Zoom button in the Zoom group on the View tab to enlarge or reduce a document's appearance.

6. **Point to the** Zoom slider [−———|————+   100%] **on the status bar, then drag to the right until the Zoom level reads** 166%

    The slide display is enlarged. Zoom tools are located on the status bar. You can drag the slider or click the Zoom In or Zoom Out buttons to zoom in or out on an area of interest. **Zooming in** (a higher percentage), makes a document appear bigger on screen but less of it fits on the screen at once; **zooming out** (a lower percentage) lets you see more of the document at a reduced size.

7. **Click the** Zoom Out button ⊟ **on the status bar to the left of the Zoom slider until the Zoom level reads** 120%

FIGURE 1-4: PowerPoint program window

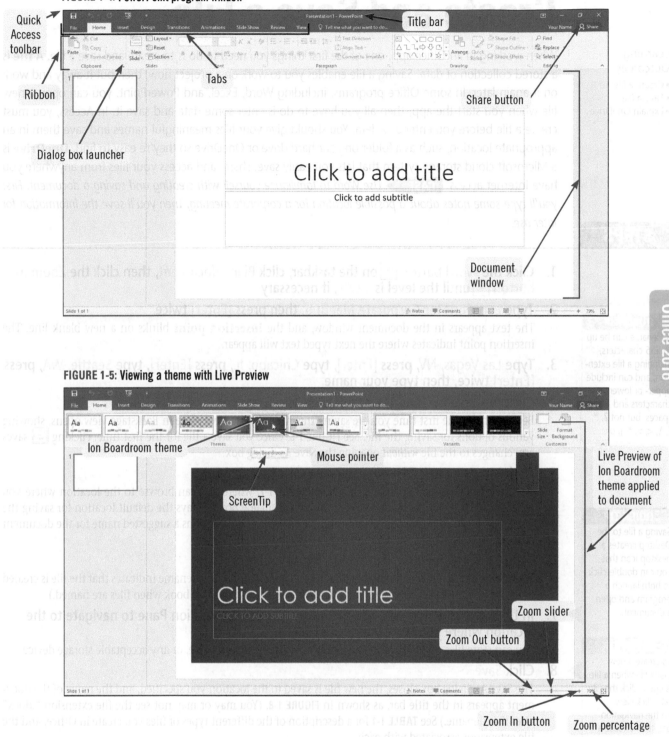

Quick Access toolbar

Ribbon

Dialog box launcher

Tabs

Title bar

Share button

Document window

FIGURE 1-5: Viewing a theme with Live Preview

Ion Boardroom theme

Mouse pointer

ScreenTip

Click to add title

Live Preview of Ion Boardroom theme applied to document

Zoom slider

Zoom Out button

Zoom In button

Zoom percentage

Using Backstage view

Backstage view in each Microsoft Office app offers "one stop shopping" for many commonly performed tasks, such as opening and saving a file, printing and previewing a document, defining document properties, sharing information, and exiting a program. Backstage view opens when you click the File tab in any Office app, and while features such as the Ribbon, Mini toolbar, and Live Preview all help you work *in* your documents, the File tab and Backstage view help you work *with* your documents. You can click commands in the navigation pane to open different places for working with your documents, such as the Open place, the Save place, and so on. You can return to your active document by clicking the Back button.

Create and Save a File

Learning
Outcomes
• Create a file
• Save a file
• Explain OneDrive

When working in an Office app, one of the first things you need to do is to create and save a file. A **file** is a stored collection of data. Saving a file enables you to work on a project now, then put it away and work on it again later. In some Office programs, including Word, Excel, and PowerPoint, you can open a new file when you start the app, then all you have to do is enter some data and save it. In Access, you must create a file before you enter any data. You should give your files meaningful names and save them in an appropriate location, such as a folder on your hard drive or OneDrive so they're easy to find. **OneDrive** is a Microsoft cloud storage system that lets you easily save, share, and access your files from anywhere you have Internet access. **CASE** *Use Word to familiarize yourself with creating and saving a document. First you'll type some notes about a possible location for a corporate meeting, then you'll save the information for later use.*

STEPS

1. **Click the** Word button 📃 **on the taskbar, click** Blank document, **then click the** Zoom In button ➕ **until the level is** 120%, **if necessary**

2. **Type** Locations for Corporate Meeting, **then press [Enter] twice**
   The text appears in the document window, and the **insertion point** blinks on a new blank line. The insertion point indicates where the next typed text will appear.

QUICK TIP
A filename can be up to 255 characters, including a file extension, and can include upper- or lowercase characters and spaces, but not ?, ", /, \, <, >, *, |, or :.

3. **Type** Las Vegas, NV, **press [Enter], type** Chicago, IL, **press [Enter], type** Seattle, WA, **press [Enter] twice, then type your name**

4. **Click the** Save button 💾 **on the Quick Access toolbar**
   Because this is the first time you are saving this new file, the Save place in Backstage view opens, showing various options for saving the file. See **FIGURE 1-6**. Once you save a file for the first time, clicking 💾 saves any changes to the file *without* opening the Save As dialog box.

5. **Click** Browse
   The Save As dialog box opens, as shown in **FIGURE 1-7**, where you can browse to the location where you want to save the file. The Address bar in the Save As dialog box displays the default location for saving the file, but you can change it to any location. The File name field contains a suggested name for the document based on text in the file, but you can enter a different name.

QUICK TIP
Saving a file to the Desktop creates a desktop icon that you can double-click to both launch a program and open a document.

6. **Type** OF 1-Possible Corporate Meeting Locations
   The text you type replaces the highlighted text. (The "OF 1-" in the filename indicates that the file is created in Office Module 1. You will see similar designations throughout this book when files are named.)

7. **In the Save As dialog box, use the Address bar or Navigation Pane to navigate to the location where you store your Data Files**
   You can store files on your computer, a network drive, your OneDrive, or any acceptable storage device.

QUICK TIP
To create a new blank file when a file is open, click the File tab, click New on the navigation bar, then choose a template.

8. **Click** Save
   The Save As dialog box closes, the new file is saved to the location you specified, and the name of the document appears in the title bar, as shown in **FIGURE 1-8**. (You may or may not see the file extension ".docx" after the filename.) See **TABLE 1-1** for a description of the different types of files you create in Office, and the file extensions associated with each.

TABLE 1-1: Common filenames and default file extensions

file created in	is called a	and has the default extension
Word	document	.docx
Excel	workbook	.xlsx
PowerPoint	presentation	.pptx
Access	database	.accdb

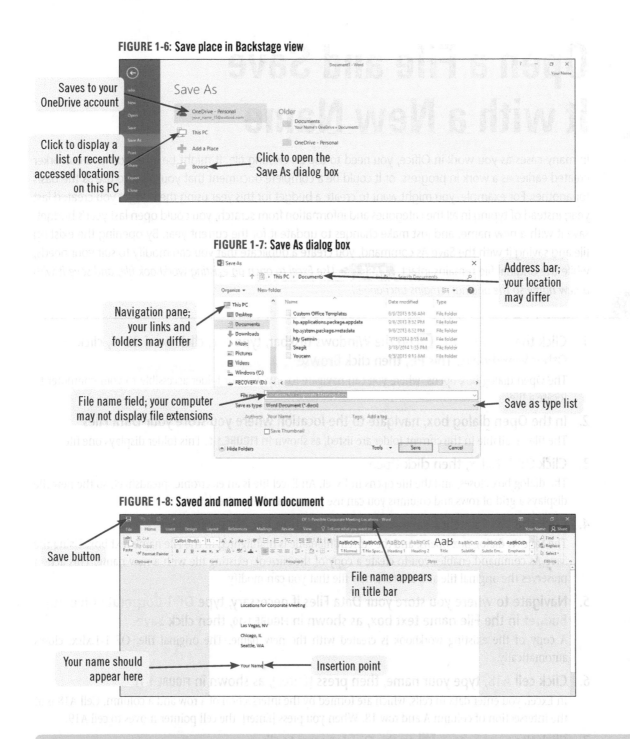

FIGURE 1-6: Save place in Backstage view

Saves to your OneDrive account

Click to display a list of recently accessed locations on this PC

Click to open the Save As dialog box

FIGURE 1-7: Save As dialog box

Address bar; your location may differ

Navigation pane; your links and folders may differ

File name field; your computer may not display file extensions

Save as type list

FIGURE 1-8: Saved and named Word document

Save button

File name appears in title bar

Your name should appear here

Insertion point

Saving files to OneDrive

All Office programs include the capability to incorporate feedback—called **online collaboration**—across the Internet or a company network. Using **cloud computing** (work done in a virtual environment), you can store your work in the cloud. Using OneDrive, a file storage service from Microsoft, you and your colleagues can create and store documents in the cloud and make the documents available anywhere there is Internet access to whomever you choose. To use OneDrive, you need a Microsoft Account, which you obtain at onedrive.live.com. Pricing and storage plans vary based on the type of Microsoft account you have. When you are logged into your Microsoft account and you

save a file in any of the Office apps, the first option in the Save As screen is your OneDrive. Double-click your OneDrive option, and the Save As dialog box opens displaying a location in the address bar unique to your OneDrive account. Type a name in the File name text box, then click Save and your file is saved to your OneDrive. To sync your files with OneDrive, you'll need to download and install the OneDrive for Windows app. Then, when you open Explorer, you'll notice a new folder called OneDrive has been added to your folder. In this folder is a sub-folder called Documents. This means if your Internet connection fails, you can work on your files offline.

Learning
Outcomes
• Open an existing
  file
• Save a file with a
  new name

Open a File and Save It with a New Name

In many cases as you work in Office, you need to use an existing file. It might be a file you or a coworker created earlier as a work in progress, or it could be a complete document that you want to use as the basis for another. For example, you might want to create a budget for this year using the budget you created last year; instead of typing in all the categories and information from scratch, you could open last year's budget, save it with a new name, and just make changes to update it for the current year. By opening the existing file and saving it with the Save As command, you create a duplicate that you can modify to suit your needs, while the original file remains intact. **CASE** > *Use Excel to open an existing workbook file, and save it with a new name so the original remains unchanged.*

STEPS

1. **Click the Start button ⊞ on the Windows taskbar, type exc, click Excel 2016, click Open Other Workbooks, This PC, then click Browse**

   The Open dialog box opens, where you can navigate to any drive or folder accessible to your computer to locate a file.

2. **In the Open dialog box, navigate to the location where you store your Data Files**

   The files available in the current folder are listed, as shown in **FIGURE 1-9**. This folder displays one file.

3. **Click OF 1-1.xlsx, then click Open**

   The dialog box closes, and the file opens in Excel. An Excel file is an electronic spreadsheet, so the new file displays a grid of rows and columns you can use to enter and organize data.

4. **Click the File tab, click Save As on the navigation bar, then click Browse**

   The Save As dialog box opens, and the current filename is highlighted in the File name text box. Using the Save As command enables you to create a copy of the current, existing file with a new name. This action preserves the original file and creates a new file that you can modify.

5. **Navigate to where you store your Data Files if necessary, type OF 1-Corporate Meeting Budget in the File name text box, as shown in FIGURE 1-10, then click Save**

   A copy of the existing workbook is created with the new name. The original file, OF 1-1.xlsx, closes automatically.

6. **Click cell A18, type your name, then press [Enter], as shown in FIGURE 1-11**

   In Excel, you enter data in cells, which are formed by the intersection of a row and a column. Cell A18 is at the intersection of column A and row 18. When you press [Enter], the cell pointer moves to cell A19.

7. **Click the Save button 🖫 on the Quick Access toolbar**

   Your name appears in the workbook, and your changes to the file are saved.

Exploring File Open options

You might have noticed that the Open button in the Open dialog box includes a list arrow to the right of the button. In a dialog box, if a button includes a list arrow you can click the button to invoke the command, or you can click the list arrow to see a list of related commands that you can apply to the currently selected file. The Open list arrow includes several related commands, including Open Read-Only and Open as Copy.

Clicking Open Read-Only opens a file that you can only save with a new name; you cannot make changes to the original file. Clicking Open as Copy creates and opens a copy of the selected file and inserts the word "Copy" in the file's title. Like the Save As command, these commands provide additional ways to use copies of existing files while ensuring that original files do not get changed by mistake.

FIGURE 1-9: Open dialog box

FIGURE 1-10: Save As dialog box

FIGURE 1-11: Your name added to the workbook

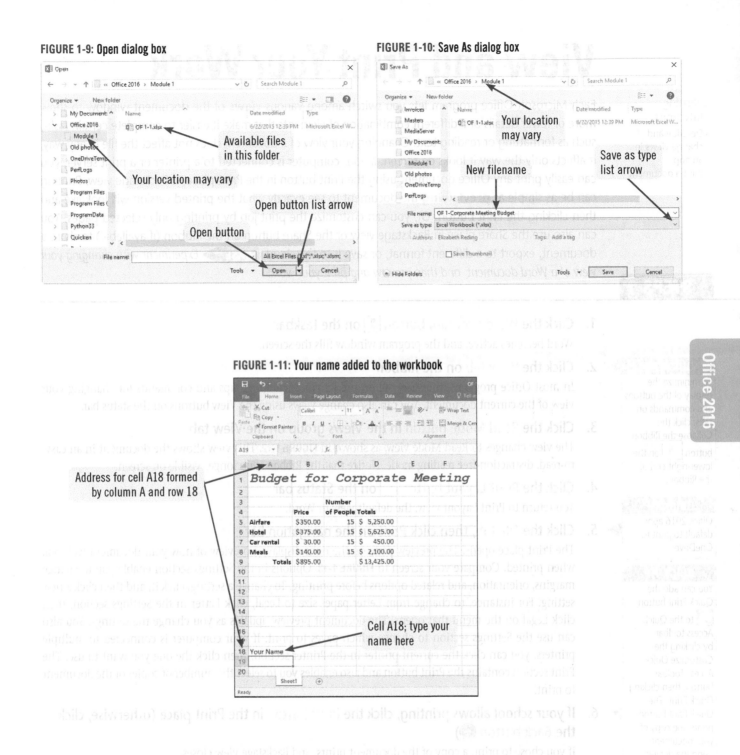

Working in Compatibility Mode

Not everyone upgrades to the newest version of Office. As a general rule, new software versions are **backward compatible**, meaning that documents saved by an older version can be read by newer software. To open documents created in older Office versions, Office 2016 includes a feature called Compatibility Mode. When you use Office 2016 to open a file created in an earlier version of Office, "Compatibility Mode" appears in the title bar, letting you know the file was created in an earlier but usable version of the program. If you are working with someone who

may not be using the newest version of the software, you can avoid possible incompatibility problems by saving your file in another, earlier format. To do this in an Office program, click the File tab, click Save As on the navigation bar, then click Browse. In the Save As dialog box, click the Save as type list arrow in the Save As dialog box, then click an option in the list. For example, if you're working in Excel, click Excel 97-2003 Workbook format in the Save as type list to save an Excel file so it can be opened in Excel 97 or Excel 2003.

View and Print Your Work

Each Microsoft Office program lets you switch among various **views** of the document window to show more or fewer details or a different combination of elements that make it easier to complete certain tasks, such as formatting or reading text. Changing your view of a document does not affect the file in any way, it affects only the way it looks on screen. If your computer is connected to a printer or a print server, you can easily print any Office document using the Print button in the Print place in Backstage view. Printing can be as simple as **previewing** the document to see exactly what the printed version will look like and then clicking the Print button. Or, you can customize the print job by printing only selected pages. You can also use the Share place in Backstage view or the Share button on the Ribbon (if available) to share a document, export to a different format, or save it to the cloud. **CASE** ▸ *Experiment with changing your view of a Word document, and then preview and print your work.*

STEPS

1. **Click the** Word program button ▦ **on the taskbar**
   Word becomes active, and the program window fills the screen.

2. **Click the** View tab **on the Ribbon**
   In most Office programs, the View tab on the Ribbon includes groups and commands for changing your view of the current document. You can also change views using the View buttons on the status bar.

3. **Click the** Read Mode button **in the Views group on the View tab**
   The view changes to Read Mode view, as shown in **FIGURE 1-12**. This view shows the document in an easy-to-read, distraction-free reading mode. Notice that the Ribbon is no longer visible on screen.

4. **Click the** Print Layout button ▤ **on the Status bar**
   You return to Print Layout view, the default view in Word.

5. **Click the** File tab, **then click** Print **on the navigation bar**
   The Print place opens. The preview pane on the right displays a preview of how your document will look when printed. Compare your screen to **FIGURE 1-13**. Options in the Settings section enable you to change margins, orientation, and related options before printing. To change a setting, click it, and then click a new setting. For instance, to change from Letter paper size to Legal, click Letter in the Settings section, then click Legal on the menu that opens. The document preview updates as you change the settings. You also can use the Settings section to change which pages to print. If your computer is connected to multiple printers, you can click the current printer in the Printer section, then click the one you want to use. The Print section contains the Print button and also enables you to select the number of copies of the document to print.

6. **If your school allows printing, click the** Print button **in the Print place (otherwise, click the** Back button ⬅**)**
   If you chose to print, a copy of the document prints, and Backstage view closes.

Customizing the Quick Access toolbar

You can customize the Quick Access toolbar to display your favorite commands. To do so, click the Customize Quick Access Toolbar button ▾ in the title bar, then click the command you want to add. If you don't see the command in the list, click More Commands to open the Quick Access Toolbar tab of the current program's Options dialog box. In the Options dialog box, use the Choose commands from list to choose a category, click the desired command in the list on the left, click Add to add it to the Quick Access toolbar, then click OK. To remove a button from the toolbar, click the name in the list on the right in the Options dialog box, then click Remove. To add a command to the Quick Access toolbar as you work, simply right-click the button on the Ribbon, then click Add to Quick Access Toolbar on the shortcut menu. To move the Quick Access toolbar below the Ribbon, click the Customize Quick Access Toolbar button, and then click Show Below the Ribbon.

FIGURE 1-12: Read Mode view

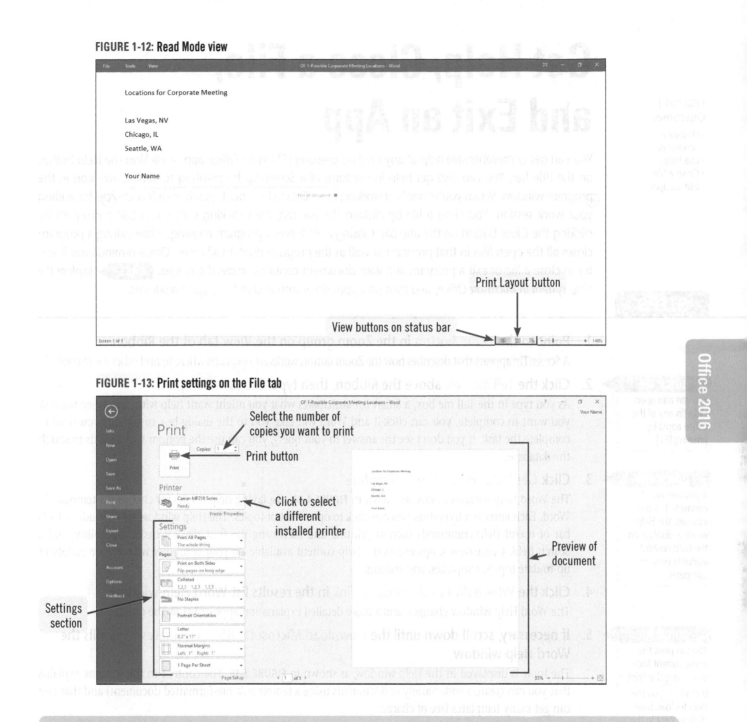

Print Layout button

View buttons on status bar

FIGURE 1-13: Print settings on the File tab

Select the number of copies you want to print

Print button

Click to select a different installed printer

Preview of document

Settings section

Creating a screen capture

A **screen capture** is a digital image of your screen, as if you took a picture of it with a camera. For instance, you might want to take a screen capture if an error message occurs and you want a Technical Support person to see exactly what's on the screen. You can create a screen capture using the Snipping Tool, an accessory designed to capture whole screens or portions of screens. To open the Snipping Tool, click the Start button on the Windows taskbar, type "sni", then click the Snipping Tool when it appears in the left panel. On the Snipping Tool toolbar, click New, then drag the pointer on the screen to select the area of the screen you want to capture. When you release the mouse button, the screen capture opens in the Snipping Tool window, and you can save, copy, or send it in an email. In Word, Excel, and PowerPoint 2016, you can capture screens or portions of screens and insert them in the current document using the Screenshot button in the Illustrations group on the Insert tab. Alternatively, you can create a screen capture by pressing [PrtScn]. (Keyboards differ, but you may find the [PrtScn] button in or near your keyboard's function keys.) Pressing this key places a digital image of your screen in the Windows temporary storage area known as the **Clipboard**. Open the document where you want the screen capture to appear, click the Home tab on the Ribbon (if necessary), then click the Paste button in the Clipboard group on the Home tab. The screen capture is pasted into the document.

Get Help, Close a File, and Exit an App

Learning
Outcomes
• Display a
  ScreenTip
• Use Help
• Close a file
• Exit an app

You can get comprehensive help at any time by pressing [F1] in an Office app or clicking the Help button on the title bar. You can also get help in the form of a ScreenTip by pointing to almost any icon in the program window. When you're finished working in an Office document, you have a few choices for ending your work session. You close a file by clicking the File tab, then clicking Close; you exit a program by clicking the Close button on the title bar. Closing a file leaves a program running, while exiting a program closes all the open files in that program as well as the program itself. In all cases, Office reminds you if you try to close a file or exit a program and your document contains unsaved changes. **CASE** ▶ *Explore the Help system in Microsoft Office, and then close your documents and exit any open programs.*

STEPS

1. **Point to the Zoom button in the Zoom group on the View tab of the Ribbon**
   A ScreenTip appears that describes how the Zoom button works and explains where to find other zoom controls.

2. **Click the Tell me box above the Ribbon, then type Choose a template**
   As you type in the Tell me box, a Smart list anticipates what you might want help with. If you see the task you want to complete, you can click it and Word will take you to the dialog box or options you need to complete the task. If you don't see the answer to your query, you can use the bottom two options to search the database.

3. **Click Get Help on "choose a template"**
   The Word Help window opens, as shown in **FIGURE 1-14**, displaying help results for choosing a template in Word. Each entry is a hyperlink you can click to open a list of topics. The Help window also includes a toolbar of useful Help commands such as printing and increasing the font size for easier readability, and a Search field. Office.com supplements the help content available on your computer with a wide variety of up-to-date topics, templates, and training.

4. **Click the Where do I find templates link in the results list Word Help window**
   The Word Help window changes, and a more detailed explanation appears below the topic.

5. **If necessary, scroll down until the Download Microsoft Office templates topic fills the Word Help window**
   The topic is displayed in the Help window, as shown in **FIGURE 1-15**. The content in the window explains that you can create a wide variety of documents using a template (a pre-formatted document) and that you can get many templates free of charge.

6. **Click the Keep Help on Top button 📌 in the lower-right corner of the window**
   The Pin Help button rotates so the pin point is pointed towards the bottom of the screen: this allows you to read the Help window while you work on your document.

7. **Click the Word document window, notice the Help window remains visible**

8. **Click a blank area of the Help window, click 📌 to Unpin Help, click the Close button ☒ in the Help window, then click the Close button ☒ in the Word program window**
   Word closes, and the Excel program window is active.

9. **Click the Close button ☒ in the Excel program window, click the PowerPoint app button 📧 on the taskbar if necessary, then click the Close button ☒ to exit PowerPoint**
   Excel and PowerPoint both close.

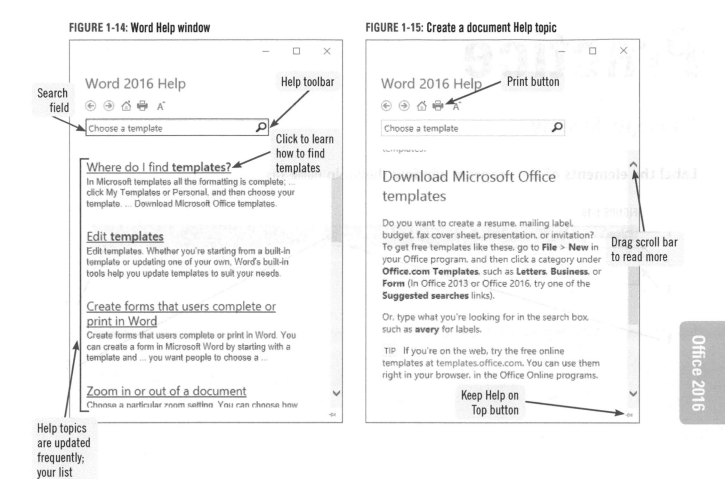

FIGURE 1-14: Word Help window

FIGURE 1-15: Create a document Help topic

Using sharing features and co-authoring capabilities

If you are using Word, Excel, or PowerPoint, you can take advantage of the Share feature, which makes it easy to share your files that have been saved to OneDrive. When you click the Share button, you will be asked to invite others to share the file. To do this, type in the name or email addresses in the Invite people text box. When you invite others, you have the opportunity to give them different levels of permission. You might want some people to have read-only privileges; you might want others to be able to make edits. Also available in Word, Excel, and PowerPoint is real-time co-authoring capabilities for files stored on OneDrive. Once a file on OneDrive is opened and all the users have been given editing privileges, all the users can make edits simultaneously. On first use, each user will be prompted to automatically share their changes.

Recovering a document

Each Office program has a built-in recovery feature that allows you to open and save files that were open at the time of an interruption such as a power failure. When you restart the program(s) after an interruption, the Document Recovery task pane opens on the left side of your screen displaying both original and recovered versions of the files that were open. If you're not sure which file to open (original or recovered), it's usually better to open the recovered file because it will contain the latest information. You can, however, open and review all versions of the file that were recovered and save the best one. Each file listed in the Document Recovery task pane displays a list arrow with options that allow you to open the file, save it as is, delete it, or show repairs made to it during recovery.

Office 2016

Practice

Concepts Review

Label the elements of the program window shown in FIGURE 1-16.

FIGURE 1-16

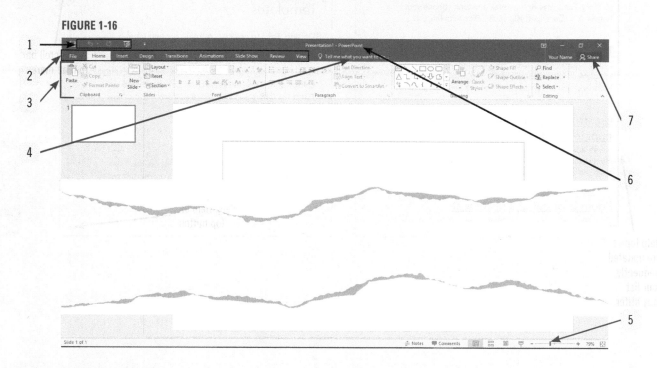

Match each project with the program for which it is best suited.

8. **Microsoft PowerPoint**   a. Corporate convention budget with expense projections
9. **Microsoft Word**   b. Presentation for city council meeting
10. **Microsoft Excel**   c. Business cover letter for a job application
11. **Microsoft Access**   d. Department store inventory

Independent Challenge 1

You just accepted an administrative position with a local independently owned insurance agent who has recently invested in computers and is now considering purchasing a subscription to Office 365. You have been asked to think of uses for the apps and you put your ideas in a Word document.

a. Start Word, create a new Blank document, then save the document as **OF 1-Microsoft Office Apps Uses** in the location where you store your Data Files.

b. Change the zoom factor to 120%, type **Microsoft Access**, press [Enter] twice, type **Microsoft Excel**, press [Enter] twice, type **Microsoft PowerPoint**, press [Enter] twice, type **Microsoft Word**, press [Enter] twice, then type your name.

c. Click the line beneath each program name, type at least two tasks you can perform using that program (each separated by a comma), then press [Enter].

d. Save the document, then submit your work to your instructor as directed.

e. Exit Word.

Creating a Presentation in PowerPoint 2016

CASE ▶ Reason2Go (R2G) is a voluntourism company that provides customers a unique experience of traveling to different countries and performing volunteer work. As a marketing representative for R2G, one of your responsibilities is to develop materials that describe the company vision, philosophy, and services. You have been asked to create a presentation using PowerPoint 2016 that describes projects R2G is currently developing in Kenya Africa.

Module Objectives

After completing this module, you will be able to:

- Define presentation software
- Plan an effective presentation
- Examine the PowerPoint window
- Enter slide text
- Add a new slide
- Apply a design theme
- Compare presentation views
- Print a PowerPoint presentation

Files You Will Need

No files needed.

Define Presentation Software

Presentation software (also called presentation graphics software) is a computer program you use to organize and present information to others. Presentations are typically in the form of a slide show. Whether you are explaining a new product or moderating a meeting, presentation software can help you effectively communicate your ideas. You can use PowerPoint to create informational slides that you print or display on a monitor, share in real time on the web, or save as a video for others to watch. **CASE** ▶ *You need to start working on your Kenya presentation. Because you are only somewhat familiar with PowerPoint, you get to work exploring its capabilities.* **FIGURE 1-1** *shows how a presentation looks printed as handouts.* **FIGURE 1-2** *shows how the same presentation might look shared on the Internet with others.*

DETAILS

You can easily complete the following tasks using PowerPoint:

• **Enter and edit text easily**

   Text editing and formatting commands in PowerPoint are organized by the task you are performing at the time, so you can enter, edit, and format text information simply and efficiently to produce the best results in the least amount of time.

• **Change the appearance of information**

   PowerPoint has many effects that can transform the way text, graphics, and slides appear. By exploring some of these capabilities, you discover how easy it is to change the appearance of your presentation.

• **Organize and arrange information**

   Once you start using PowerPoint, you won't have to spend much time making sure your information is correct and in the right order. With PowerPoint, you can quickly and easily rearrange and modify text, graphics, and slides in your presentation.

• **Include information from other sources**

   Often, when you create presentations, you use information from a variety of sources. With PowerPoint, you can import text, photographs, videos, numerical data, and other information from files created in programs such as Adobe Photoshop, Microsoft Word, Microsoft Excel, and Microsoft Access. You can also import information from other PowerPoint presentations as well as graphic images from a variety of sources such as the Internet, other computers, a digital camera, or other graphics programs. Always be sure you have permission to use any work that you did not create yourself.

• **Present information in a variety of ways**

   With PowerPoint, you can present information using a variety of methods. For example, you can print handout pages or an outline of your presentation for audience members. You can display your presentation as an on-screen slide show using your computer, or if you are presenting to a large group, you can use a video projector and a large screen. If you want to reach an even wider audience, you can broadcast the presentation or upload it as a video to the Internet so people anywhere in the world can use a web browser to view your presentation.

• **Collaborate with others on a presentation**

   PowerPoint makes it easy to collaborate or share a presentation with colleagues and coworkers using the Internet. You can use your email program to send a presentation as an attachment to a colleague for feedback. If you have a number of people that need to work together on a presentation, you can save the presentation to a shared workspace such as a network drive or OneDrive so authorized users in your group with an Internet connection can access the presentation.

FIGURE 1-1: PowerPoint handout

FIGURE 1-2: Presentation shared on the Internet

Using PowerPoint on a touch screen

You can use PowerPoint 2016 on a Windows computer with a touch-enabled monitor or any other compatible touch screen, such as a tablet computer. Using your fingers, you can use typical touch gestures to create, modify, and navigate presentations. To enable touch mode capabilities in PowerPoint, you need to add the Touch Mode button to the Quick Access toolbar. Click the Customize Quick Access Toolbar button, click

Touch/Mouse Mode, click the on the Quick Access toolbar then click Touch. In Touch mode, additional space is added around all of the buttons and icons in the Ribbon and the status bar to make them easier to touch. Common gestures that you can use in PowerPoint include double-tapping text to edit it and tapping a slide then dragging it to rearrange it in the presentation.

Plan an Effective Presentation

Before you create a presentation, you need to have a general idea of the information you want to communicate. PowerPoint is a powerful and flexible program that gives you the ability to start a presentation simply by entering the text of your message. If you have a specific design in mind that you want to use, you can start the presentation by working on the design. In most cases you'll probably enter the text of your presentation into PowerPoint first and then tailor the design to the message and audience. When preparing your presentation, you need to keep in mind not only who you are giving it to, but also how you are presenting it. For example, if you are giving a presentation using a projector, you need to know what other equipment you will need, such as a sound system and a projector. **CASE** ▶ *Use the planning guidelines below to help plan an effective presentation.* **FIGURE 1-3** *illustrates a storyboard for a well-planned presentation.*

DETAILS

In planning a presentation, it is important to:

• **Determine and outline the message you want to communicate**

The more time you take developing the message and outline of your presentation, the better your presentation will be in the end. A presentation with a clear message that reads like a story and is illustrated with appropriate visual aids will have the greatest impact on your audience. Start the presentation by providing a general description of the Kenyan projects currently being developed. See **FIGURE 1-3**.

• **Identify your audience and where and how you are giving the presentation**

Audience and delivery location are major factors in the type of presentation you create. For example, a presentation you develop for a staff meeting that is held in a conference room would not necessarily need to be as sophisticated or detailed as a presentation that you develop for a large audience held in an auditorium. Room lighting, natural light, screen position, and room layout all affect how the audience responds to your presentation. You might also broadcast your presentation over the Internet to several people who view the presentation on their computers in real time. This presentation will be broadcast over the Internet.

• **Determine the type of output**

Output choices for a presentation include black-and-white or color handouts for audience members, on-screen slide show, a video, or an online broadcast. Consider the time demands and computer equipment availability as you decide which output types to produce. Because this presentation will be broadcast over the Internet, the default output settings work just fine.

• **Determine the design**

Visual appeal, graphics, and presentation design work together to communicate your message. You can choose one of the professionally designed themes that come with PowerPoint, modify one of these themes, or create one of your own. You decide to choose one of PowerPoint's design themes for your presentation.

FIGURE 1-3: Storyboard of the presentation

Slide 1
Kenya Development Projects
Reason2Go

Slide 2
Priority Projects
-Insufficient water supply
-Sustainable farming methods

Slide 3
Reason2Go Travel
-Unique experiences

Photo

Slide 4
R2G Staff
- Advanced certification required
- All leaders with 10 or more years experience

Understanding copyright

Intellectual property is any idea or creation of the human mind. Copyright law is a type of intellectual property law that protects works of authorship, including books, webpages, computer games, music, artwork, and photographs. Copyright protects the expression of an idea, but not the underlying facts or concepts. In other words, the general subject matter is not protected, but how you express it is, such as when several people photograph the same sunset. Copyright attaches to any original work of authorship as soon as it is created, you do not have to register it with the Copyright Office or display the copyright symbol, ©. Fair use is an exception to copyright and permits the public to use copyrighted material for certain purposes without obtaining prior consent from the owner. Determining whether fair use applies to a work depends on its purpose, the nature of the work, how much of the work you want to copy, and the effect on the work's value. Unauthorized use of protected work (such as downloading a photo or a song from the web) is known as copyright infringement and can lead to legal action.

**Learning
Outcomes**
• Explain PowerPoint
window elements

Examine the PowerPoint Window

When you first start PowerPoint, you have the ability to choose what kind of presentation you want to use to start—a blank one, or one with a preformatted design. You can also open and work on an existing presentation. PowerPoint has different **views** that allow you to see your presentation in different forms. By default, the PowerPoint window opens in **Normal view**, which is the primary view that you use to write, edit, and design your presentation. Normal view is divided into areas called **panes**: the pane on the left, called the **Slides tab**, displays the slides of your presentation as small images, called **slide thumbnails**. The large pane is the Slide pane where you do most of your work on the slide. **CASE** ▶ *The PowerPoint window and the specific parts of Normal view are described below.*

STEPS

1. **Start** PowerPoint 2016

    PowerPoint starts and the PowerPoint start screen opens, as shown in **FIGURE 1-4**.

2. **Click the** Blank Presentation slide thumbnail

    The PowerPoint window opens in Normal view, as shown in **FIGURE 1-5**.

DETAILS

TROUBLE ▶
If you are unsure how to start PowerPoint, refer to the "Getting Started with Office 2016" Module in this book for specific instructions on how to start the application.

Using Figure 1-5 as a guide, examine the elements of the PowerPoint window, then find and compare the elements described below:

• The **Ribbon** is a wide band spanning the top of the PowerPoint window that organizes all of PowerPoint's primary commands. Each set of primary commands is identified by a **tab**; for example, the Home tab is selected by default, as shown in **FIGURE 1-5**. Commands are further arranged into **groups** on the Ribbon based on their function. So, for example, text formatting commands such as Bold, Underline, and Italic are located on the Home tab, in the Font group.

• The **Slides tab** is to the left. You can navigate through the slides in your presentation by clicking the slide thumbnails. You can also add, delete, or rearrange slides using this pane.

• The **Slide pane** displays the current slide in your presentation.

• The **Quick Access toolbar** provides access to common commands such as Save, Undo, Redo, and Start From Beginning. The Quick Access toolbar is always visible no matter which Ribbon tab you select. Click the Customize Quick Access Toolbar button to add or remove buttons.

• The **View Shortcuts** buttons on the status bar allow you to switch quickly between PowerPoint views.

• The **Notes button** on the status bar opens the Notes pane and is used to enter text that references a slide's content. You can print these notes and refer to them when you make a presentation or use them as audience handouts. The Notes pane is not visible in Slide Show view.

• The **Comments button** on the status bar opens the Comments pane. In the Comments pane you can create, edit, select, and delete comments.

• The **status bar**, located at the bottom of the PowerPoint window, shows messages about what you are doing and seeing in PowerPoint, including which slide you are viewing and the total number of slides. In addition, the status bar displays the Zoom slider controls, the Fit slide to current window button 🔲, and other functionality information.

• The **Zoom slider** on the lower-right corner of the status bar is used to zoom the slide in and out.

FIGURE 1-4: PowerPoint start screen

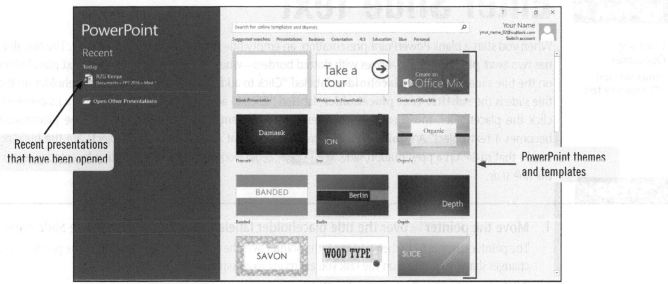

Recent presentations that have been opened

PowerPoint themes and templates

FIGURE 1-5: PowerPoint window in Normal view

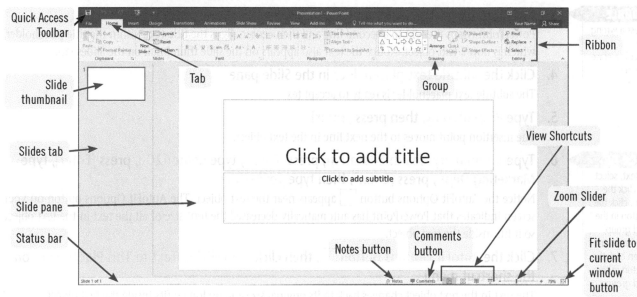

Quick Access Toolbar

Slide thumbnail

Tab

Group

Ribbon

View Shortcuts

Slides tab

Slide pane

Zoom Slider

Status bar

Notes button

Comments button

Fit slide to current window button

Viewing your presentation in gray scale or black and white

Viewing your presentation in gray scale (using shades of gray) or pure black and white is very useful when you are printing a presentation on a black-and-white printer and you want to make sure your presentation prints correctly. To see how your color presentation looks in gray scale or black and white, click the View tab, then click either the Grayscale or Black and White button in the Color/Grayscale group. Depending on which button you select, the Grayscale or the Black and White tab appears, and the Ribbon displays different settings that you can customize. If you don't like the way an individual object looks in black and white or gray scale, you can change its color. Click the object while still in Grayscale or Black and White view, then choose an option in the Change Selected Object group on the Ribbon.

Enter Slide Text

Learning Outcomes
- Enter slide text
- Change slide text

When you start a blank PowerPoint presentation, an empty title slide appears in Normal view. The title slide has two **text placeholders**—boxes with dotted borders—where you enter text. The top text placeholder on the title slide is the **title placeholder**, labeled "Click to add title". The bottom text placeholder on the title slide is the **subtitle text placeholder**, labeled "Click to add subtitle". To enter text in a placeholder, click the placeholder and then type your text. After you enter text in a placeholder, the placeholder becomes a text object. An **object** is any item on a slide that can be modified. Objects are the building blocks that make up a presentation slide. **CASE** *Begin working on your presentation by entering text on the title slide.*

STEPS

1. **Move the pointer ꝅ over the title placeholder labeled** Click to add title **in the Slide pane**

   The pointer changes to Ɪ when you move the pointer over the placeholder. In PowerPoint, the pointer often changes shape, depending on the task you are trying to accomplish.

2. **Click the** title placeholder **in the Slide pane**

   The **insertion point**, a blinking vertical line, indicates where your text appears when you type in the placeholder. A **selection box** with a dashed line border and **sizing handles** appears around the placeholder, indicating that it is selected and ready to accept text. When a placeholder or object is selected, you can change its shape or size by dragging one of the sizing handles. See **FIGURE 1-6**.

3. **Type** Community Development Projects Kenya

   PowerPoint wraps the text to a second line and then center-aligns the title text within the title placeholder, which is now a text object. Notice the text also appears on the slide thumbnail on the Slides tab.

4. **Click the** subtitle text placeholder **in the Slide pane**

   The subtitle text placeholder is ready to accept text.

5. **Type** Presented by, **then press** [Enter]

   The insertion point moves to the next line in the text object.

6. **Type** Community Health Education, **press** [Enter], **type** Reason2Go, **press** [Enter], **type** Marketing Dept., **press** [Enter], **then type** your name

   Notice the AutoFit Options button ⊞ appears near the text object. The AutoFit Options button on your screen indicates that PowerPoint has automatically decreased the font size of all the text in the text object so it fits inside the text object.

7. **Click the** AutoFit Options button ⊞, **then click** Stop Fitting Text to This Placeholder **on the shortcut menu**

   The text in the text object changes back to its original size and no longer fits inside the text object.

8. **In the subtitle text object, position** Ɪ **to the right of** Education, **drag left to select the entire line of text, press** [Backspace], **then click outside the text object in a blank area of the slide**

   The Community Health Education line of text is deleted and the AutoFit Options button menu closes, as shown in **FIGURE 1-7**. Clicking a blank area of the slide deselects all selected objects on the slide.

9. **Click the** Save button 🖫 **on the Quick Access toolbar to open Backstage view, then save the presentation as** PPT 1-R2G **in the location where you store your Data Files**

   In Backstage view, you have the option of saving your presentation to your computer or OneDrive. Notice that PowerPoint automatically entered the title of the presentation as the filename in the Save As dialog box.

FIGURE 1-6: Title text placeholder selected

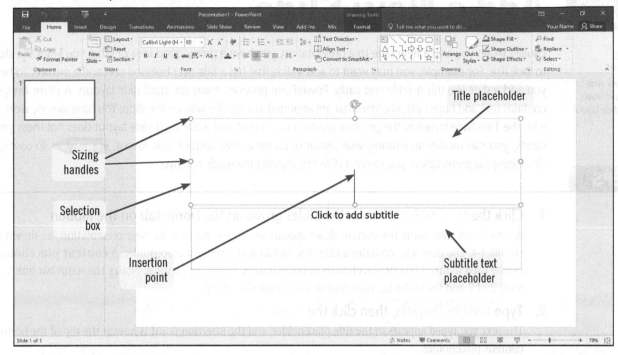

FIGURE 1-7: Text on title slide

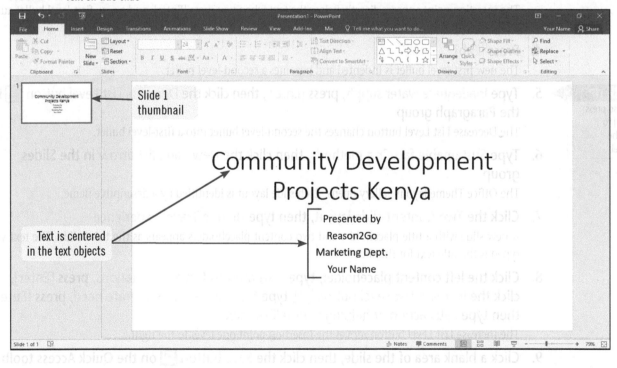

Inking a slide

In Slide View, you can add freehand pen and highlighter marks, also known as **inking**, to the slides of your presentation to emphasize information. To begin inking, go to the slide you want mark up, click the Review tab, then click the Start Inking button in the Ink group. The Pens tab appears on the Ribbon and the Pen tool appears on the slide ready for you to draw using your mouse. To customize your pen, select a different pen color, style, or thickness from options in the Pens group. Click the Highlighter button in the Write group to insert highlighter strokes on your slide. To erase inking on the slide, click the Eraser button in the Write group.

Add a New Slide

Learning Outcomes
• Add a new slide
• Indent text levels
• Modify slide layout

Usually when you add a new slide to a presentation, you have a pretty good idea of what you want the slide to look like. For example, you may want to add a slide that has a title over bulleted text and a picture. To help you add a slide like this quickly and easily, PowerPoint provides many standard slide layouts. A **slide layout** contains text and object placeholders that are arranged in a specific way on the slide. You have already worked with the Title Slide layout in the previous lesson. In the event that a standard slide layout does not meet your needs, you can modify an existing slide layout or create a new, custom slide layout. **CASE** ▸ *To continue developing the presentation, you create a slide that explains the needs in Kenya.*

STEPS

1. **Click the** New Slide button **in the Slides group on the Home tab on the Ribbon**
   A new blank slide (now the current slide) appears as the second slide in your presentation, as shown in **FIGURE 1-8**. The new slide contains a title placeholder and a content placeholder. A **content placeholder** can be used to insert text or objects such as tables, charts, videos, or pictures. Notice the status bar indicates Slide 2 of 2 and the Slides tab now contains two slide thumbnails.

2. **Type** Priority Projects, **then click the** bottom content placeholder
   The text you typed appears in the title placeholder, and the insertion point is now at the top of the bottom content placeholder.

3. **Type** Well water production, **then press** [Enter]
   The insertion point appears directly below the text when you press [Enter], and a new first-level bullet automatically appears.

4. **Press** [Tab]
   The new first-level bullet is indented and becomes a second-level bullet.

QUICK TIP
You can also press [Shift][Tab] to decrease the indent level.

5. **Type** Inadequate water supply, **press** [Enter], **then click the** Decrease List Level button ⬅ **in the Paragraph group**
   The Decrease List Level button changes the second-level bullet into a first-level bullet.

6. **Type** Sustainable farming methods, **then click the** New Slide list arrow **in the Slides group**
   The Office Theme layout gallery opens. Each slide layout is identified by a descriptive name.

7. **Click the** Two Content slide layout, **then type** Unique Travel Experience
   A new slide with a title placeholder and two content placeholders appears as the third slide. The text you typed is the title text for the slide.

8. **Click the left content placeholder, type** Adventurous travel destinations, **press** [Enter], **click the** Increase List Level button ➡, **type** Serve others in desperate need, **press** [Enter], **then type** Satisfaction of helping your fellow man
   The Increase List Level button moves the insertion point one level to the right.

9. **Click a blank area of the slide, then click the** Save button 🖫 **on the Quick Access toolbar**
   The Save button saves all of the changes to the file. Compare your screen with **FIGURE 1-9**.

FIGURE 1-8: New blank slide in Normal view

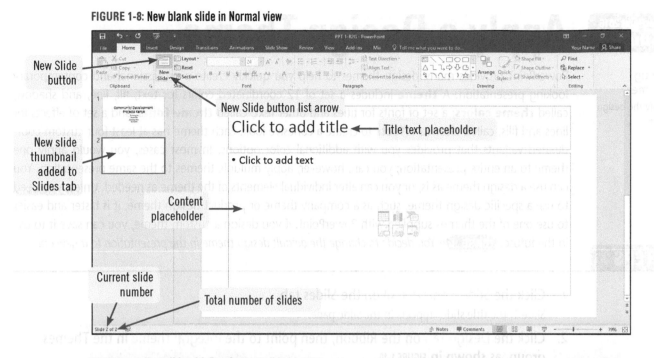

New Slide button

New slide thumbnail added to Slides tab

New Slide button list arrow

Title text placeholder

Content placeholder

Current slide number

Total number of slides

FIGURE 1-9: New slide with Two Content slide layout

Decrease List Level button

Increase List Level button

Unique Travel Experience

First-level bullet

Second-level bullet

Two content placeholders based on the slide layout

Entering and printing notes

You can add notes to your slides when there are certain facts you want to remember during a presentation or when there is additional information you want to hand out to your audience. Notes do not appear on the slides when you run a slide show. Use the Notes pane in Normal view or Notes Page view to enter notes for your slides. To open or close the Notes pane, click the Notes button on the status bar. To enter text notes on a slide, click in the Notes pane, then type. If you want to insert graphics as notes, you must use Notes Page view. To open Notes Page view, click the View tab on the Ribbon, then click

the Notes Page button in the Presentation Views group. You can print your notes by clicking the File tab on the Ribbon to open Backstage view. Click Print, click the Full Page Slides list arrow in the Settings group (this button retains the last setting for what was printed previously so it might differ) to open the gallery, and then click Notes Pages. Once you verify your print settings, click the Print button. If you don't enter any notes in the Notes pane, and print the notes pages, the slides print as large thumbnails with blank space below the thumbnails to hand write notes.

PowerPoint 2016

Apply a Design Theme

Learning Outcomes
• Modify the design theme

PowerPoint provides many design themes to help you quickly create a professional and contemporary looking presentation. A **theme** includes a set of 12 coordinated colors for text, fill, line, and shadow, called **theme colors**; a set of fonts for titles and other text, called **theme fonts**; and a set of effects for lines and fills, called **theme effects** to create a cohesive look. Each theme has at least four custom coordinated variants that provides you with additional color options. In most cases, you would apply one theme to an entire presentation; you can, however, apply multiple themes to the same presentation. You can use a design theme as is, or you can alter individual elements of the theme as needed. Unless you need to use a specific design theme, such as a company theme or product design theme, it is faster and easier to use one of the themes supplied with PowerPoint. If you design a custom theme, you can save it to use in the future. **CASE** ▶ *You decide to change the default design theme in the presentation to a new one.*

STEPS

1. **Click the** Slide 1 thumbnail **on the Slides tab**
   Slide 1, the title slide, appears in the Slide pane.

2. **Click the** Design tab **on the Ribbon, then point to the** Integral theme **in the Themes group, as shown in** FIGURE 1-10
   The Design tab appears, and a Live Preview of the Integral theme is displayed on the selected slide. A **Live Preview** allows you to see how your changes affect the slides before actually making the change. The Live Preview lasts about 1 minute, and then your slide reverts back to its original state. The first (far left) theme thumbnail identifies the current theme applied to the presentation, in this case, the default design theme called the Office Theme. The number of themes you can see in the Themes group depends on your monitor resolution and screen size.

3. **Slowly move your pointer** ▷ **over the other design themes, then click the** Themes group down scroll arrow
   A Live Preview of the theme appears on the slide each time you pass your pointer over the theme thumbnails, and a ScreenTip identifies the theme names.

4. **Move** ▷ **over the** design themes, **then click the** Wisp theme
   The Wisp design theme is applied to all the slides in the presentation. Notice the new slide background color, graphic elements, fonts, and text color. You decide this theme isn't right for this presentation.

QUICK TIP
One way to apply multiple themes to the same presentation is to click the Slide Sorter button on the status bar, select a slide or a group of slides, then click the theme.

5. **Click the** More button ⊽ **in the Themes group**
   The Themes gallery window opens. At the top of the gallery window in the This Presentation section is the current theme applied to the presentation. Notice that just the Wisp theme is listed here because when you changed the theme in the last step, you replaced the default theme with the Wisp theme. The Office section identifies all of the standard themes that come with PowerPoint.

6. **Right-click the** Slice theme **in the Office section, then click** Apply to Selected Slides
   The Slice theme is applied only to Slide 1. You like the Slice theme better, and decide to apply it to all slides.

7. **Right-click the** Slice theme **in the Themes group, then click** Apply to All Slides
   The Slice theme is applied to all three slides. Preview the next slides in the presentation to see how it looks.

8. **Click the** Next Slide button ⊽ **at the bottom of the vertical scroll bar**
   Compare your screen to FIGURE 1-11.

9. **Click the** Previous Slide button ⊼ **at the bottom of the vertical scroll bar, then save your changes**

FIGURE 1-10: Slide showing a different design theme

Current theme applied

Office theme

Design tab

Screentip

Integral theme

More button

Themes group down scroll arrow

Variants

New font type

New graphic elements

COMMUNITY DEVELOPMENT PROJECTS KENYA

Presented by
Reason2Go
Marketing Dept.
Your Name

FIGURE 1-11: Presentation with Slice theme applied

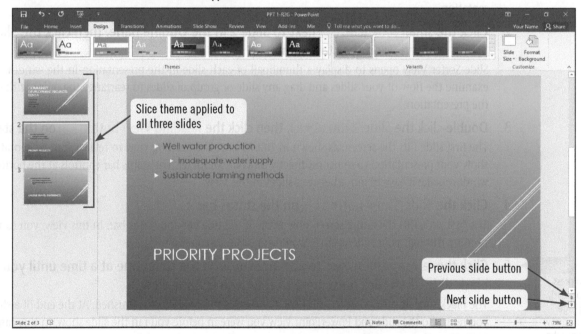

Slice theme applied to all three slides

- Well water production
  - Inadequate water supply
- Sustainable farming methods

PRIORITY PROJECTS

Previous slide button

Next slide button

Customizing themes

You are not limited to using the standard themes PowerPoint provides; you can also modify a theme to create your own custom theme. For example, you might want to incorporate your school's or company's colors on the slide background of the presentation or be able to type using fonts your company uses for brand recognition. To change an existing theme, click the View tab on the Ribbon, then click one of the Master buttons in the Master Views group. Click the Theme Colors button, the Theme Fonts button, or the Theme Effects button in the Background group to make changes to the theme, save this new theme for future use by clicking the Themes button in the Edit Themes group, then click Save Current Theme. You also have the ability to create a new font theme or color theme from scratch by clicking the Theme Fonts button or the Theme Colors button and then clicking Customize Fonts or Customize Colors. You work in the Create New Theme Fonts or Create New Theme Colors dialog box to define the custom theme fonts or colors.

Compare Presentation Views

Learning Outcomes
• Open PowerPoint views

PowerPoint has six primary views: Normal view, Outline view, Slide Sorter view, Notes Page view, Slide Show view, and Reading view. Each PowerPoint view displays your presentation in a different way and is used for different purposes. Normal view is the primary editing view where you add text, graphics, and other elements to the slides. Outline view is the view you use to focus on the text of your presentation. Slide Sorter view is primarily used to rearrange slides; however, you can also add slide effects and design themes in this view. You use Notes Page view to type notes that are important for each slide. Slide Show view displays your presentation over the whole computer screen and is designed to show your presentation to an audience. Similar to Slide Show view, Reading view is designed to view your presentation on a computer screen. To move easily among the PowerPoint views, use the View Shortcuts buttons located on the status bar and the View tab on the Ribbon. **TABLE 1-1** provides a brief description of the PowerPoint views. **CASE** *Examine each of the PowerPoint views, starting with Normal view.*

STEPS

1. **Click the View tab on the Ribbon, then click the Outline View button in the Presentation Views group**

   The presentation text is in the Outline pane on the left side of the window, as shown in **FIGURE 1-12**. Notice the status bar identifies the number of the slide you are viewing and the total number of slides in the presentation.

2. **Click the small slide icon ▢ next to Slide 2 in the Outline pane, then click the Slide Sorter button ▦ on the status bar**

   Slide Sorter View opens to display a thumbnail of each slide in the presentation in the window. You can examine the flow of your slides and drag any slide or group of slides to rearrange the order of the slides in the presentation.

3. **Double-click the Slide 1 thumbnail, then click the Reading View button 📖 on the status bar**

   The first slide fills the screen, as shown in **FIGURE 1-13**. Use Reading view to review your presentation or to show your presentation to someone directly on your computer. The status bar controls at the bottom of the window make it easy to move between slides in this view.

4. **Click the Slide Show button ▭ on the status bar**

   The first slide fills the entire screen now without the title bar and status bar. In this view, you can practice running through your slides as they would appear in a slide show.

QUICK TIP
You can also press [Enter], [Spacebar], [Page Up], [Page Down], or the arrow keys to advance the slide show.

5. **Click the left mouse button to advance through the slides one at a time until you see a black slide, then click once more to return to Outline view**

   The black slide at the end of the slide show indicates the slide show is finished. At the end of a slide show, you return to the slide and PowerPoint view you were in before you ran the slide show, in this case, Slide 1 in Outline view.

6. **Click the Notes Page button in the Presentation Views group**

   Notes Page view appears, showing a reduced image of the current slide above a large text placeholder. You can enter text in this placeholder and then print the notes page for your own use.

7. **Click the Normal button in the Presentation Views group, then click the Home tab on the Ribbon**

FIGURE 1-12: Outline view

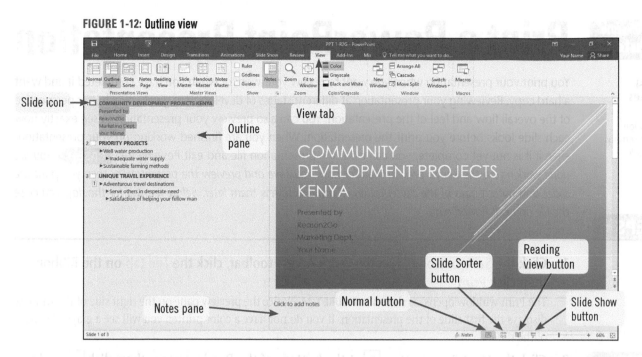

Slide icon →

View tab

Outline pane

Slide Sorter button

Reading view button

Normal button

Notes pane

Slide Show button

FIGURE 1-13: Reading view

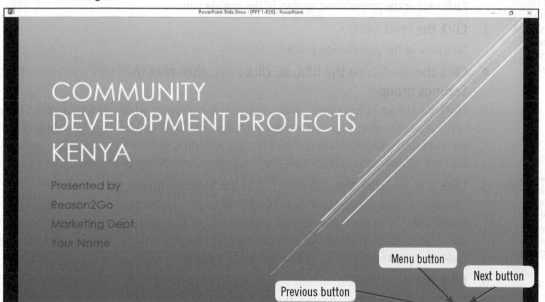

Menu button

Next button

Previous button

TABLE 1-1: PowerPoint views

view name	button	button name	displays
Normal		Normal	The Slide pane and the Slides tab at the same time
Outline View	(no View Shortcuts button)		An outline of the presentation and the Slide pane at the same time
Slide Sorter		Slide Sorter	Thumbnails of all slides
Slide Show		Slide Show	Your presentation on the whole computer screen
Reading View		Reading View	Your presentation in a large window on your computer screen
Notes Page	(no View Shortcuts button)		A reduced image of the current slide above a large text box

Creating a Presentation in PowerPoint 2016

Print a PowerPoint Presentation

Learning Outcomes
- Print a presentation
- Set print settings
- Modify color settings

You print your presentation when you want to review your work or when you have completed it and want a hard copy. Reviewing your presentation at different stages of development gives you a better perspective of the overall flow and feel of the presentation. You can also preview your presentation to see exactly how each slide looks before you print the presentation. When you are finished working on your presentation, even if it is not yet complete, you can close the presentation file and exit PowerPoint. **CASE** ▸ *You are done working on the Kenya presentation for now. You save and preview the presentation, then you print the slides and notes pages of the presentation so you can review them later. Before leaving for the day, you close the file and exit PowerPoint.*

STEPS

1. **Click the** Save button 🖫 **on the Quick Access toolbar, click the** File tab **on the Ribbon, then click** Print

   The Print window opens, as shown in **FIGURE 1-14**. Notice the preview pane on the right side of the window displays the first slide of the presentation. If you do not have a color printer, you will see a grayscale image of the slide.

QUICK TIP

To quickly print the presentation with the current Print options, add the Quick Print button to the Quick Access toolbar.

2. **Click the** Next Page button ▶ **at the bottom of the Preview pane, then click** ▶ **again**

   Each slide in the presentation appears in the preview pane.

3. **Click the** Print button

   Each slide in the presentation prints.

4. **Click the** File tab **on the Ribbon, click** Print, **then click the** Full Page Slides button **in the Settings group**

   The Print Layout gallery opens. In this gallery you can specify what you want to print (slides, handouts, notes pages, or outline), as well as other print options. To save paper when you are reviewing your slides, you can print in handout format, which lets you print up to nine slides per page. The options you choose in the Print window remain there until you change them or close the presentation.

QUICK TIP

To print slides appropriate in size for overhead transparencies, click the Design tab, click the Slide Size button in the Customize group, click Customize Slide Size, click the Slides sized for list arrow, then click Overhead.

5. **Click** 3 Slides, **click the** Color button **in the Settings group, then click** Pure Black and White

   PowerPoint removes the color and displays the slides as thumbnails next to blank lines, as shown in **FIGURE 1-15**. Using the Handouts with three slides per page printing option is a great way to print your presentation when you want to provide a way for audience members to take notes. Printing pure black-and-white prints without any gray tones can save printer toner.

6. **Click the** Print button

   The presentation prints one page showing all the slides of the presentation as thumbnails next to blank lines.

7. **Click the** File tab **on the Ribbon, then click** Close

   If you have made changes to your presentation, a Microsoft PowerPoint alert box opens asking you if you want to save changes you have made to your presentation file.

8. **Click** Save, **if necessary, to close the alert box**

   Your presentation closes.

9. **Click the** Close button ✕ **in the Title bar**

   The PowerPoint program closes, and you return to the Windows desktop.

FIGURE 1-14: Print window

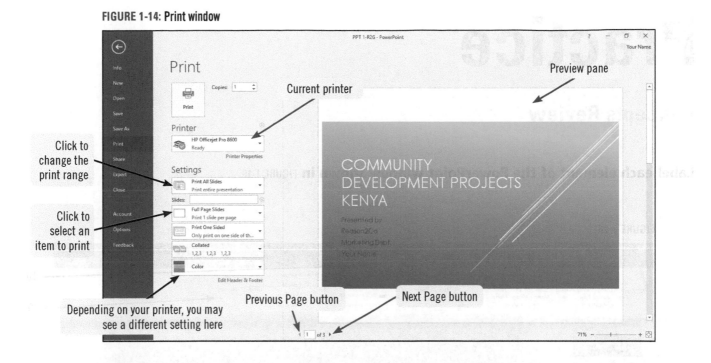

Preview pane

Current printer

Click to change the print range

Click to select an item to print

Depending on your printer, you may see a different setting here

Previous Page button

Next Page button

FIGURE 1-15: Print window with changed settings

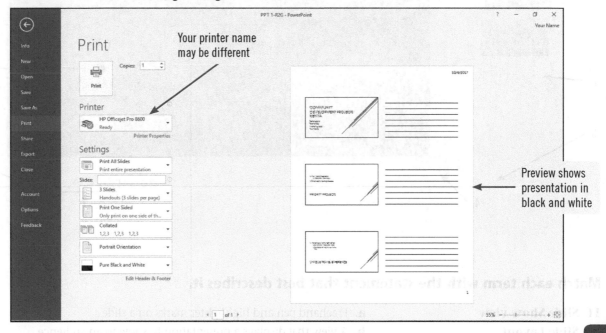

Your printer name may be different

Preview shows presentation in black and white

Microsoft Office Online Apps

Some Office programs, PowerPoint for example, include the capability to incorporate feedback—called online collaboration—across the Internet or a company network. Using **cloud computing** (work done in a virtual environment), you can take advantage of web programs called Microsoft Office Online Apps, which are simplified versions of the programs found in the Microsoft Office 2016 suite. Because these programs are online, they take up no computer disk space and are accessed using Microsoft OneDrive, a free service from Microsoft. Using Microsoft OneDrive, you and your colleagues can create and store documents in the "cloud" and make the documents available to whomever you grant access. To use Microsoft OneDrive, you need to create a free Microsoft account, which you obtain at the Microsoft website.

Practice

Concepts Review

Label each element of the PowerPoint window shown in FIGURE 1-16.

FIGURE 1-16

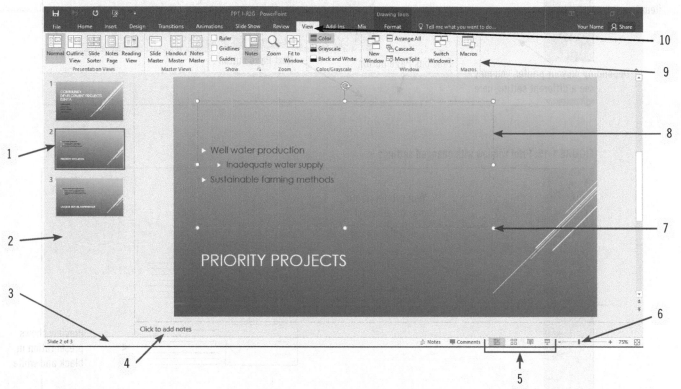

Match each term with the statement that best describes it.

11. Slide Show view	**a.** Freehand pen and highlighter marks on a slide
12. Slide Layout	**b.** A view that displays a presentation to show to an audience
13. Inking	**c.** Allows you to change the size of the slide in the window
14. Theme	**d.** Set of coordinated colors, fonts, and effects
15. Zoom slider	**e.** Placeholders arranged in a specific way on the slide
16. Text placeholder	**f.** Box with dotted border where you enter text

Select the best answer from the list of choices.

17. The view that fills the entire computer screen with each slide in the presentation is called:
    a. Outline view.
    b. Normal view.
    c. Slide Show view.
    d. Fit to window view.

18. You can enter slide text in the Slide Pane and in the _____.
    a. Reading pane
    b. Notes Page view
    c. Outline view
    d. Slides tab

19. What is the function of the slide layout?
    a. Defines how all the elements on a slide are arranged.
    b. Enables you to apply a template to the presentation.
    c. Puts all your slides in order.
    d. Shows you which themes you can apply.

20. Which of the following is not included in a design theme?
    a. Pictures
    b. Normal view
    c. Fonts
    d. Colors

21. Which button indents the insertion point to the right?
    a. Right Indent Level
    b. Increase List Level
    c. Decrease Indent Level
    d. Move Margin

22. Which status bar feature allows you to quickly switch between views?
    a. Zoom Slider
    b. View Shortcuts
    c. Fit slide to current window button
    d. Switch view button

23. What can you drag to adjust the size of an object?
    a. Rotate handle
    b. Object border point
    c. Sizing handle
    d. Selection box

24. What are the basic building blocks of any presentation?
    a. Placeholders
    b. Objects
    c. Slides
    d. Graphics

Skills Review

1. **Examine the PowerPoint window.**
   a. Start PowerPoint, if necessary then open a new blank presentation.
   b. Identify as many elements of the PowerPoint window as you can without referring to the lessons in this module.
   c. Be able to describe the purpose or function of each element.
   d. For any elements you cannot identify, refer to the lessons in this module.

2. **Enter slide text.**
   a. In the Slide pane in Normal view, enter the text **Nelsonville** in the title placeholder.
   b. In the subtitle text placeholder, enter **Wyoming Ghost Town Preservation Society**.
   c. On the next line of the placeholder, enter your name.
   d. Deselect the text object.
   e. Save the presentation using the filename **PPT 1-Nelsonville** to location where you store your Data Files.

Skills Review (continued)

3. Add a new slide.

   a. Create a new slide.

   b. Using **FIGURE 1-17**, enter text on the slide.

   c. Create another new slide.

   d. Using **FIGURE 1-18**, enter text on the slide.

   e. Save your changes.

4. Apply a design theme.

   a. Click the Design tab.

   b. Click the Themes group More button, then point to all of the themes.

   c. Locate the Ion Boardroom theme, then apply it to the selected slide.

   d. Select Slide 1.

   e. Locate the Wisp theme, then apply it to Slide 1.

   f. Apply the Wisp theme to all of the slides in the presentation.

   g. Use the Next Slide button to move to Slide 3, then save your changes.

5. Compare presentation views.

   a. Click the View tab, then click the Outline View button in the Presentation Views group.

   b. Click the Slide Sorter button in the Presentation Views group.

   c. Click the Notes Page button in the Presentation Views group, then click the Previous Slide button twice.

   d. Click the Reading View button in the Presentation Views group, then click the Next button on the status bar.

   e. Click the Normal button on the status bar, then click the Slide Show button.

   f. Advance the slides until a black screen appears, then click to end the presentation.

   g. Save your changes.

6. Print a PowerPoint presentation.

   a. Print all the slides as handouts, 3 Slides, in color.

   b. Print the presentation outline.

   c. Close the file, saving your changes.

   d. Exit PowerPoint.

FIGURE 1-17

Nelsonville's Settlers

- First wagon train left Tennessee in Aug. 1854
  - Expedition led by the Thomas Leslie, James Rowley, and Benjamin Lane families
  - 18 separate families made the trip
  - Wagon train split into two groups due to illness
- First wagons arrived in Wyoming Nov. 1854
  - During trip 5 people died and 1 baby delivered
  - Settlers defended themselves against 2 Indian raids in Nebraska
  - Wyoming area settled known by locals as "Four Trees Crossing"

FIGURE 1-18

Nelsonville Hotel & Bar History

- Built by John Nelson in 1868
  - Constructed from local lodgepole and ponderosa pine
  - Sold cattle and land for construction capital
- Continuously operated from 1870 to 1929
  - Featured 14 double rooms and 1 bridal suite
  - Restaurant, bath house, and barber shop eventually added to property
  - Featured gambling tables until 1911

Independent Challenge 1

You work for RuraLink Systems, a business that offers rural broadband Internet service and network server management. One of your jobs at the company is to present the company's services to local government and community meetings. Your boss has asked you to create a company profile presentation that describes company goals and services.

a. Start PowerPoint then open a new blank presentation.

b. In the title placeholder on Slide 1, type **RuraLink Systems**.

c. In the subtitle placeholder, type your name, press [Enter], then type today's date.

d. Apply the Ion Boardroom design theme to the presentation.

e. Save your presentation with the filename **PPT 1-RuraLink** to the location where you store your Data Files.

f. Use **FIGURE 1-19** and **FIGURE 1-20** to add two more slides to your presentation. (*Hint*: Slide 3 uses the Comparison layout.)

g. Use the buttons on the View tab to switch between all of PowerPoint's views.

h. Print the presentation using handouts, 3 Slides, in black and white.

i. Save and close the file, then exit PowerPoint.

FIGURE 1-19

RuraLink Service Goals

▶ Prompt & reliable service
▶ Provide only necessary services to complete job
▶ Work done on time and within budget
▶ Comply with all relevant regulatory agencies
▶ Superior network server management
▶ 100% Satisfaction guarantee

FIGURE 1-20

Basic Services

Installation Services
▶ Location assessment
▶ Free estimates
▶ 50% off full installation
▶ Latest technology provided
▶ Guaranteed workmanship

Client Services
▶ 24-hr customer service
▶ 24-hr emergency service
▶ Complete documentation back-up services available

Independent Challenge 2

You have recently been promoted to sales manager at General Hardwood Industries, which sells and distributes specialty hardwood products used in flooring, cabinets, and furniture. Part of your job is to present company sales figures at a yearly sales meeting. Use the following information as the basis for units of wood sold nationally in your presentation: 501 units cherry, 429 units birch, 95 units hickory, 742 units mahogany, 182 units Brazilian walnut, 401 units American walnut, and 269 units pine. Assume that General Hardwood has five sales regions throughout the country: Pacific Northwest, West, South, Midwest, and Northeast. Also, assume the sales in each region rose between 1.2% and 3.6% over last year, and gross sales reached $31 million. The presentation should have at least five slides.

a. Spend some time planning the slides of your presentation. What is the best way to show the information provided? What other information could you add that might be useful for this presentation?

b. Start PowerPoint.

c. Give the presentation an appropriate title on the title slide, and enter today's date and your name in the subtitle placeholder.

d. Add slides and enter appropriate slide text.

e. On the last slide of the presentation, include the following information:

   General Hardwood Industries
   "Your specialty hardwood store"

f. Apply a design theme. A typical slide might look like the one shown in **FIGURE 1-21**.

g. Switch views. Run through the slide show at least once.

h. Save your presentation with the filename **PPT 1-General** where you store your Data Files.

i. Close the presentation and exit PowerPoint.

FIGURE 1-21

Overall View

- This year's sales
  - $31 million gross sales
- By region
  - Pacific Northwest +2.2%
  - West +2.7%
  - South +1.2%
  - Midwest +3.0%
  - Northeast +2.1%

Independent Challenge 3

You work for Janic Corporation, an international trade company that distributes products made in the Midwest. The marketing manager has asked you to plan and create a PowerPoint presentation that describes the primary products Janic exports and the top 3 importing countries; Saudi Arabia, Mexico, and Japan. Describe the top exports, which include tractors, fresh and frozen pork meat, soybeans, corn, and aircraft engine parts. Use the Internet, if possible, to research information that will help you formulate your ideas. The presentation should have at least five slides.

a. Spend some time planning the slides of your presentation.

b. Start PowerPoint then open a new blank presentation.

c. Give the presentation an appropriate title on the title slide, and enter today's date and your name in the subtitle placeholder.

d. Add slides and enter appropriate slide text.

e. On the last slide of the presentation, type the following information:

   Janic Corp.
   Est. 1948
   Headquarters: Independence, MO

f. Apply a design theme.

g. Switch views. Run through the slide show at least once.

h. Save your presentation with the filename **PPT 1-Janic** to the location where you store your Data Files.

i. Close the presentation and exit PowerPoint.

Independent Challenge 4: Explore

You are a member of the Chattanooga Service Organization (CSO), a non profit organization in Chattanooga, TN. This organization raises money throughout the year to support community needs such as schools, youth organizations, and other worthy causes. This year CSO has decided to support the Penhale Youth Center by hosting a regional barbeque cook-off, called the Ultimate BBQ Cook-Off. The competition includes over 20 cooking teams from a five-state region. Create a presentation that describes the event.

a. Spend some time planning the slides of your presentation. Assume the following: the competition is a 2-day event; event advertising will be multistate wide; musical groups will be invited; there will be events and games for kids; the event will be held at the county fairgrounds. Use the Internet, if possible, to research information that will help you formulate your ideas.

b. Start PowerPoint then open a new blank presentation.

c. Give the presentation an appropriate title on the title slide, and enter your name and today's date in the subtitle placeholder.

d. Add slides and enter appropriate slide text. You must create at least three slides.

e. Apply a Design Theme. Typical slides might look like the ones shown in **FIGURE 1-22** and **FIGURE 1-23**.

f. View the presentation.

g. Save your presentation with the filename **PPT 1-CSO** to the location where you store your Data Files.

h. Close the presentation and exit PowerPoint.

FIGURE 1-22

Schedule

Sat & Sun
- 9:00am – Open gates
- 10:00am – Music on Stage 1
- 10:30am – Special kid events in Roundhouse
- 10:30am – Food prep demonstrations
- 11:30am – Music on Stage 1
- 12:00pm – Food testing and judging begins
- 2:00pm – Special guest on main stage

FIGURE 1-23

Judging Times & Categories

Saturday – Prelims
- 12:00pm – Sauces
- 1:15pm – Chicken
- 2:00pm – Brisket
- 3:15pm – Ribs

Sunday – Finals
- 12:00pm – Sauces
- 12:30pm – Chicken
- 2:30pm – Brisket
- 3:30pm – Ribs
- 5:00pm – Winner's Cook-off Round

Visual Workshop

Create the presentation shown in **FIGURE 1-24** and **FIGURE 1-25**. Make sure you include your name on the title slide. Save the presentation as **PPT 1-Neptune** to the location where you store your Data Files. Print the slides.

FIGURE 1-24

NEPTUNE INDUSTRIES   Your Name
Senior Project Manager

FIGURE 1-25

PRODUCT OVERVIEW

Product designation: Genford XDS-2000
- Turf reduction device
- Primary guidance system: global positioning system

Systems tested
- Integrated on-board computer system
- Engine and hydraulics
- Turf reduction components
- Obstacle detection system

Modifying a Presentation

You continue working on your Kenya Africa projects presentation. In this module, you'll enter text using Outline view, then you'll format text, create a SmartArt graphic, draw and modify objects, and add slide footer information in the presentation.

Module Objectives

After completing this module, you will be able to:

- Enter text in Outline view
- Format text
- Convert text to SmartArt
- Insert and modify shapes

- Rearrange and merge shapes
- Edit and duplicate shapes
- Align and group objects
- Add slide footers

Files You Will Need

PPT 2-1.pptx	PPT 2-4.pptx
PPT 2-2.pptx	PPT 2-5.pptx
PPT 2-3.pptx	

Enter Text in Outline View

Learning Outcomes
• Enter text in Outline view
• Create a new slide

You can enter presentation text by typing directly on the slide in the Slide pane, or, if you need to focus on the text of the presentation, you can enter text in Outline view. Text in Outline view is organized so the headings, or slide titles, appear at the top of the outline. Each subpoint, or each line of bulleted text, appears as one or more indented lines under the title. Each indent in the outline creates another level of bulleted text on the slide. **CASE** ▶ *You switch to Outline view to enter text for two more slides for your presentation.*

STEPS

1. **Start PowerPoint, open the presentation** PPT 2-1.pptx **from the location where you store your Data Files, then save it as** PPT 2-R2G.pptx
   A presentation with the new name appears in the PowerPoint window.

2. **Click the** Slide 2 thumbnail **in the Slides tab, click the** New Slide button list arrow **in the Slides group, then click** Title and Content
   A new slide, Slide 3, with the Title and Content layout appears as the current slide below Slide 2.

3. **Click the** View tab **on the Ribbon, then click the** Outline View button **in the Presentation Views group**
   The text of the presentation appears in the Outline pane next to the Slide pane. The slide icon and the insertion point for Slide 3 are highlighted, indicating it is selected and ready to accept text. Text that you enter next to a slide icon becomes the title for that slide.

4. **Type** Water: The Strategic Commodity, **press** [Enter], **then press** [Tab]
   When you pressed [Enter] after typing the slide title, you created a new slide. However, because you want to enter bulleted text on Slide 3, you then pressed [Tab] so the text you type will be entered as bullet text on Slide 3. See **FIGURE 2-1**.

5. **Type** Economic efficiency, **press** [Enter], **type** Social fairness, **press** [Enter], **type** Sustainability, **press** [Enter], **type** Population demands, **then press** [Enter]
   Each time you press [Enter], the insertion point moves down one line.

6. **Press** [Shift][Tab]
   Because you are working in Outline view, a new slide with the same layout, Slide 4, is created when you press [Shift][Tab].

7. **Type** Water: Developmental Essentials, **press** [Ctrl][Enter], **type** Household water safety, **press** [Enter], **type** Catchment area, **press** [Enter], **type** Water quality, **press** [Enter], **then type** Conflict resolution
   Pressing [Ctrl][Enter] while the insertion point is in the title text object moves the cursor into the content placeholder.

8. **Position the pointer on the** Slide 3 icon ▢ **in the Outline pane**
   The pointer changes to ✥. The Water: The Strategic Commodity slide, Slide 3, is out of order.

9. **Drag** ▢ **down until a horizontal indicator line appears above the Slide 5 icon, then release the mouse button**
   The third slide moves down and switches places with the fourth slide, as shown in **FIGURE 2-2**.

10. **Click the** Normal button ▣ **on the status bar, then save your work**
    The Outline pane closes, and the Slides tab is now visible in the window.

FIGURE 2-1: Outline view showing new slide

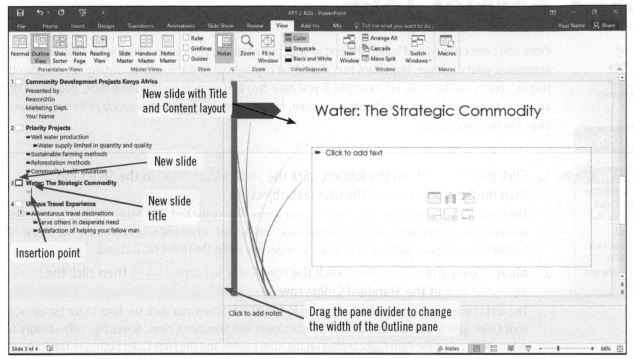

New slide with Title and Content layout

Water: The Strategic Commodity

New slide

New slide title

Insertion point

Drag the pane divider to change the width of the Outline pane

FIGURE 2-2: Outline view showing moved slide

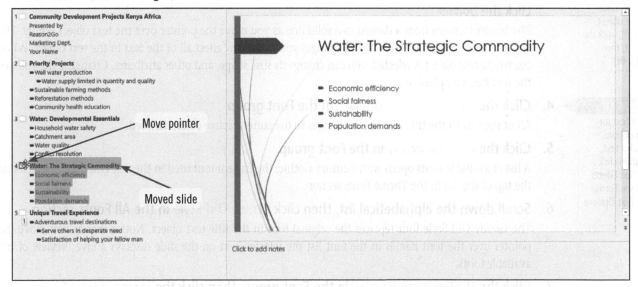

Move pointer

Moved slide

Water: The Strategic Commodity

- Economic efficiency
- Social fairness
- Sustainability
- Population demands

Using proofing tools for other languages

If you have a presentation in another language, how would you check the spelling and grammar of that presentation? Every version of PowerPoint contains a language pack with a primary language, such as English, Italian, or Arabic. Each language pack includes additional languages other than the primary language. For example, the English language pack also includes French and Spanish. So, let's say you have an English version of PowerPoint and you want to check the spelling of a presentation that is written in French. To check the spelling of a French presentation, click a text object on a slide, click the Review tab on the Ribbon, click the Language button in the Language group, then click Set Proofing Language to open the Language dialog box. Click one of the French options from the list, then click OK. Only languages in the list with a spelling symbol are available to use for checking spelling and grammar. Now when you check the spelling, PowerPoint will do so in French. If your version of PowerPoint does not have the language you want to use, you can purchase additional language packs from Microsoft.

Format Text

Learning Outcomes
• Modify text characteristics

Once you have entered and edited the text in your presentation, you can modify the way the text looks to emphasize your message. Important text should be highlighted in some way to distinguish it from other text or objects on the slide. For example, if you have two text objects on the same slide, you could draw attention to one text object by changing its color, font, or size. **CASE** *You decide to format the text on Slide 5 of the presentation.*

STEPS

QUICK TIP
To show or hide the Mini toolbar, click the File tab on the Ribbon, click Options, then click the Show Mini Toolbar on selection check box.

1. **Click the** Home tab **on the Ribbon, click the** Slide 5 thumbnail **in the Slides tab, then double-click** Travel **in the title text object**

   The word "Travel" is selected, and a Mini toolbar appears above the text. The **Mini toolbar** contains basic text-formatting commands, such as bold and italic, and appears when you select text using the mouse. This toolbar makes it quick and easy to format text, especially when the Home tab is closed.

2. **Move** 🔓 **over the** Mini toolbar, **click the** Font Color list arrow 🔺▾, **then click the** Dark Red color box **in the Standard Colors row**

   The text changes color to dark red, as shown in **FIGURE 2-3**. When you click the Font Color list arrow, the Font Color gallery appears showing the Theme Colors and Standard Colors. ScreenTips help identify font colors. Notice that the Font Color button on the Mini toolbar and the Font Color button in the Font group on the Home tab change color to reflect the new color choice, which is now the active color.

QUICK TIP
To select an unselected text object, press [Shift], click the text object, then release [Shift].

3. **Move the pointer over the** title text object border **until the pointer changes to** 🔾, **then click the** border

   The border changes from a dashed to a solid line as you move the pointer over the text object border. The entire title text object is selected, and changes you make now affect all of the text in the text object. When the whole text object is selected, you can change its size, shape, and other attributes. Changing the color of the text helps emphasize it.

QUICK TIP
For more text formatting options, right-click a text object, then click Format Text Effects to open the Format Shape - Text Options pane.

4. **Click the** Font Color button 🔺▾ **in the Font group**

   All of the text in the title text object changes to the current active color, dark red.

5. **Click the** Font list arrow **in the Font group**

   A list of available fonts opens with Century Gothic, the current font used in the title text object, selected at the top of the list in the Theme Fonts section.

6. **Scroll down the alphabetical list, then click** Goudy Old Style **in the All Fonts section**

   The Goudy Old Style font replaces the original font in the title text object. Notice that as you move the pointer over the font names in the font list the selected text on the slide displays a Live Preview of the available fonts.

7. **Click the** Underline button 🔲 **in the Font group, then click the** Increase Font Size button 🔲 **in the Font group**

   All of the text now displays an underline and increases in size to 40.

8. **Click the** Character Spacing button 🔲▾ **in the Font group, then click** Tight

   The spacing between the letters in the title decreases. Compare your screen to **FIGURE 2-4**.

9. **Click a blank area of the slide outside the text object to deselect it, then save your work**

   Clicking a blank area of the slide deselects all objects that are selected.

FIGURE 2-3: Selected word with Mini toolbar open

FIGURE 2-4: Formatted text

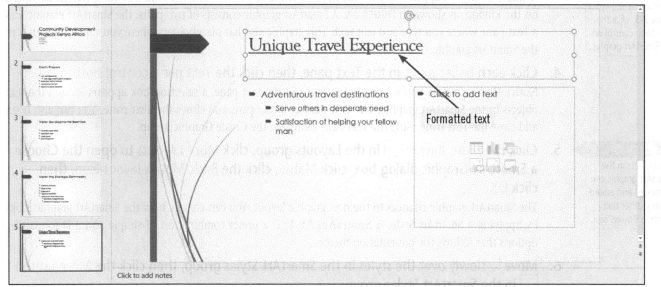

Replacing text and fonts

As you review your presentation, you may decide to replace certain text or fonts throughout the entire presentation using the Replace command. Text can be a word, phrase, or sentence. To replace specific text, click the Home tab on the Ribbon, then click the Replace button in the Editing group. In the Replace dialog box, enter the text you want to replace, then enter the text you want to use as its replacement. You can also use the Replace command to replace one font for another. Simply click the Replace button list arrow in the Editing group, then click Replace Fonts to open the Replace Font dialog box.

Modifying a Presentation

Convert Text to SmartArt

Learning
Outcomes
• Create a SmartArt
  graphic
• Modify the
  SmartArt design

Sometimes when you are working with text it just doesn't capture your attention. The ability to convert text to a SmartArt graphic provides a creative way to convey a message using text and graphics. A **SmartArt** graphic is a professional-quality diagram that graphically illustrates text. For example, you can show steps in a process or timeline, show proportional relationships, or show how parts relate to a whole. You can create a SmartArt graphic from scratch or create one by converting existing text you have entered on a slide. **CASE** *You want the presentation to appear visually dynamic, so you convert the text on Slide 3 to a SmartArt graphic.*

STEPS

1. **Click the** Slide 3 thumbnail **in the Slides tab, click** Household **in the text object, then click the** Convert to SmartArt Graphic button **in the Paragraph group**

   A gallery of SmartArt graphic layouts opens. As with many features in PowerPoint, you can preview how your text will look prior to applying the SmartArt graphic layout by using PowerPoint's Live Preview feature. You can review each SmartArt graphic layout and see how it changes the appearance of the text.

2. **Move** 🖑 **over the** SmartArt graphic layouts **in the gallery**

   Notice how the text becomes part of the graphic and the color and font changes each time you move the pointer over a different graphic layout. SmartArt graphic names appear in ScreenTips.

TROUBLE
If the Text pane is not open as shown in Figure 2-5, click the Text pane control on the SmartArt graphic.

3. **Click the** Basic Process layout **in the SmartArt graphics gallery**

   A SmartArt graphic appears on the slide in place of the text object, and the SmartArt Tools Design tab opens on the Ribbon, as shown in **FIGURE 2-5**. A SmartArt graphic consists of two parts: the SmartArt graphic and a Text pane where you type and edit text. This graphic also has placeholders where you can add pictures to the SmartArt graphic.

4. **Click each** bullet point **in the Text pane, then click the** Text pane control button ⟩

   Notice that each time you select a bullet point in the text pane, a selection box appears around the text objects in the SmartArt graphic. The Text pane control opens and closes the Text pane. You can also open and close the Text pane using the Text Pane button in the Create Graphic group.

QUICK TIP
Text objects in the SmartArt graphic can be moved and edited like any other text object in PowerPoint.

5. **Click the** More button ⊽ **in the Layouts group, click** More Layouts **to open the Choose a SmartArt Graphic dialog box, click** Matrix, **click the** Basic Matrix layout icon, **then click** OK

   The SmartArt graphic changes to the new graphic layout. You can change how the SmartArt graphic looks by applying a SmartArt Style. A **SmartArt Style** is a preset combination of simple and 3-D formatting options that follows the presentation theme.

6. **Move** 🖑 **slowly over the styles in the SmartArt Styles group, then click the** More button ⊽ **in the SmartArt Styles group**

   A Live Preview of each style is displayed on the SmartArt graphic. The SmartArt styles are organized into sections; the top group offers suggestions for the best match for the document, and the bottom group shows you all of the possible 3-D styles that are available.

QUICK TIP
Click the Convert button in the Reset group, then click Convert to Text to revert the SmartArt graphic to a standard text object.

7. **Move** 🖑 **over the styles in the gallery, click** Intense Effect **in the Best Match for Document section, then click in a blank area of the slide outside the SmartArt graphic**

   Notice how this new style adds a shadow to each object to achieve a dimensional effect. Compare your screen to **FIGURE 2-6**.

8. **Click the** Slide 4 thumbnail **in the Slides tab, then save your work**

   Slide 4 appears in the Slide pane.

FIGURE 2-5: Text converted to a SmartArt graphic

Text Pane button

More button

SmartArt graphic

Text pane control

Text pane

FIGURE 2-6: Final SmartArt graphic

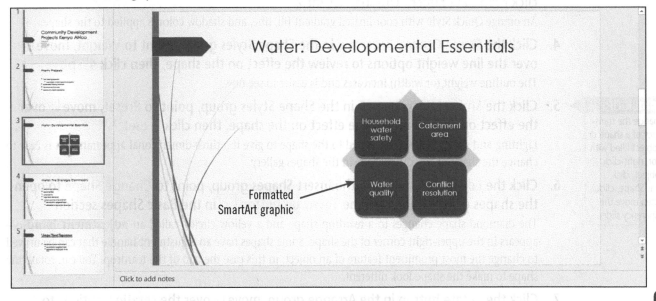

Formatted SmartArt graphic

Choosing SmartArt graphics

When choosing a SmartArt graphic to use on your slide, remember that you want the SmartArt graphic to communicate the message of the text effectively; not every SmartArt graphic layout achieves that goal. You must consider the type of text you want to illustrate. For example, does the text show steps in a process, does it show a continual process, or does it show nonsequential information? The answer to this question will dictate the type of SmartArt graphic layout you should choose. Also, the amount of text you want to illustrate will have an effect on the SmartArt graphic layout you choose. Most of the time key points will be the text you use in a SmartArt graphic. Finally, some SmartArt graphic layouts are limited by the number of shapes they can accommodate, so be sure to choose a graphic layout that can illustrate your text appropriately. Experiment with the SmartArt graphic layouts until you find the right one, and have fun in the process!

Insert and Modify Shapes

Learning
Outcomes
• Create a shape
• Modify a shape's
  style

In PowerPoint you can insert many different types of shapes including lines, geometric figures, arrows, stars, callouts, and banners to enhance your presentation. You can modify many aspects of a shape including its fill color, line color, and line style, as well as add shadows and 3-D effects. A quick way to alter the appearance of a shape is to apply a Quick Style. A **Quick Style** is a set of formatting options, including line style, fill color, and effects. **CASE** ▶ *You decide to draw some shapes on Slide 4 of your presentation that identify strategies for increasing water supply.*

STEPS

1. **Click the More button ▼ in the Drawing group, click the Diamond button ◇ in the Basic Shapes section, then position ┼ in the blank area of Slide 4 below the slide title**
    ScreenTips help you identify the shapes.

TROUBLE
If your shape is not approximately the same size as the one shown in Figure 2-7, press [Shift], then drag one of the corner sizing handles to resize the object.

2. **Press and hold [Shift], drag ┼ down and to the right to create the shape, as shown in FIGURE 2-7, release the mouse button, then release [Shift]**
    A diamond shape appears on the slide, filled with the default theme color. Pressing [Shift] while you create the object maintains the object proportions as you change its size. A **rotate handle**—circular arrow—appears on top of the shape, which you can drag to manually rotate the shape. To change the style of the shape, apply a Quick Style from the Shape Styles group.

3. **Click the Drawing Tools Format tab on the Ribbon, click the ▼ in the Shape Styles group, move ⬚ over the styles in the gallery to review the effects on the shape, then click Moderate Effect - Orange, Accent 2**
    An orange Quick Style with coordinated gradient fill, line, and shadow color is applied to the shape.

4. **Click the Shape Outline list arrow in the Shape Styles group, point to Weight, move ⬚ over the line weight options to review the effect on the shape, then click 4½ pt**
    The outline weight (or width) increases and is easier to see now.

QUICK TIP
To change the transparency of a shape or text object filled with a color, right-click the object, click Format Shape, click Fill, then move the Transparency slider.

5. **Click the Shape Effects button in the Shape Styles group, point to Preset, move ⬚ over the effect options to review the effect on the shape, then click Preset 7**
    Lighting and shadow effects are added to the shape to give it a three-dimensional appearance. It is easy to change the shape to any other shape in the shapes gallery.

6. **Click the Edit Shape button in the Insert Shapes group, point to Change Shape to open the shapes gallery, then click the Teardrop button ◯ in the Basic Shapes section**
    The diamond shape changes to a teardrop shape and a yellow circle—called an **adjustment handle**—appears in the upper-right corner of the shape. Some shapes have an adjustment handle that can be moved to change the most prominent feature of an object, in this case the end of the teardrop. You can rotate the shape to make the shape look different.

7. **Click the Rotate button in the Arrange group, move ⬚ over the rotation options to review the effect on the shape, then click Flip Horizontal**
    Notice that the adjustment handle is now on the top left of the shape, indicating that the shape has flipped horizontally, or rotated 180 degrees, as shown in FIGURE 2-8. You prefer the diamond shape, and you decide the shape looks better rotated back the way it was before.

8. **Click the Undo button list arrow ↺ ▾ in the Quick Access Toolbar, click Change Shape, click a blank area of the slide, then save your work**
    The last two commands you performed are undone, and the shape changes back to a diamond and is flipped back to its original position. Clicking a blank area of the slide deselects all selected objects.

FIGURE 2-7: Diamond shape added to slide

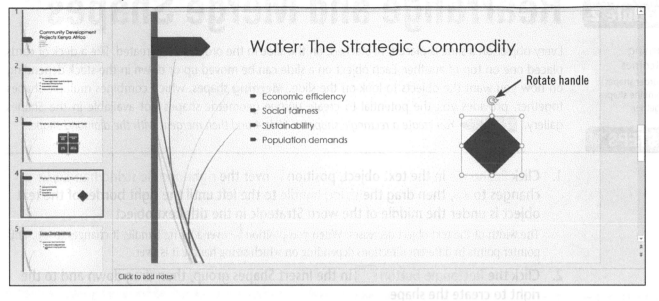

FIGURE 2-8: Rotated teardrop shape

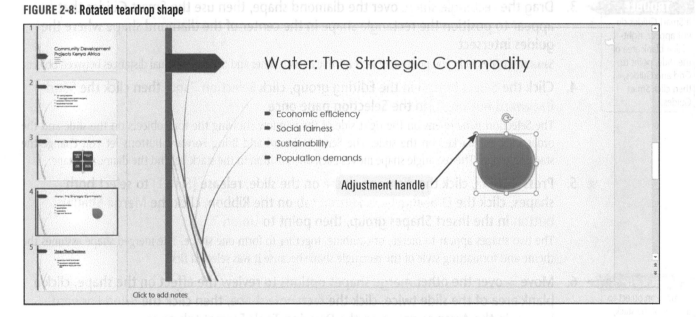

Using the Eyedropper to match colors

As you develop your presentation and work with different shapes and pictures, sometimes from other sources, there may be a certain color that is not in the theme colors of the presentation that you want to capture and apply to objects in your presentation. To capture a color on a specific slide, select any object on the slide, click any button list arrow with a color feature, such as the Shape Fill button or the Shape Outline button on the Drawing Tools Format tab, then click Eyedropper. Move the 🖋 over the color you want to capture and pause, or hover. As you hover over a color, a Live Preview of the color appears and the RGB (Red Green Blue) values, called coordinates, appear in a ScreenTip. Click when you see the color you want to capture. The new color now appears in any color gallery under Recent Colors. If you decide not to capture a new color, press [Esc] to close the Eyedropper without making any change.

Rearrange and Merge Shapes

Learning Outcomes
• Reorder shapes
• Combine shapes together

Every object on a slide is placed, or stacked, on the slide in the order it was created, like a deck of cards placed one on top of another. Each object on a slide can be moved up or down in the stack depending on how you want the objects to look on the slide. **Merging** shapes, which combines multiple shapes together, provides you the potential to create unique geometric shapes not available in the Shapes gallery. **CASE** *You create a rectangle shape on Slide 4 and then merge it with the diamond shape.*

STEPS

1. **Click Economic in the text object, position ⬚ over the right-middle sizing handle, ⬚ changes to ↔, then drag the sizing handle to the left until the right border of the text object is under the middle of the word Strategic in the title text object**

   The width of the text object decreases. When you position ⬚ over a sizing handle, it changes to ↔. This pointer points in different directions depending on which sizing handle it is over.

2. **Click the Rectangle button ⬚ in the Insert Shapes group, then drag down and to the right to create the shape**

   Compare your screen to **FIGURE 2-9**. A rectangle shape appears on the slide, filled with the default theme color. You can move shapes by dragging them on the slide.

3. **Drag the rectangle shape over the diamond shape, then use the Smart Guides that appear to position the rectangle shape in the center of the diamond shape where the guides intersect**

   Smart Guides help you position objects relative to each other and determine equal distances between objects.

4. **Click the Select button in the Editing group, click Selection Pane, then click the Send Backward button ▼ in the Selection pane once**

   The Selection pane opens on the right side of the window showing the four objects on the slide and the order they are stacked on the slide. The Send Backward and Bring Forward buttons let you change the stacking order. The rectangle shape moves back one position in the stack behind the diamond shape.

5. **Press [SHIFT], click the diamond shape on the slide, release [SHIFT] to select both shapes, click the Drawing Tools Format tab on the Ribbon, click the Merge Shapes button in the Insert Shapes group, then point to Union**

   The two shapes appear to merge, or combine, together to form one shape. The merged shape assumes the theme and formatting style of the rectangle shape because it was selected first.

6. **Move ⬚ over the other merge shapes options to review the effect on the shape, click a blank area of the slide twice, click the rectangle shape, then click the Bring Forward button in the Arrange group on the Drawing Tools Format tab once**

   Each merge option produces a different result. The rectangle shape moves back to the top of the stack. Now, you want to see what happens when you select the diamond shape first before you merge the two shapes together.

7. **Click the diamond shape, press [SHIFT], click the rectangle shape, release [SHIFT], click the Merge Shapes button in the Insert Shapes group, then point to Union**

   The merged shape adopts the theme and formatting style of the diamond shape.

8. **Point to each of the merge shapes options, then click Subtract**

   The two shapes merge into one shape. This merge option deletes the area of all shapes from the first shape you selected, so in this case the area of the rectangle shape is deleted from the diamond shape. The merged shape is identified as Freeform 5 in the Selection pane. See **FIGURE 2-10**.

9. **Click the Selection Pane button in the Arrange group, click a blank area of the slide, then save your work**

FIGURE 2-9: Rectangle shape added to slide

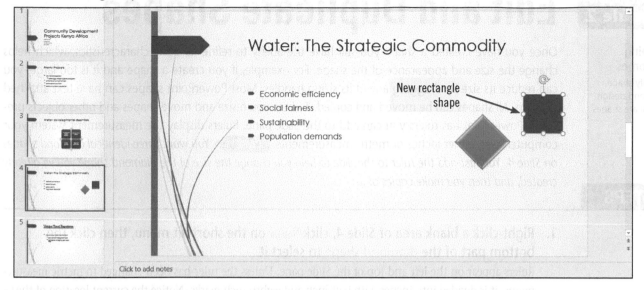

FIGURE 2-10: New Merged shape

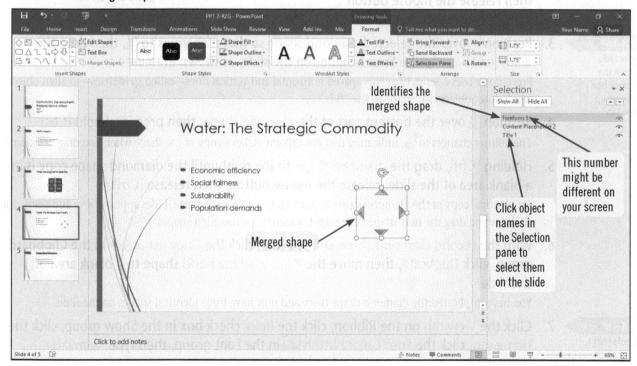

Changing the size and position of shapes

Usually when you resize a shape you can simply drag one of the sizing handles around the outside of the shape, but sometimes you may need to resize a shape more precisely. When you select a shape, the Drawing Tools Format tab appears on the Ribbon, offering you many different formatting options including some

sizing commands located in the Size group. The Width and Height commands in the Size group allow you to change the width and height of a shape. You also have the option to open the Format Shape pane, which allows you to change the size of a shape, as well as the rotation, scale, and position of a shape on the slide.

Edit and Duplicate Shapes

Learning Outcomes
• Modify shape, size, and design
• Duplicate shapes

Once you have created a shape you still have the ability to refine its basic characteristics, which helps change the size and appearance of the shape. For example, if you create a shape and it is too large, you can reduce its size by dragging any of its sizing handles. Most PowerPoint shapes can have text attached to them. All shapes can be moved and copied. To help you resize and move shapes and other objects precisely, PowerPoint has rulers you can add to the Slide pane. Rulers display the measurement system your computer uses, either inches or metric measurements. **CASE** *You want three identical diamond shapes on Slide 4. You first add the ruler to the slide to help you change the size of the diamond shape you've already created, and then you make copies of it.*

STEPS

1. **Right-click a blank area of Slide 4, click Ruler on the shortcut menu, then click the bottom part of the diamond shape to select it**

   Rulers appear on the left and top of the Slide pane. Unless the ruler has been changed to metric measurements, it is divided into inches with half-inch and eighth-inch marks. Notice the current location of the ⊾ is identified on both rulers by a small dotted red line in the ruler.

2. **Drag the middle left sizing handle on the diamond shape to the left approximately ½", then release the mouse button**

   The diamond shape is now slightly larger in diameter.

QUICK TIP
To display or hide gridlines, click the Gridlines check box in the Show group on the View tab.

3. **Position ⊾ over the selected diamond shape so that it changes to ⁺⁞₃, then drag the diamond shape to the Smart Guides on the slide, as shown in FIGURE 2-11**

   PowerPoint uses a series of evenly spaced horizontal and vertical lines—called **gridlines**—to align objects, which force objects to "snap" to the grid.

4. **Position ⁺⁞₃ over the bottom part of the diamond shape, then press and hold [Ctrl]**

   The pointer changes to ⁺⁞₃, indicating that PowerPoint makes a copy of the shape when you drag the mouse.

5. **Holding [Ctrl], drag the diamond shape to the right until the diamond shape copy is in a blank area of the slide, release the mouse button, then release [Ctrl]**

   An identical copy of the diamond shape appears on the slide and Smart Guides appear above and below the shape as you drag the new shape to the right, which helps you align shapes.

6. **With the second diamond shape still selected, click the Copy list arrow in the Clipboard group, click Duplicate, then move the duplicated diamond shape to a blank area of the slide**

   You have duplicated the diamond shape twice and now have three identical shapes on the slide.

QUICK TIP
Press and hold [Alt] to temporarily turn the snap-to-grid feature off while dragging objects on the slide or dragging a sizing handle to make precise adjustments.

7. **Click the View tab on the Ribbon, click the Ruler check box in the Show group, click the Home tab, click the Font Color button 🔺 in the Font group, then type Rainwater Harvesting**

   The ruler closes, and the text you type appears in the selected diamond shape and becomes a part of the shape. Now if you move or rotate the shape, the text moves with it. Compare your screen with **FIGURE 2-12**.

8. **Click the left diamond shape, click 🔺, type Salt Removal, click the right diamond shape, click 🔺, type Continuous Water Use, click in a blank area of the slide, then save your work**

   All three diamond shapes include text.

FIGURE 2-11: Merged shape moved on slide

FIGURE 2-12: Duplicated shapes

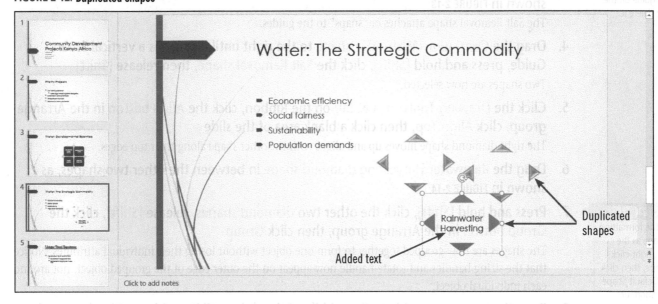

Editing points of a shape

If you want to customize the form (or outline) of any shape in the shapes gallery, you can modify its edit points. To display a shape's edit points, select the shape you want to modify, click the Drawing Tools Format tab on the Ribbon, click the Edit Shape button in the Insert Shapes group, then click Edit Points. Black edit points appear on the shape. To change the form of a shape, drag a black edit point. When you click a black edit point, white square edit points appear on either side of the black edit point, which allow you to change the curvature of a line between two black edit points. When you are finished with your custom shape, you can save it as picture and reuse it in other presentations or other files. To save the shape as a picture, right-click the shape, then click Save as Picture.

Align and Group Objects

Learning Outcomes
• Move shapes using guides
• Align and group shapes

After you are finished creating and modifying your objects, you can position them accurately on the slide to achieve the look you want. Using the Align commands in the Arrange group, you can align objects relative to each other by snapping them to the gridlines on a slide or to guides that you manually position on the slide. The Group command groups two or more objects into one object, which secures their relative position to each other and makes it easy to edit and move them. **CASE** ▶ *You are ready to position and group the diamond shapes on Slide 4 to finish the slide.*

STEPS

1. **Right-click a blank area of the slide, point to** Grid and Guides **on the shortcut menu, then click** Guides

   The guides appear as dotted lines on the slide and usually intersect at the center of the slide. Guides help you position objects precisely on the slide.

2. **Position** ☐ **over the** horizontal guide **in a blank area of the slide, notice the pointer change to** ⟺**, press and hold the mouse button until the pointer changes to a measurement guide box, then drag the** guide **up until the guide position box reads** 1.33

3. **Drag the** vertical guide **to the left until the guide position box reads** .33**, then drag the** Salt Removal shape **so that the top and left edges of the shape touch the guides, as shown in** FIGURE 2-13

   The Salt Removal shape attaches or "snaps" to the guides.

4. **Drag the** Continuous Water Use shape **to the right until it touches a vertical Smart Guide, press and hold** [Shift]**, click the** Salt Removal shape**, then release** [Shift]

   Two shapes are now selected.

5. **Click the** Drawing Tools Format tab **on the Ribbon, click the** Align button **in the Arrange group, click** Align Top**, then click a blank area of the slide**

   The right diamond shape moves up and aligns with the other shape along their top edges.

6. **Drag the** Rainwater Harvesting diamond shape **in between the other two shapes, as shown in** FIGURE 2-14

7. **Press and hold** [Shift]**, click the other two** diamond shapes**, release** [Shift]**, click the** Group button **in the Arrange group, then click** Group

   The shapes are now grouped together to form one object without losing their individual attributes. Notice that the sizing handles and rotate handle now appear on the outer edge of the grouped object, not around each individual object.

8. **Drag the** horizontal guide **to the middle of the slide until its guide position box reads** 0.00**, then drag the** vertical guide **to the middle of the slide until its guide position box reads** 0.00

9. **Click the** View tab **on the Ribbon, click the** Guides check box **in the Show group, click a blank area of the slide, then save your work**

   The guides are no longer displayed on the slide.

FIGURE 2-13: Repositioned shape

FIGURE 2-14: Repositioned shapes

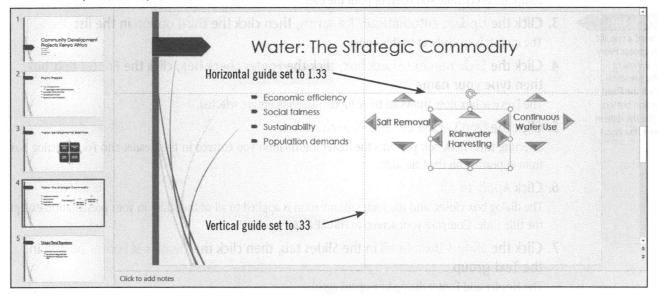

Distributing objects

There are two ways to distribute objects in PowerPoint: relative to each other and relative to the slide edge. If you choose to distribute objects relative to each other, PowerPoint evenly divides the empty space between all of the selected objects. When distributing objects in relation to the slide, PowerPoint evenly splits the empty space from slide edge to slide edge between the selected objects. To distribute objects relative to each other, click the Align button in the Arrange group on the Drawing Tools Format tab, then click Align Selected Objects. To distribute objects relative to the slide, click the Align button in the Arrange group on the Drawing Tools Format tab, then click Align to Slide.

Add Slide Footers

Learning Outcomes
• Add footer text to slides

Footer text, such as a company, school, or product name, the slide number, or the date, can give your slides a professional look and make it easier for your audience to follow your presentation. Slides do not have headers. However, notes or handouts can include both header and footer text. You can review footer information that you apply to the slides in the PowerPoint views and when you print the slides. Notes and handouts header and footer text is visible when you print notes pages, handouts, and the outline. **CASE** *You add footer text to the slides of the Kenya Africa presentation to make it easier for the audience to follow.*

STEPS

QUICK TIP
The placement of the footer text objects on the slide is dependent on the presentation theme.

1. **Click the** Insert tab **on the Ribbon, then click the** Header & Footer button **in the Text group**

   The Header and Footer dialog box opens, as shown in **FIGURE 2-15**. The Header and Footer dialog box has two tabs: a Slide tab and a Notes and Handouts tab. The Slide tab is selected. There are three types of footer text, Date and time, Slide number, and Footer. The bold rectangles in the Preview box identify the default position of the three types of footer text placeholders on the slides.

2. **Click the** Date and time check box **to select it**

   The date and time options are now available to select. The Update automatically date and time option button is selected by default. This option updates the date and time to the date and time set by your computer every time you open or print the file.

QUICK TIP
If you want a specific date to appear every time you view or print the presentation, click the Fixed date option button, then type the date in the Fixed text box.

3. **Click the** Update automatically list arrow, **then click the** third option **in the list**

   The month is spelled out in this option.

4. **Click the** Slide number check box, **click the** Footer check box, **click the** Footer text box, **then type your name**

   The Preview box now shows all three footer placeholders are selected.

5. **Click the** Don't show on title slide check box

   Selecting this check box prevents the footer information you entered in the Header and Footer dialog box from appearing on the title slide.

6. **Click** Apply to All

   The dialog box closes, and the footer information is applied to all of the slides in your presentation except the title slide. Compare your screen to **FIGURE 2-16**.

7. **Click the** Slide 1 thumbnail **in the Slides tab, then click the** Header & Footer button **in the Text group**

   The Header and Footer dialog box opens again.

8. **Click the** Don't show on title slide check box **to deselect it, click the** Footer check box, **then select the text in the Footer text box**

TROUBLE
If you click Apply to All in Step 9, click the Undo button on the Quick Access toolbar and repeat Steps 7, 8, and 9.

9. **Type** Striving Toward a Sustainable Future, **click** Apply, **then save your work**

   Only the text in the Footer text box appears on the title slide. Clicking Apply applies this footer information to just the current slide.

10. **Submit your presentation to your instructor, then exit PowerPoint**

FIGURE 2-15: Header and Footer dialog box

Header and Footer   ?   ✕

| Slide | Notes and Handouts |

Include on slide

☐ Date and time

  ◉ Update automatically

  10/6/2017

  Language: Calendar type:

  English (United States)   Gregorian

  ○ Fixed

  10/6/2017

☐ Slide number

☐ Footer

☐ Don't show on title slide

Preview

Shows where footer text appears on the slide

Apply   Apply to All   Cancel

FIGURE 2-16: Footer information added to presentation

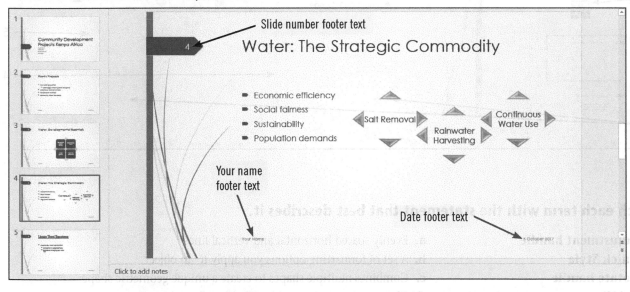

Slide number footer text

Water: The Strategic Commodity

- Economic efficiency
- Social fairness
- Sustainability
- Population demands

Salt Removal   Rainwater Harvesting   Continuous Water Use

Your name footer text

Date footer text

Click to add notes

Creating superscript and subscript text

Superscript or subscript text is a number, figure, symbol, or letter that appears smaller than other text and is positioned above or below the normal line of text. A common superscript in the English language is the sign indicator next to number, such as 1st or 3rd. Other examples of superscripts are the trademark symbol™ and the copyright symbol©. To create superscript text in PowerPoint, select the text, number, or symbol, then press [CTRL] [SHIFT] [+] at the same time. Probably the most familiar subscript text are the numerals in chemical compounds and formulas, for example, H_2O and CO_2. To create subscript text, select the text, number, or symbol, then press [CTRL] [=] at the same time. To change superscript or subscript text back to normal text, select the text, then press [CTRL] [Spacebar].

Practice

Concepts Review

Label each element of the PowerPoint window shown in FIGURE 2-17.

FIGURE 2-17

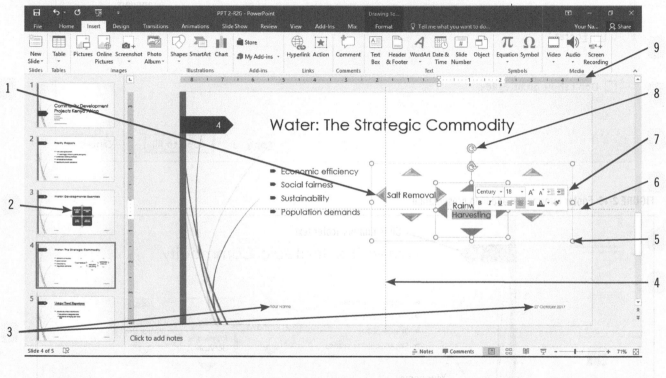

Match each term with the statement that best describes it.

10. **Adjustment handle**
11. **Quick Style**
12. **Rotate handle**
13. **Gridlines**
14. **Merge**
15. **Smart Guides**

a. Evenly spaced horizontal and vertical lines
b. A set of formatting options you apply to an object
c. Combines multiple shapes to create a unique geometric shape
d. Changes the most prominent feature of an object
e. Helps you determine equal distances between objects
f. Drag to turn an object

Select the best answer from the list of choices.

16. What is *not* true about grouped objects?
  a. Grouped objects have one rotate handle.
  b. Grouped objects act as one object but maintain their individual attributes.
  c. Sizing handles appear around the grouped object.
  d. Each object is distributed relative to the slide edges.

17. A professional-quality diagram that visually illustrates text best describes which of the following?
  a. A SmartArt Style
  b. A merged shape
  c. A subscript
  d. A SmartArt graphic

18. Which of the following statements is *not* true about Outline view?
  a. Pressing [Enter] moves the insertion point down one line.
  b. Text you enter next to the slide icon becomes a bullet point for that slide.
  c. Headings are the same as slide titles.
  d. Added slides use the same layout as the previous slide.

19. What do you have to drag to customize the form or outline of a shape?
  a. Anchor points
  b. Edit points
  c. Slide edges
  d. Shape area

20. Why would you use the Eyedropper tool?
  a. To format an object with a new style
  b. To soften the edges of a shape
  c. To capture and apply a new color to an object
  d. To change the fill color of an object

21. What appears just above text when it is selected?
  a. Mini toolbar
  b. QuickStyles
  c. Adjustment handle
  d. AutoFit Options button

22. Which of the following statements about merged shapes is *not* true?
  a. Merged shapes can be added to the shapes gallery.
  b. A merged shape assumes the theme of the shape that is selected first.
  c. The stacking order of shapes changes the way a merged shape looks.
  d. A merged shape is a combination of multiple shapes.

Skills Review

FIGURE 2-18

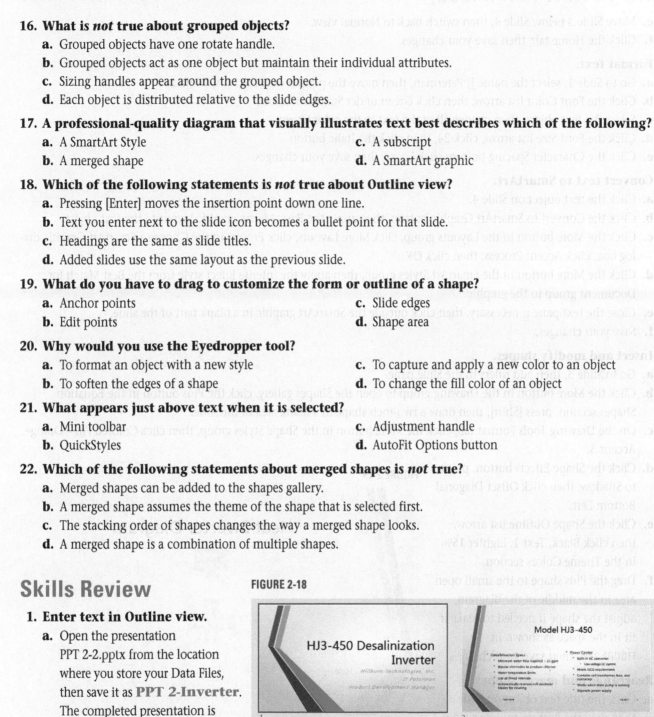

1. Enter text in Outline view.
  a. Open the presentation PPT 2-2.pptx from the location where you store your Data Files, then save it as **PPT 2-Inverter**. The completed presentation is shown in **FIGURE 2-18**.
  b. Create a new slide after Slide 2 with the Title and Content layout.
  c. Open Outline view, then type **Diffusion Desalinization**.
  d. Press [Enter], press [Tab], type **Main Feed**, press [Enter], type **Circulating Pump**, press [Enter], type **Primary Heaters**, press [Enter], then type **Diffusion Tower**.

e. Move Slide 3 below Slide 4, then switch back to Normal view.

f. Click the Home tab, then save your changes.

2. Format text.

a. Go to Slide 1, select the name JJ Peterman, then move the pointer over the Mini Toolbar.

b. Click the Font Color list arrow, then click Green under Standard Colors.

c. Select the text object, then change all of the text to the color Green.

d. Click the Font Size list arrow, click 24, then click the Italic button.

e. Click the Character Spacing button, click Loose, then save your changes.

3. Convert text to SmartArt.

a. Click the text object on Slide 4.

b. Click the Convert to SmartArt Graphic button, then apply the Basic Matrix graphic layout to the text object.

c. Click the More button in the Layouts group, click More Layouts, click Process in the Choose a SmartArt Graphic dialog box, click Accent Process, then click OK.

d. Click the More button in the SmartArt Styles group, then apply the Intense Effect style from the Best Match for Document group to the graphic.

e. Close the text pane if necessary, then click outside the SmartArt graphic in a blank part of the slide.

f. Save your changes.

4. Insert and modify shapes.

a. Go to Slide 3, then add rulers to the Slide pane.

b. Click the More button in the Drawing group to open the Shapes gallery, click the Plus button in the Equation Shapes section, press [Shift], then draw a two-inch shape in a blank area of the slide.

c. On the Drawing Tools Format tab, click the More button in the Shape Styles group, then click Colored Fill – Orange, Accent 3.

d. Click the Shape Effects button, point to Shadow, then click Offset Diagonal Bottom Left.

e. Click the Shape Outline list arrow, then click Black, Text 1, Lighter 15% in the Theme Colors section.

f. Drag the Plus shape to the small open area in the middle of the diagram, adjust the shape if needed to make it fit in the space as shown in FIGURE 2-19, then save your changes.

FIGURE 2-19

5. Rearrange and merge shapes.

a. Click the title text object on Slide 3, then drag the bottom-middle sizing handle up above the shapes.

b. Click the More button in the Insert Shapes group, click the Hexagon button in the Basic Shapes section, press and hold [Shift], then draw a 1-inch shape.

c. Drag the hexagon shape over top of the plus shape and center it, then open the Selection pane.

d. Send the hexagon shape back one level, press [Shift], click the plus shape, then click the Merge Shapes button in the Insert Shapes group on the Drawing Tools Format tab.

e. Point to each of the merge shapes options, click a blank area of the slide twice, then click the plus shape.

Skills Review (continued)

    f. Send the plus shape back one level, press [Shift], click the hexagon shape, click the Merge Shapes button, then click Combine.

    g. Close the Selection pane, then save your work.

6. Edit and duplicate shapes.

    a. Select the up-angled shape to the right of the merged shape, then using [Ctrl] make one copy of the shape.

    b. Use Smart Guides to align the new up-angled shape just to the right of the original shape.

    c. Click the Rotate button in the Arrange group, click Flip Vertical, click the Undo button, click the Rotate button, then click Flip Horizontal.

    d. Type **Bypass**, click the up-angled shape to the right of the merged shape, type **Water**, click the down-angled shape to the left of the merged shape, then type **Flow**.

    e. Click the Heat Source arrow shape above the merged shape, then drag the bottom-middle sizing handle down until the arrow touches the merged shape.

    f. Click a blank area of the slide, add the guides to the Slide pane, then save your changes.

7. Align and group objects.

    a. Move the vertical guide to the left until 3.42 appears, drag a selection box to select the five small purple triangle shapes at the bottom of the slide, then click the Drawing Tools Format tab.

    b. Click the Align button in the Arrange group, click Align Middle, click the Align button, then click Distribute Horizontally.

    c. Click the Rotate button in the Arrange group, click Rotate Left 90°, click the Group button in the Arrange group, then click Group.

    d. Move the grouped triangle shape object to the guide in the blank space on the down-angled shape to the left of the merged shape.

    e. Duplicate the grouped triangle shape object, then rotate the new object to the left 90°.

    f. Duplicate the rotated grouped triangle shape object, then move the two new triangle shape objects on the slide as shown in **FIGURE 2-20**.

    g. Set the guides back to 0.00, remove the guides from your screen, remove the rulers, then save your work.

FIGURE 2-20

Heat Inverter Diagram

Heat Source

Water   Bypass

Flow

Holding Tank

8. Add slide footers.

    a. Open the Header and Footer dialog box.

    b. On the Slide tab, click the Date and time check box to select it, then click the Fixed option button.

    c. Add the slide number to the footer, then type your name in the Footer text box.

    d. Apply the footer to all of the slides except the title slide.

    e. Open the Header and Footer dialog box again, then click the Notes and Handouts tab.

    f. Click the Date and time check box, then type today's date in the Fixed text box.

    g. Type the name of your class in the Header text box, then click the Page number check box.

    h. Type your name in the Footer text box.

    i. Apply the header and footer information to all the notes and handouts, then save your changes.

    j. Submit your presentation to your instructor, close the presentation, then exit PowerPoint.

Independent Challenge 1

You are the director of the Center for the Arts in Rapid City, South Dakota, and one of your many duties is to raise funds to cover operation costs. One of the primary ways you do this is by speaking to businesses, community clubs, and other organizations throughout the region. Every year you speak to many organizations, where you give a short presentation detailing what the theater center plans to do for the coming season. You need to continue working on the presentation you started already.

a. Start PowerPoint, open the presentation PPT 2-3.pptx from the location where you store your Data Files, and save it as **PPT 2-Arts**.

b. Use Outline view to enter the following as bulleted text on the Commitment to Excellence slide:
Excellence
Testing
Study
Diligence

c. Apply the Ion design theme to the presentation.

d. Change the font color of each play name on Slide 3 to Gold, Accent 3.

e. Change the bulleted text on Slide 5 to the Trapezoid List SmartArt Graphic, then apply the Polished SmartArt style.

f. Add your name and slide number as a footer on the slides, then save your changes.

g. Submit your presentation to your instructor, close your presentation, then exit PowerPoint.

Independent Challenge 2

You are a manager for J Barrett Inc., a financial services company. You have been asked by your boss to develop a presentation outlining important details and aspects of the mortgage process to be used at a financial seminar.

a. Start PowerPoint, open the presentation PPT 2-4.pptx from the location where you store your Data Files, and save it as **PPT 2-Broker**.

b. Apply the Facet design theme to the presentation.

c. On Slide 3, press [Shift], select the three shapes, Banks, Mortgage Bankers, and Private Investors, release [Shift], then using the Align command align them to their left edges.

d. Select the blank shape, type **Borrower**, press [Shift], select the Mortgage Broker and Mortgage Bankers shapes, release [Shift], then using the Align command distribute them horizontally and align them to the middle.

e. Select all of the shapes, then apply Intense Effect – Orange, Accent 4 from the Shape Styles group.

f. Create a diamond shape, then merge it with the Borrower shape as shown in **FIGURE 2-21**. (*Hint*: Use the Fragment Merge option.)

g. Using the Arrow shape from the Shapes gallery, draw a 6-pt arrow between all of the shapes. (*Hint*: Draw one arrow shape, change the line weight using the Shape Outline list arrow, then duplicate the shape.)

h. Group all the shapes together.

i. Add the page number and your name as a footer on the notes and handouts, then save your changes.

j. Submit your presentation to your instructor, close your presentation, then exit PowerPoint.

FIGURE 2-21

Independent Challenge 3

You are an independent distributor of natural foods in Birmingham, Alabama. Your business, Southern Whole Foods, has grown progressively since its inception 5 years ago, but sales have leveled off over the last 9 months. In an effort to increase your market share, you decide to purchase J&R Foods, a natural food dealer, which would allow your company to expand into surrounding states. Use PowerPoint to develop a presentation you can use to gain a financial backer for the acquisition. Create your own information for the presentation.

a. Start PowerPoint, create a new presentation, then apply the Wood Type design theme to the presentation.
b. Type **A Plan for Growth** as the main title on the title slide, and **Southern Whole Foods** as the subtitle.
c. Save the presentation as **PPT 2-Southern** to the location where you store your Data Files.
d. Add five more slides with the following titles: Slide 2, **Trends**; Slide 3, **Growth**; Slide 4, **Funding**; Slide 5, **History**; Slide 6, **Management Team**.
e. Enter appropriate text into the text placeholders of the slides. Use both the Slide pane and Outline view to enter text.
f. Convert text on one slide to a SmartArt graphic, then apply the SmartArt graphic style Inset Effect.
g. Create two shapes, format the shapes, then merge the shapes together.
h. View the presentation as a slide show, then view the slides in Slide Sorter view.
i. Add the slide number and your name as a footer on the slides, then save your changes.
j. Submit your presentation to your instructor, close your presentation, then exit PowerPoint.

Independent Challenge 4: Explore

Your computer instructor at Basset City College has been asked by the department head to convert her Computer Basics 101 course into an accelerated night course designed for adult students. Your instructor has asked you to help her create a presentation for the class that she can post on the Internet. Most of the basic text information is already on the slides, you primarily need to add a theme and other object formatting.

a. Start PowerPoint, open the presentation PPT 2-5.pptx from the location where you store your Data Files, and save it as **PPT 2-Basset**.
b. Add a new slide after the Course Facts slide with the same layout, type **Course Details** in the title text placeholder, then enter the following as bulleted text in Outline view:
   Information systems
   Networking
   Applied methods
   Technology solutions
   Software design
   Applications
c. Apply the Retrospect design theme to the presentation.
d. Select the title text object on Slide 1 (*Hint*: Press [Shift] to select the whole object), then change the text color to Orange.
e. Change the font of the title text object to Biondi, then decrease the font size to 48.
f. Click the subtitle text object on Slide 1, then change the character spacing to Very Loose.
g. Change the text on Slide 4 to a SmartArt graphic. Use an appropriate diagram type for a list.
h. Change the style of the SmartArt diagram using one of the SmartArt Styles, then view the presentation in Slide Show view.
i. Add the slide number and your name as a footer on the notes and handouts, then save your changes.
j. Submit your presentation to your instructor, close your presentation, then exit PowerPoint.

Visual Workshop

Create the presentation shown in **FIGURE 2-22** and **FIGURE 2-23**. Add today's date as the date on the title slide. Save the presentation as **PPT 2-Nebraska Trade** to the location where you store your Data Files. (*Hint*: The SmartArt style used for the SmartArt is a 3D style.) Review your slides in Slide Show view, then add your name as a footer to the notes and handouts. Submit your presentation to your instructor, save your changes, close the presentation, then exit PowerPoint.

FIGURE 2-22

FIGURE 2-23

Inserting Objects into a Presentation

CASE In this module, you continue working on the presentation by inserting text from Microsoft Word. You also add visual elements into the presentation including a photograph, a table, and a chart. You format these objects using PowerPoint's powerful object-editing features.

Module Objectives

After completing this module, you will be able to:

- Insert text from Microsoft Word
- Insert and style a picture
- Insert a text box
- Insert a chart

- Enter and edit chart data
- Insert slides from other presentations
- Insert a table
- Insert and format WordArt

Files You Will Need

PPT 3-1.pptx	PPT 3-10.pptx
PPT 3-2.docx	PPT 3-11.pptx
PPT 3-3.jpg	PPT 3-12.jpg
PPT 3-4.pptx	PPT 3-13.pptx
PPT 3-5.pptx	PPT 3-14.docx
PPT 3-6.docx	PPT 3-15.jpg
PPT 3-7.jpg	PPT 3-16.jpg
PPT 3-8.pptx	PPT 3-17.jpg
PPT 3-9.pptx	PPT 3-18.jpg

Insert Text from Microsoft Word

Learning Outcomes
• Create slides using Outline view
• Move and delete slides

It is easy to insert documents saved in Microsoft Word format (.docx), Rich Text Format (.rtf), plain text format (.txt), and HTML format (.htm) into a PowerPoint presentation. If you have an outline saved in a document file, you can import it into PowerPoint to create a new presentation or create additional slides in an existing presentation. When you import a document into a presentation, PowerPoint creates an outline structure based on the styles in the document. For example, a Heading 1 style in the Word document becomes a slide title and a Heading 2 style becomes the first level of text in a bulleted list. If you insert a plain text format document into a presentation, PowerPoint creates an outline based on the tabs at the beginning of the document's paragraphs. Paragraphs without tabs become slide titles, and paragraphs with one tab indent become first-level text in bulleted lists. **CASE** ▸ *You have a Microsoft Word document with information about the new Kenyan well project tour that you want to insert into your presentation.*

STEPS

QUICK TIP
While in Normal view you can click the Normal button in the status bar to go to Outline view.

1. **Start PowerPoint, open the presentation** PPT 3-1.pptx **from the location where you store your Data Files, save it as** PPT 3-R2G, **click the** View tab **on the Ribbon, then click the** Outline View button **in the Presentation Views group**

2. **Click the** Slide 6 icon ☐ **in the Outline pane, click the** Home tab **on the Ribbon, click the** New Slide button list arrow **in the Slides group, then click** Slides from Outline
   Slide 6 appears in the Slide pane. The Insert Outline dialog box opens. Before you insert an outline into a presentation, you need to determine where you want the new slides to be placed. You want the text from the Word document inserted as new slides after Slide 6.

3. **Navigate to the location where you store your Data Files, click the Word document file** PPT 3-2.docx, **then click** Insert
   Six new slides (7, 8, 9, 10, 11, and 12) are added to the presentation, and the new Slide 7 appears in the Slide pane. See **FIGURE 3-1**.

4. **Click the** down scroll arrow ▾ **in the Outline pane and read the text for all the new slides, then click the** Normal button 🖳 **on the status bar**
   The information on Slides 7 and 12 refer to information not needed for this presentation.

5. **Click the** Slide 7 thumbnail **in the Slides tab, press [Ctrl], click the** Slide 12 thumbnail, **then click the** Cut button **in the Clipboard group**
   Slides 7 and 12 are deleted, and the next slide down (Suggested Itinerary) becomes the new Slide 10 and appears in the Slide pane.

6. **Drag the** Slide 10 thumbnail **in the Slides tab above Slide 8**
   Slide 10 becomes Slide 8. The inserted slides have a different slide layout and font style than the other slides. You want the text of the inserted outline to adopt the theme fonts of the presentation.

QUICK TIP
You can also use Slide Sorter view to move slides around in the presentation.

7. **Click the** Slide 7 thumbnail **in the Slides tab, press [Shift], click the** Slide 10 thumbnail, **release [Shift], click the** Reset button **in the Slides group, click the** Layout button **in the Slides group, then click the** Title and Content slide layout
   The new slides now follow the presentation design and font themes. Compare your screen to **FIGURE 3-2**.

8. **Click the** Save button 🖫 **on the Quick Access toolbar**

FIGURE 3-1: Outline pane showing imported text

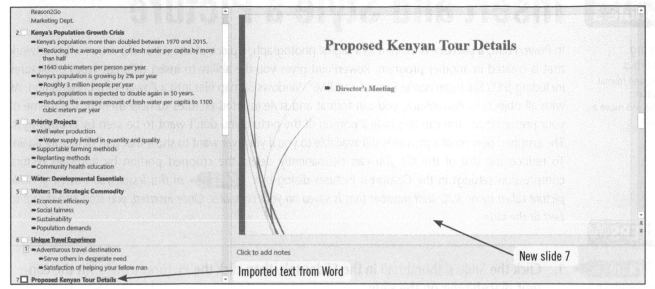

FIGURE 3-2: Slides reset to Wisp theme default settings

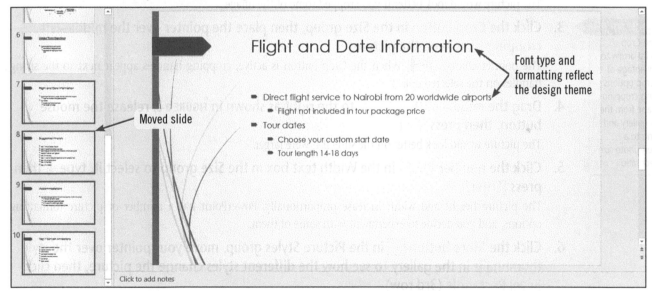

Sending a presentation using email

You can send a copy of a presentation over the Internet to a reviewer to edit and add comments. You can use Microsoft Outlook to send your presentation. Although your email program allows you to attach files, you can send a presentation using Outlook from within PowerPoint. Click the File tab, click Share, click Email in the center pane, then click Send as

Attachment. Outlook opens and automatically creates an email with a copy of the presentation attached to it. You can also attach and send a PDF copy or an XPS copy of the presentation using your email program. Both of these file formats preserve document formatting, enable file sharing, and can be viewed online and printed.

Insert and Style a Picture

Learning Outcomes
- Insert and format a picture
- Resize and move a picture

In PowerPoint, a **picture** is defined as a digital photograph, a piece of line art or clip art, or other artwork that is created in another program. PowerPoint gives you the ability to insert different types of pictures including JPEG File Interchange Format and BMP Windows Bitmap files into a PowerPoint presentation. As with all objects in PowerPoint, you can format and style inserted pictures to help them fit the theme of your presentation. You can also hide a portion of the picture you don't want to be seen by **cropping** it. The cropped portion of a picture is still available to you if you ever want to show that part of picture again. To reduce the size of the file you can permanently delete the cropped portion by applying picture compression settings in the Compress Pictures dialog box. **CASE** *In this lesson you insert a JPG file picture taken by an R2G staff member that is saved on your computer. Once inserted, you crop and style it to best fit the slide.*

STEPS

1. **Click the Slide 6 thumbnail in the Slides tab, then click the Pictures icon 🖼 in the content placeholder on the slide**

   The Insert Picture dialog box opens displaying the pictures available in the default Pictures folder.

2. **Navigate to location where you store your Data Files, select the picture file PPT 3-3.jpg, then click Insert**

   The picture fills the content placeholder on the slide, and the Picture Tools Format tab opens on the Ribbon. The picture would look better if you cropped some of the image.

3. **Click the Crop button in the Size group, then place the pointer over the middle-left cropping handle on the picture**

   The pointer changes to ⊣. When the Crop button is active, cropping handles appear next to the sizing handles on the selected object.

4. **Drag the middle of the picture to the right as shown in FIGURE 3-3, release the mouse button, then press [Esc]**

   The picture would look better on the slide if it were larger.

5. **Click the number (3.08) in the Width text box in the Size group to select it, type 4, then press [Enter]**

   The picture height and width increase proportionally. PowerPoint has a number of picture formatting options, and you decide to experiment with some of them.

6. **Click the More button ⤓ in the Picture Styles group, move your pointer over the style thumbnails in the gallery to see how the different styles change the picture, then click Bevel Rectangle (3rd row)**

   The picture now has rounded corners and a background shadow.

7. **Click the Corrections button in the Adjust group, move your pointer over the thumbnails to see how the picture changes, then click Sharpen: 25% in the Sharpen/Soften section**

   The picture clarity is better.

8. **Click the Artistic Effects button in the Adjust group, move your pointer over the thumbnails to see how the picture changes, then click a blank area of the slide**

   The artistic effects are all interesting, but none of them will work well for this picture.

9. **Drag the picture to the center of the blank area of the slide to the right of the text object, click a blank area on the slide, then save your changes**

   Compare your screen to FIGURE 3-4.

FIGURE 3-3: Using the cropping pointer to crop a picture

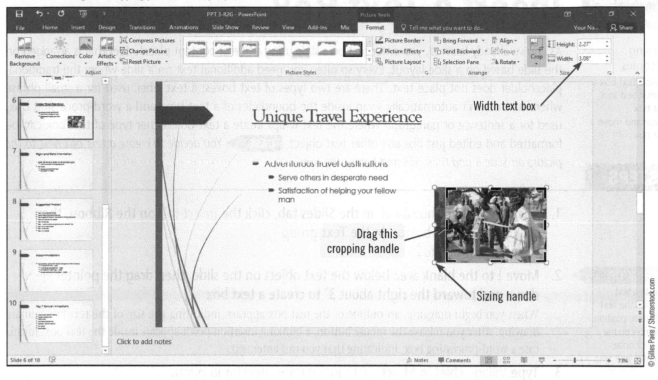

FIGURE 3-4: Cropped and styled picture

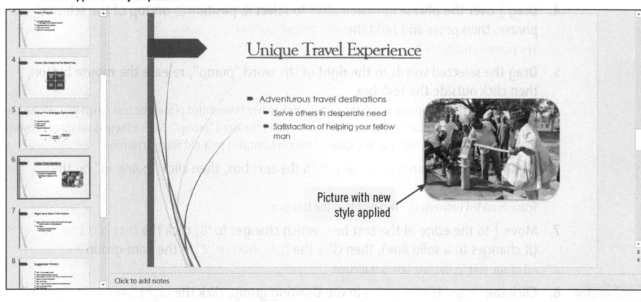

Inserting a screen recording

Using the Screen Recording button in the Media group on the Insert tab, you can record your computer screen with audio and insert the recording to a slide. For example, if you want to make a recording of an Internet video, locate and display the video on your computer screen. In PowerPoint on the slide where you want to insert the recording, click the Screen Recording button.

On the toolbar, click the Select Area button, drag a selection box around the video, click the Audio button if necessary, then click the Record button on the toolbar. Click the video play button. When finished recording, click Windows Logo+[Shift]+Q to stop recording. PowerPoint opens and the recording appears on your slide. Click the Play button to review your recording.

Inserting Objects into a Presentation

Insert a Text Box

Learning Outcomes
- Insert a text box
- Format text in a text box
- Resize and move a text box

As you've already learned, you enter text on a slide using a title or content placeholder that is arranged on the slide based on a slide layout. Every so often you need additional text on a slide where the traditional placeholder does not place text. There are two types of text boxes: a text label, used for a small phrase where text doesn't automatically wrap inside the boundaries of a text box, and a word-processing box, used for a sentence or paragraph where the text wraps inside a text box. Either type of text box can be formatted and edited just like any other text object. **CASE** *You decide to create a text box next to the picture on Slide 6 and then edit and format the text.*

STEPS

1. **Click the** Slide 6 thumbnail **in the Slides tab, click the** Insert tab **on the Ribbon, then click the** Text Box button **in the Text group**
   The pointer changes to ↓.

2. **Move** ↓ **to the blank area below the text object on the slide, then drag the pointer** ✛ **down and toward the right about 3" to create a text box**
   When you begin dragging, an outline of the text box appears, indicating the size of the text box you are drawing. After you release the mouse button, a blinking insertion point appears inside the text box, in this case a word-processing box, indicating that you can enter text.

3. **Type** Village chief in March 2017 inaugurates new hand pump
   Notice the text box increases in size as your text wraps to additional lines inside the text box. Your screen should look similar to **FIGURE 3-5**. After entering the text, you decide to edit the sentence.

4. **Drag** I **over the phrase** in March 2017 **to select it, position** ⇖ **on top of the selected phrase, then press and hold the** left mouse button
   The pointer changes to ⇖.

5. **Drag the selected words to the right of the word "pump", release the mouse button, then click outside the text box**
   A grey insertion line appears as you drag, indicating where PowerPoint places the text when you release the mouse button. The phrase "in March 2017" moves after the word "pump". Notice there is no space between the words "pump" and "in" and the spelling error is identified by a red wavy underline.

6. **Right-click the** red underlined words **in the text box, then click "pump in" on the shortcut menu**
   Space is added between the two words in the text box.

7. **Move** I **to the edge of the text box, which changes to** ✣, **click the** text box border **(it changes to a solid line), then click the** Italic button I **in the Font group**
   All of the text in the text box is italicized.

8. **Click the** Shape Fill list arrow **in the Drawing group, click the** Light Green, Background 2, Darker 10% color box, **click the** Shape Outline list arrow **in the Drawing group, then click the** Dark Red, Accent 1, Lighter 40% color box
   The text object is now filled with a light green color and has a red outline.

9. **Position** ✣ **over the text box edge, drag the** text box **to the Smart Guide on the slide as shown in FIGURE 3-6, then save your changes**

FIGURE 3-5: New text object

FIGURE 3-6: Formatted text object

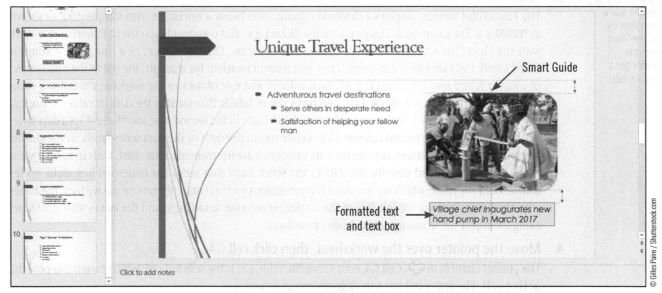

Changing text box defaults

You can change the default formatting characteristics of text boxes you create using the Text Box button on the Insert tab. To change the formatting defaults for text boxes, select an existing formatted text box, or create a new one and format it using any of PowerPoint's formatting commands. When you are ready to change the text box defaults of a text box that is not selected, press [Shift], right-click the formatted text box, release [Shift], then click Set as Default Text Box on the shortcut menu. Any new text boxes you create now will display the formatting characteristics of this formatted text box.

Insert a Chart

Frequently, the best way to communicate numerical information is with a visual aid such as a chart. A **chart** is the graphical representation of numerical data. PowerPoint uses Excel to create charts. Every chart has a corresponding **worksheet** that contains the numerical data displayed by the chart. When you insert a chart object into PowerPoint, you are embedding it. An **embedded object** is one that is a part of your presentation (just like any other object you insert into PowerPoint) except that an embedded object's data source can be opened, in this case using Excel, for editing purposes. Changes you make to an embedded object in PowerPoint using the features in PowerPoint do not affect the data source for the data. **CASE** ▶ *You insert a chart on a new slide.*

STEPS

1. **Click the** Slide 2 thumbnail **in the Slides tab, then press** [Enter]

   Pressing [Enter] adds a new slide to your presentation with the slide layout of the selected slide, in this case the Title and Content slide layout.

2. **Click the** Title placeholder, **type** Population Growth Comparison, **then click the** Insert Chart icon ▦ **in the Content placeholder**

   The Insert Chart dialog box opens as shown in **FIGURE 3-7**. Each chart type includes a number of 2D and 3D styles. The Clustered Column chart is the default 2D chart style. For a brief explanation of common chart types, refer to **TABLE 3-1**.

3. **Click** OK

   The PowerPoint window displays a clustered column chart below a worksheet with sample data, as shown in **FIGURE 3-8**. The Chart Tools Design tab on the Ribbon contains commands you use in PowerPoint to work with the chart. The worksheet consists of rows and columns. The intersection of a row and a column is called a **cell**. Cells are referred to by their row and column location; for example, the cell at the intersection of column A and row 1 is called cell A1. Each column and row of data in the worksheet is called a **data series**. Cells in column A and row 1 contain **data series labels** that identify the data or values in the column and row. "Category 1" is the data series label for the data in the second row, and "Series 1" is a data series label for the data in the second column. Cells below and to the right of the data series labels, in the shaded blue portion of the worksheet, contain the data values that are represented in the chart. Cells in row 1 appear in the chart **legend** and describe the data in the series. Each data series has corresponding **data series markers** in the chart, which are graphical representations such as bars, columns, or pie wedges. The boxes with the numbers along the left side of the worksheet are **row headings**, and the boxes with the letters along the top of the worksheet are **column headings**.

4. **Move the pointer over the worksheet, then click cell** C4

   The pointer changes to ✛. Cell C4, containing the value 1.8, is the selected cell, which means it is now the **active cell**. The active cell has a thick green border around it.

5. **Click the** Close button ✕ **on the worksheet title bar, then click the** Quick Layout button **in the Chart Layouts group**

   The worksheet window closes, and the Quick Layout gallery opens.

6. **Move** ▷ **over the layouts in the gallery, then click** Layout 1

   This new layout moves the legend to the right side of the chart and increases the size of the data series markers.

7. **Click in a blank area of the slide to deselect the chart, then save your changes**

   The Chart Tools Design tab is no longer active.

FIGURE 3-7: Insert Chart dialog box

Default chart

FIGURE 3-8: Worksheet open showing chart data

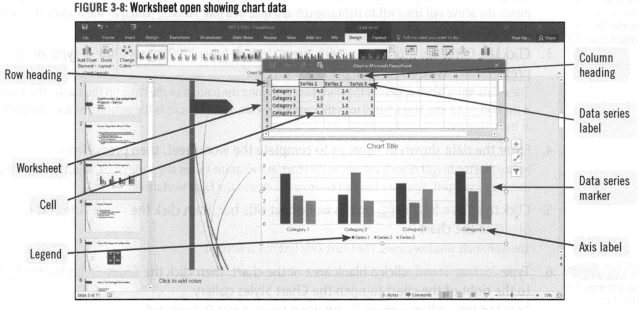

Row heading

Worksheet

Cell

Legend

Column heading

Data series label

Data series marker

Axis label

TABLE 3-1: Chart types

chart type	icon looks like	use to
Column		Track values over time or across categories
Line		Track values over time
Pie		Compare individual values to the whole
Bar		Compare values in categories or over time
Area		Show contribution of each data series to the total over time
X Y (Scatter)		Compare pairs of values
Stock		Show stock market information or scientific data
Surface		Show value trends across two dimensions
Radar		Show changes in values in relation to a center point
Combo		Use multiple types of data markers to compare values

Inserting Objects into a Presentation

Enter and Edit Chart Data

Learning Outcomes
- Change chart data values and labels
- Format a chart

After you insert a chart into your presentation, you need to replace the sample information with the correct data. If you have the data you want to chart in an Excel worksheet, you can import it from Excel; otherwise, you can type your own data into the worksheet on the slide. As you enter data and make other changes in the worksheet, the chart on the slide automatically reflects the new changes. **CASE** ▸ *You enter and format population data you have gathered comparing the growth trends of three African countries.*

STEPS

1. **Click the chart on Slide 3, click the Chart Tools Design tab on the Ribbon, then click the Edit Data button in the Data group**
   The chart is selected and the worksheet opens in a separate window. The information in the worksheet needs to be replaced with the correct data.

2. **Click the Series 1 cell, type Kenya, press [Tab], type Uganda, press [Tab], then type S. Africa**
   The data series labels you enter in the worksheet are displayed in the legend on the chart. Pressing [Tab] moves the active cell from left to right one cell at a time in a row. Pressing [Enter] in the worksheet moves the active cell down one cell at a time in a column.

3. **Click the Category 1 cell, type 1990, press [Enter], type 2000, press [Enter], type 2010, press [Enter], type 2015, then press [Enter]**
   These data series labels appear in the worksheet and along the bottom of the chart on the x-axis. The x-axis is the horizontal axis also referred to as the **category axis**, and the y-axis is the vertical axis also referred to as the **value axis**.

4. **Enter the data shown in FIGURE 3-9 to complete the worksheet, then press [Enter]**
   Notice that the height of each column in the chart, as well as the values along the y-axis, adjust to reflect the numbers you typed. You have finished entering the data in the Excel worksheet.

5. **Click the Close button ☒ on the worksheet title bar, then click the Chart Title text box object in the chart**
   The worksheet window closes. The Chart Title text box is selected.

6. **Type 25 Year Trend, click a blank area of the chart, then click the Chart Styles button ✐ to the right of the chart to open the Chart Styles gallery**
   The Chart Styles gallery opens on the left side of the chart with Style selected.

7. **Scroll down the gallery, click Style 6, click Color at the top of the Chart Styles gallery, then click the Color 3 palette in the Colorful section**
   The new chart style and color gives the column data markers a professional look as shown in **FIGURE 3-10**.

8. **Click a blank area on the slide, then save the presentation**
   The Chart Styles gallery closes.

FIGURE 3-9: Worksheet data for the chart

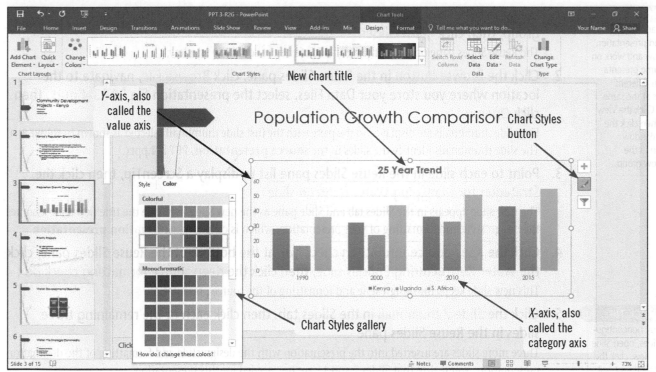

New data

FIGURE 3-10: Formatted chart

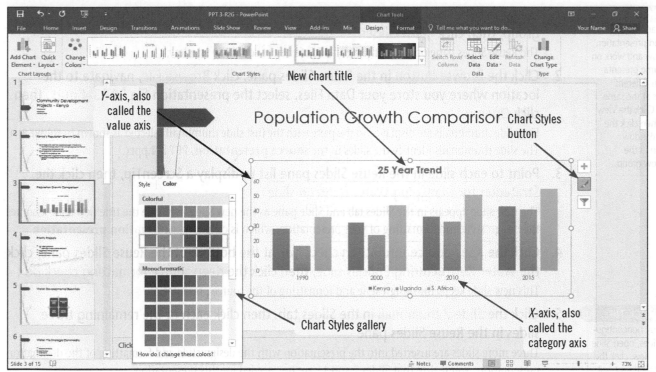

Adding a hyperlink to a chart

You can add a hyperlink to any object in PowerPoint, including a chart. Select that chart, click the Insert tab on the Ribbon, then click the Hyperlink button in the Links group. If you are linking to another file, click the Existing File or Web Page button, locate the file you want to link to the chart, then click OK. Or, if you want to link to another slide in the presentation, click the Place in This Document button, click the slide in the list, then click OK. Now, during a slide show you can click the chart to open the linked object. To remove the link, click the chart, click the Hyperlink button in the Links group, then click Remove Link.

Insert Slides from Other Presentations

To save time and energy, you can insert one or more slides you already created in other presentations into an existing presentation or one you are currently working on. One way to share slides between presentations is to open an existing presentation, copy the slides you want to the Clipboard, and then paste them into your open presentation. However, PowerPoint offers a simpler way to transfer slides directly between presentations. By using the Reuse Slides pane, you can insert slides from another presentation or a network location called a Slide Library. A **Slide Library** is folder that you and others can access to open, modify, and review presentation slides. Newly inserted slides automatically take on the theme of the open presentation, unless you decide to use slide formatting from the original source presentation. **CASE** *You decide to insert slides you created for another presentation into the Kenya presentation.*

STEPS

QUICK TIP
You can also open a
second presentation
window and work on
the same presenta-
tion in different
places at the same
time. Click the View
tab, then click the
New Window
button in the
Window group.

1. **Click the** Slide 6 thumbnail **in the Slides tab, click the** New Slide list arrow **in the Slides group, then click** Reuse Slides

   The Reuse Slides pane opens on the right side of the pre sentation window.

2. **Click the** Browse button **in the Reuse Slides pane, click** Browse File, **navigate to the location where you store your Data Files, select the presentation file** PPT 3-4.pptx, **then click** Open

   Five slide thumbnails are displayed in the pane with the first slide thumbnail selected as shown in **FIGURE 3-11**. The slide thumbnails identify the slides in the **source presentation**, PPT 3-4.pptx.

3. **Point to each slide in the Reuse Slides pane list to display a ScreenTip, then click the** Strategies for Managing Water Demand slide

   The new slide appears in the Slides tab and Slide pane as the new Slide 7. Notice the title new slide assumes the design style and formatting of your presentation, which is called the **destination presentation**.

4. **Click the** Keep source formatting check box **at the bottom of the Reuse Slides pane, click the** Water Restructuring Policies slide, **then click the** Keep source formatting check box

   This new slide keeps the design style and formatting of the source presentation.

QUICK TIP
To copy noncontigu-
ous slides, open Slide
Sorter view, click the
first slide thumbnail,
press and hold [Ctrl],
click each additional
slide thumbnail,
release [Ctrl],
then click the
Copy button.

5. **Click the** Slide 7 thumbnail **in the Slides tab, then click each of the remaining three slides in the Reuse Slides pane**

   Three more slides are inserted into the presentation with the design style and formatting of the destination presentation. You realize that Slides 7 and 11 are not needed for this presentation.

6. **Click the** Slide 11 thumbnail **in the Slides tab, press [Ctrl], click the** Slide 7 thumbnail, **release [Ctrl], right-click the** Slide 7 thumbnail, **then click** Delete Slide **in the shortcut menu**

   Slides 7 and 11 are deleted.

7. **Click the** Reuse Slides pane Close button ⊠, **click a blank area of the slide, then save the presentation**

   The Reuse Slides pane closes. Compare your screen to **FIGURE 3-12**.

FIGURE 3-11: Presentation window with Reuse Slides pane open

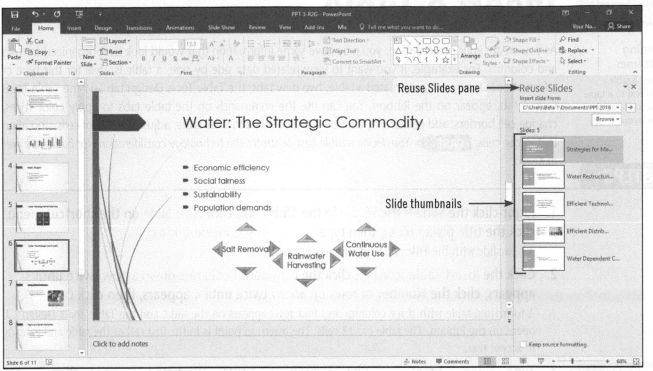

FIGURE 3-12: New slides added to presentation

Working with multiple windows

Another way to work with information in multiple presentations is to arrange the presentation windows on your monitor so you see each window side by side. Open each presentation, click the View tab on the Ribbon in any presentation window, then click the Arrange All button in the Window group. Each presentation you have open is placed next to each other so you can easily drag, or transfer, information between the presentations.

If you are working with more than two open presentations, you can overlap the presentation windows on top of one another. Open all the presentations you want, then click the Cascade Windows button in the Window group. Now you can easily jump from one presentation to another by clicking on the presentation title bar or any part of the presentation window.

Insert a Table

Learning Outcomes
- Insert a table
- Add text to a table
- Change table size and layout

As you create your presentation, you may have some information that would look best organized in rows and columns. For example, if you want to view related data side by side, a table is ideal for this type of information. Once you have created a table, two new tabs, the Table Tools Design tab and the Table Tools Layout tab, appear on the Ribbon. You can use the commands on the table tabs to apply color styles, change cell borders, add cell effects, add rows and columns to your table, adjust the size of cells, and align text in the cells. **CASE** ▶ *You decide a table best illustrates the technology considerations for building a well in Kenya.*

STEPS

1. **Right-click the** Slide 9 thumbnail **in the Slides tab, click** New Slide **on the shortcut menu, click the** title placeholder, **then type** Technology Considerations

   A new slide with the Title and Content layout appears.

2. **Click the** Insert Table icon ⊞, **click the** Number of columns down arrow **twice until** 3 **appears, click the** Number of rows up arrow **twice until** 4 **appears, then click** OK

   A formatted table with three columns and four rows appears on the slide, and the Table Tools Design tab opens on the Ribbon. The table has 12 cells. The insertion point is in the first cell of the table and is ready to accept text.

   QUICK TIP
   Press [Tab] when the insertion point is in the last cell of a table to create a new row.

3. **Type** Financial, **press** [Tab], **type** Maintenance, **press** [Tab], **type** Population, **then press** [Tab]

   The text you typed appears in the top three cells of the table. Pressing [Tab] moves the insertion point to the next cell; pressing [Enter] moves the insertion point to the next line in the same cell.

4. **Enter the rest of the table information shown in** FIGURE 3-13

   The table would look better if it were formatted differently.

5. **Click the** More button ▼ **in the Table Styles group, scroll to the bottom of the gallery, then click** Medium Style 3

   The background and text color change to reflect the table style you applied.

   QUICK TIP
   Change the height or width of any table cell by dragging its borders.

6. **Click the** Financial **cell in the table, click the** Table Tools Layout tab **on the Ribbon, click the** Select button **in the Table group, click** Select Row, **then click the** Center button ▤ **in the Alignment group**

   The text in the top row is centered horizontally in each cell.

7. **Click the** Select button **in the Table group, click** Select Table, **then click the** Center Vertically button ▤ **in the Alignment group**

   The text in the entire table is aligned in the center of each cell.

   QUICK TIP
   To change the cell color behind text, click the Shading list arrow in the Table Styles group, then choose a color.

8. **Click the** Table Tools Design tab, **click the** Effects button **in the Table Styles group, point to** Cell Bevel, **then click** Soft Round (2nd row)

   The 3D effect makes the cells of the table stand out. The table would look better in a different place on the slide.

9. **Place the pointer** ⬚ **over the top edge of the table, drag the table straight down so it is placed as shown in** FIGURE 3-14, **click a blank area of the slide, then save the presentation**

   The slide looks better with more space between the table and the slide title.

FIGURE 3-13: Inserted table with data

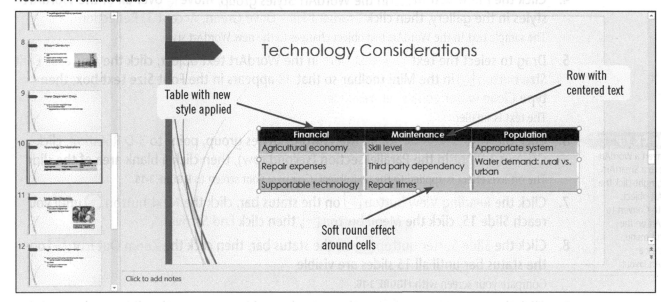

FIGURE 3-14: Formatted table

Setting permissions

In PowerPoint, you can set specific access permissions for people who review or edit your work so you have better control over your content. For example, you may want to give a user permission to edit or change your presentation but not allow them to print it. You can also restrict a user by permitting them to view the presentation without the ability to edit or print the presentation, or you can give the user full access or control of the presentation. To use this feature, you first must have access to an information rights management company. Then, to set user access permissions, click the File tab, click the Protect Presentation button, point to Restrict Access, then click an appropriate option.

Insert and Format WordArt

Learning
Outcomes
• Create, format,
  and resize WordArt

As you work to create an interesting presentation, your goal should include making your slides visually appealing. Sometimes plain text can come across as dull and unexciting in a presentation. **WordArt** is a set of decorative text styles, or text effects, you can apply to any text object to help direct the attention of your audience to a certain piece of information. You can use WordArt in two different ways: you can apply a WordArt text style to an existing text object that converts the text into WordArt, or you can create a new WordArt object. The WordArt text styles and effects include text shadows, reflections, glows, bevels, 3D rotations, and transformations. **CASE** ▸ *Create a new WordArt text object on Slide 4.*

STEPS

QUICK TIP
To format any text
with a WordArt style,
select the text, click
the Drawing Tools
Format tab on the
Ribbon, then click a
WordArt style option
in the WordArt
Styles group.

1. **Click the** Slide 4 thumbnail **in the Slides tab, click the** Insert tab **on the Ribbon, then click the** WordArt button **in the Text group**

   The WordArt gallery appears displaying 20 WordArt text styles.

2. **Click** Fill – Orange, Accent 2, Outline – Accent 2 **(first row)**

   A text object appears in the middle of the slide displaying sample text with the WordArt style you just selected. The Drawing Tools Format tab is open on the Ribbon.

3. **Click the edge of the** WordArt text object, **then when the pointer changes to** ⭲, **drag the text object to the blank area of the slide**

4. **Click the** More button ▾ **in the WordArt Styles group, move** ▷ **over all of the WordArt styles in the gallery, then click** Gradient Fill – Olive Green, Accent 1, Reflection

   The sample text in the WordArt text object changes to the new WordArt style.

5. **Drag to select the text** Your text here **in the WordArt text object, click the** Decrease Font Size button A˅ **in the Mini toolbar so that** 48 **appears in the Font Size text box, then type** Clean water equals self-reliance

   The text is smaller.

QUICK TIP
To convert a WordArt
object to a SmartArt
object, right-click the
WordArt object,
point to Convert to
SmartArt on the
shortcut menu,
then click a
SmartArt layout.

6. **Click the** Text Effects button **in the WordArt Styles group, point to** 3-D Rotation, **click** Off Axis 1 Right **in the Parallel section (second row), then click a blank area of the slide**

   The off-axis effect is applied to the text object. Compare your screen to **FIGURE 3-15**.

7. **Click the** Reading View button 🕮 **on the status bar, click the** Next button ⊙ **until you reach Slide 15, click the** Menu button 🗐, **then click** End Show

8. **Click the** Slide Sorter button ⊞ **on the status bar, then click the** Zoom Out icon ⊟ **on the status bar until all 15 slides are visible**

   Compare your screen with **FIGURE 3-16**.

9. **Click the** Normal button 🖳 **on the status bar, add your name, the slide number and the date as a footer to the slides, save your changes, submit your presentation to your instructor, then exit PowerPoint**

FIGURE 3-15: WordArt inserted on slide

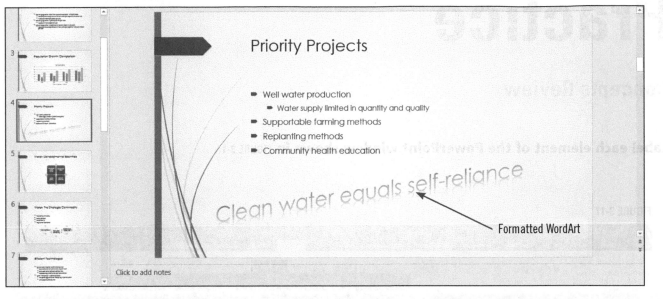

FIGURE 3-16: Completed presentation in Slide Sorter view

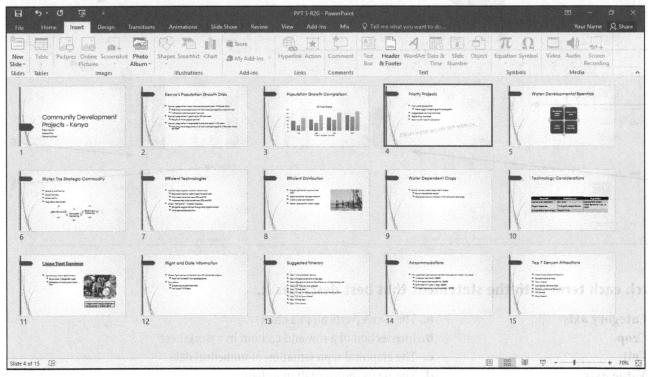

Saving a presentation as a video

You can save your PowerPoint presentation as a full-fidelity video, which incorporates all slide timings, transitions, animations, and narrations. The video can be distributed using a disc, the web, or email. Depending on how you want to display your video, you have three resolution settings from which to choose: Presentation Quality, Internet Quality, and Low Quality. The Large setting, Presentation Quality (1920 X 1080), is used for viewing on a computer monitor, projector, or other high-definition displays. The Medium setting, Internet Quality (1280 X 720), is used for uploading to the web or copying to a standard DVD. The Small setting, Low Quality (852 X 480), is used on portable media players. To save your presentation as a video, click the File tab, click Export, click Create a Video, choose your settings, then click the Create Video button.

Practice

Concepts Review

Label each element of the PowerPoint window shown in FIGURE 3-17.

FIGURE 3-17

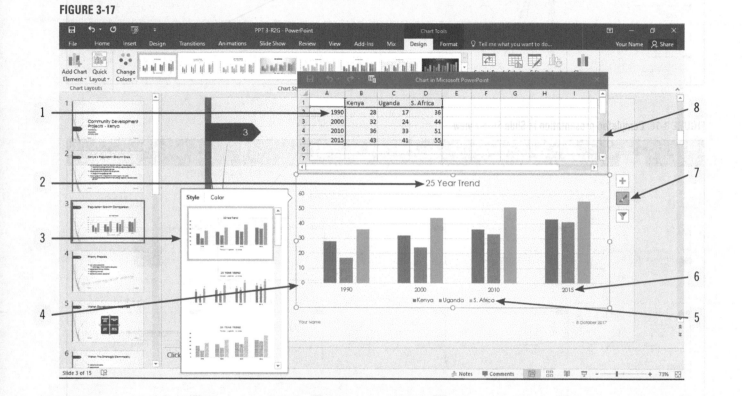

Match each term with the statement that best describes it.

9. Category axis
10. Crop
11. Cell
12. Value axis
13. Chart

a. The *y*-axis (vertical) in a chart
b. Intersection of a row and column in a worksheet
c. The graphical representation of numerical data
d. The *x*-axis (horizontal) in a chart
e. Hide a portion of a picture

Select the best answer from the list of choices.

14. _____ is the network folder that you can open in the Reuse Slides pane to insert slides from other presentations.
    a. Slide Library
    b. Slide Exchange
    c. Export Exchange
    d. Slide Room

15. Use a(n) _____ object to best illustrate information you want to compare side by side.
    a. WordArt
    b. Table
    c. SmartArt
    d. Equation

16. An object that has its own data source and becomes a part of your presentation after you insert it best describes which of the following?
    a. Embedded object
    b. WordArt
    c. Table
    d. Screenshot

17. Each column and row of data in a worksheet are _____.
    a. Data series labels
    b. Headings
    c. Data series
    d. Data markers

18. The slide thumbnails in the Reuse Slides pane identify the slides of the _____ presentation.
    a. destination
    b. default
    c. source
    d. open

19. _____ to permanently delete a cropped portion of a picture.
    a. Use the Crop to Fit feature
    b. Change the aspect ratio
    c. Change the picture's artistic effect
    d. Apply picture compression

20. _____ is created by inserting text from Word document that does not have tabs.
    a. A new presentation
    b. A slide title
    c. A first level text in a bulleted list
    d. A Heading 1 style

Skills Review

1. **Insert text from Microsoft Word.**
   a. Open PPT 3-5.pptx from the location where you store your Data Files, then save it as **PPT 3-Tsar Tour**. You will work to create the completed presentation as shown in FIGURE 3-18.
   b. Click Slide 2 in the Slides tab, then use the Slides from Outline command to insert the file PPT 3-6.docx from the location where you store your Data Files.
   c. In the Slides tab, drag Slide 7 above Slide 6, then delete Slide 9, "Budapest, Hungary".
   d. Select Slides 3, 4, 5, 6, 7, and 8 in the Slides tab, reset the slides to the default theme settings, then save your work.

FIGURE 3-18

Skills Review (continued)

2. Insert and style a picture.

a. Select Slide 2 in the Slides tab, then insert the picture PPT 3-7.jpg from the location where you store your Data Files.

b. Crop the right side of the picture up to the building, then increase the size of the picture so it is 5" wide.

c. Drag the picture to the right so it is in the center of the blank area of the slide.

d. Click the Color button, change the color tone to Temperature: 11200 K, then save your changes.

3. Insert a text box.

a. On Slide 2, insert a text box below the picture.

b. Type **Catherine palace**.

c. Select the text object, then click the More button in the Shape Styles group on the Drawing Tools Format tab.

d. Click Moderate Effect – Orange, Accent 5, then fit the text box to the text by dragging its sizing handles.

e. Center the text object under the picture using Smart Guides.

f. In the main text object, type the word **on** before the word **Volga**, then move the word **cruise** before the word **on**.

4. Insert a chart.

a. Create a new slide after Slide 8 with a Title Only layout and title it **Sales by Quarter**.

b. On the Insert tab, click the Chart button in the Illustrations group, click Pie in the left column, then insert a Pie chart.

c. Close the worksheet, drag the top-middle sizing handle of the chart down under the slide title, then apply the Layout 1 quick layout to the chart.

5. Enter and edit chart data.

a. Show the worksheet, enter the data shown in **TABLE 3-2** into the worksheet, then close the worksheet.

b. Type **Tsar River Tour Sales** in the chart title text object.

c. Click the Chart Styles button next to the chart, then change the chart style to Style 12.

d. Click Color in the Charts Styles gallery, then change the color to Color 3 in the Colorful section.

e. Close the Charts Styles gallery, then save your changes.

TABLE 3-2

	Sales
1st Qtr	11
2nd Qtr	31
3rd Qtr	37
4th Qtr	21

6. Insert slides from other presentations.

a. Go to Slide 8, then open the Reuse Slides pane.

b. Open PPT 3-8.pptx from the location where you store your Data Files.

c. Insert the fourth slide thumbnail, insert the second slide thumbnail, and then insert the third slide thumbnail.

d. Close the Reuse Slides pane, then save your work.

7. Insert a table.

a. Add a new slide after Slide 11 with the Title and Content layout.

b. Add the slide title **Stateroom Special Features**.

c. Insert a table with three columns and four rows.

d. Enter the information shown in **TABLE 3-3**, then change the table style to Light Style 2 – Accent 2.

e. In the Table Tools Layout tab, center the text in the top row.

f. Open the Table Tools Design tab, click the Effects button, point to Cell Bevel, then apply the Convex effect.

g. Move the table to the center of the blank area of the slide, then save your changes.

TABLE 3-3

Deluxe Stateroom	Veranda Suite	Master Suite
160 sq. ft.	225 sq. ft.	400 sq. ft.
Private bathroom	Glass sliding door	Queen bed
Large picture window	Walk-in closet	Panoramic veranda

Skills Review (continued)

8. Insert and format WordArt.

a. Go to Slide 5, then, insert a WordArt text object using the style Fill – Yellow, Accent 3, Sharp Bevel.

b. Type **A Golden Ring City**, apply the Triangle Down Transform text effect (first row in the Warp section) to the text object, then move the text object to the middle of the blank area of the slide.

c. View the presentation in Slide Show view, add your name as a footer to all the slides, then save your changes.

d. Submit your presentation to your instructor, close your presentation, and exit PowerPoint.

Independent Challenge 1

You are a financial management consultant for Pitlock, Bryer & Mansouetti, located in Bradenton, Florida. One of your responsibilities is to create standardized presentations on different financial investments for use on the company website. As part of the presentation for this meeting, you insert a chart, add a WordArt object, and insert slides from another presentation.

a. Open PPT 3-9.pptx from the location where you store your Data Files, then save it as **PPT 3-BIP**.

b. Add your name as the footer on all of the slides, then apply the Frame Design Theme.

c. Insert a clustered column chart on Slide 2, then enter the data in **TABLE 3-4** into the worksheet.

d. Close the worksheet, format the chart using Style 14, then resize and move the chart to the blank area beside the text object.

e. Type **Annualized Return** in the chart title text object.

f. Open the Reuse Slides pane, open PPT 3-10.pptx from the location where you store your Data Files, then insert Slides 2, 3, and 4.

g. Close the Reuse Slides pane, move Slide 5 above Slide 4, then select Slide 3.

h. Insert a WordArt object using the Fill - Orange, Accent 4, Soft Bevel style, type **Invest early**, press [Enter], type **for**, press [Enter], then type **the long haul**.

TABLE 3-4

	Stocks	Bonds	Mutual funds
1 Year	5.3%	1.9%	3.8%
3 Year	4.8%	3.7%	6.7%
5 Year	3.2%	2.2%	8.3%
10 Year	2.6%	3.4%	7.2%

i. Click the Text Effects button, point to Transform, then apply the Button text effect from the Follow Path section.

j. Move the WordArt object to a blank area of the slide, click the Text Effects button, point to Shadow, then apply an Outer shadow effect.

k. View the presentation slide show, make any necessary changes, then save your work. See **FIGURE 3-19**.

l. Submit the presentation to your instructor, then close the presentation, and exit PowerPoint.

FIGURE 3-19

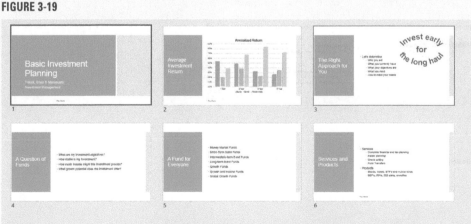

Independent Challenge 2

You work for the Boston Port Group in the commercial container division. You have been asked to enhance a marketing presentation that is going to promote the port facilities. You work on completing a presentation by inserting a picture, a text box, and a table.

a. Start PowerPoint, open PPT 3-11.pptx from the location where you store your Data Files, and save it as **PPT 3-Port**.

b. Add your name and today's date to Slide 1 in the Subtitle text box.

c. Apply the Droplet theme to the presentation.

d. On Slide 5, click the Pictures icon in the content placeholder, then insert the file PPT 3-12.jpg from the location where you store your Data Files.

e. Apply the Simple Frame, Black picture style to the picture, click the Color button, then change the color saturation to Saturation: 0%.

f. Change the size of the picture so its width is 5.2" using the Width text box in the Size group.

g. Insert a text box on the slide below the picture, type **Largest volume port on East Coast**, then format the text and text box with three formatting commands.

h. Go to Slide 2, select the picture, click the Picture Effects button, point to Soft Edges, then click 5 Point.

i. Open the Artistic Effects gallery, then apply the Cement effect to the picture.

j. Go to Slide 4, create a new table, then enter the data in **TABLE 3-5**. Format the table using at least two formatting commands. Be able to identify which formatting commands you applied to the table.

k. View the final presentation in Slide Show view. Make any necessary changes (refer to **FIGURE 3-20**).

l. Save the presentation, submit the presentation to your instructor, close the file, and exit PowerPoint.

TABLE 3-5

Total	August	September
Total containers	25,524.0	22,417.0
Loaded containers	15,283.0	14,016.0
Empty containers	10,241.0	8,401.0
Total tons	375,240	334,180

FIGURE 3-20

Independent Challenge 3

You work for World Partners Inc., a company that produces instructional software to help people learn foreign languages. Once a year, World Partners holds a meeting with their biggest client, the United States Department of Homeland Security, to brief the government on new products and to receive feedback on existing products. Your supervisor has started a presentation and has asked you to look it over and add other elements to make it look better.

a. Start PowerPoint, open PPT 3-13.pptx from the location where you store your Data Files, and save it as **PPT 3-World**.

b. Add an appropriate design theme to the presentation.

c. Insert the Word outline PPT 3-14.docx after the Product Revisions slide, then reset the new slides to the design theme.

d. Insert and format a text object and a WordArt object.

e. Insert an appropriate table on a slide of your choice. Use your own information, or use text from a bulleted list on one of the slides.

f. Add your name as footer text on the slides, then save the presentation.

g. Submit your presentation to your instructor, close the file, then exit PowerPoint.

Independent Challenge 4: Explore

As an international exchange student at your college, one of your assignments in your Intercultural Communication Studies class is to present information on a student exchange you took last semester. You need to create a pictorial presentation that highlights a trip to a different country. Create a presentation using your own pictures. If you don't have access to any appropriate pictures, use the three pictures provided in the Data Files for this unit: PPT 3-15.jpg, PPT 3-16.jpg, and PPT 3-17.jpg. (*NOTE: To complete steps below, your computer must be connected to the Internet.*)

a. Start PowerPoint, create a new blank presentation, and save it as **PPT 3-Exchange** to the location where you store your Data Files.

b. Locate and insert the pictures you want to use. Place one picture on each slide using the Content with Caption slide layout, then apply a picture style to each picture.

c. Click the Crop list arrow, and use one of the other cropping options to crop a picture.

d. Add information about each picture in the text placeholder, and enter a slide title. If you use the pictures provided, research Costa Rica, using the Internet for relevant information to place on the slides.

e. Apply an appropriate design theme, then apply an appropriate title and your name to the title slide.

f. View the final presentation slide show (refer to FIGURE 3-21).

g. Add a slide number and your class name as footer text to all of the slides, save your work, then submit your presentation to your instructor.

h. Close the file, and exit PowerPoint.

FIGURE 3-21

© Tami Freed/Shutterstock; © Ruth Choi/Shutterstock; © Mihai-Bogdan Lazar/Shutterstock

Visual Workshop

Create a one-slide presentation that looks like **FIGURE 3-22**. The slide layout used is a specific layout designed for pictures. Insert the picture file PPT 3-18.jpg to complete this presentation. Add your name as footer text to the slide, save the presentation as **PPT 3-TCM** to the location where you store your Data Files, then submit your presentation to your instructor.

FIGURE 3-22

© tcly/Shutterstock

Finishing a Presentation

CASE You have reviewed your work and are pleased with the slides you created so far for the Reason2Go presentation. Now you are ready to add some final enhancements to the slides to make the PowerPoint presentation interesting to watch.

Module Objectives

After completing this module, you will be able to:

- Modify masters
- Customize the background and theme
- Use slide show commands
- Set slide transitions and timings
- Animate objects
- Use proofing and language tools
- Inspect a presentation
- Create an Office Mix

Files You Will Need

PPT 4-1.pptx	PPT 4-6.jpg
PPT 4-2.jpg	PPT 4-7.pptx
PPT 4-3.pptx	PPT 4-8.pptx
PPT 4-4.jpg	PPT 4-9.jpg
PPT 4-5.pptx	PPT 4-10.jpg

Modify Masters

Learning
Outcomes
• Navigate Slide
  Master view
• Add and modify
  a picture

Each presentation in PowerPoint has a set of **masters** that store information about the theme and slide layouts. Masters determine the position and size of text and content placeholders, fonts, slide background, color, and effects. There are three Master views: Slide Master view, Notes Master view, and Handout Master view. Changes made in Slide Master view are reflected on the slides in Normal view; changes made in Notes Master view are reflected in Notes Page view, and changes made in Handout Master view appear when you print your presentation using a handout printing option. The primary benefit to modifying a master is that you can make universal changes to your whole presentation instead of making individual repetitive changes to each of your slides. **CASE** ▶ *You want to add the R2G company logo to every slide in your presentation, so you open your presentation and insert the logo on the slide master.*

STEPS

1. **Start PowerPoint, open the presentation** PPT 4-1.pptx **from the location where you store your Data Files, save the presentation as** PPT 4-R2G, **then click the** View tab **on the Ribbon**
   The title slide for the presentation appears.

QUICK TIP
You can press and hold [Shift] and click the Normal button on the status bar to display the slide master.

2. **Click the** Slide Master button **in the Master Views group, scroll to the top of the Master Thumbnails pane, then click the** Wisp Slide Master thumbnail **(first thumbnail)**
   The Slide Master view appears with the slide master displayed in the Slide pane as shown in **FIGURE 4-1**. A new tab, the Slide Master tab, appears next to the Home tab on the Ribbon. The slide master is the Wisp theme slide master. Each theme comes with its own slide master. Each master text placeholder on the slide master identifies the font size, style, color, and position of text placeholders on the slides in Normal view. For example, for the Wisp theme, the Master title placeholder positioned at the top of the slide uses a black, 36 pt, Century Gothic font. Slide titles use this font style and formatting. Each slide master comes with associated slide layouts located below the slide master in the Master Thumbnails pane. Slide layouts follow the information on the slide master, and changes you make are reflected in all of the slide layouts.

QUICK TIP
You can make sure the current master remains with the presentation by clicking the Preserve button in the Edit Master group.

3. **Point to each of the** slide layouts **in the Master Thumbnails pane, then click the** Title and Content Layout thumbnail
   As you point to each slide layout, a ScreenTip appears identifying each slide layout by name and lists if any slides in the presentation are using the layout. Slides 2–9 and 12–15 are using the Title and Content Layout.

4. **Click the** Wisp Slide Master thumbnail, **click the** Insert tab **on the Ribbon, then click the** Pictures button **in the Images group**
   The Insert Picture dialog box opens.

5. **Select the picture file** PPT 4-2.jpg **from the location where you store your Data Files, then click** Insert
   The R2G logo picture is placed on the slide master and will now appear on all slides in the presentation. The picture is too large and would look better with a transparent background.

6. **Click** 2.45" **in the** Width text box **in the Size group, type** 1.75, **press** [Enter], **click the** Color button **in the Adjust group, then click** Set Transparent Color
   The pointer changes to ⬟.

QUICK TIP
To reset the background color of a picture to its original state, click the Reset Picture button in the Adjust group.

7. **Click the** lime green color **in the logo picture, drag the** logo **as shown in FIGURE 4-2, then click a blank area of the slide**
   The picture background color is now transparent.

8. **Click the** Normal button 🖳 **on the status bar, then save your changes**

FIGURE 4-1: Slide Master view

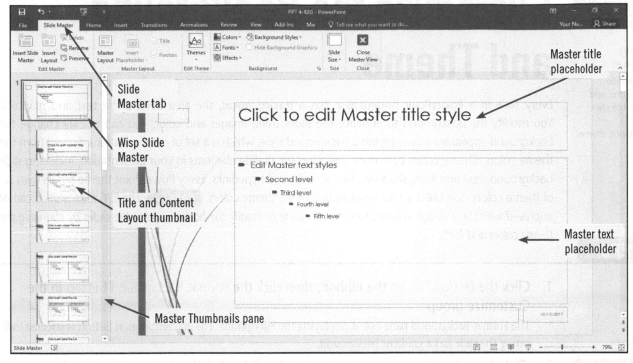

FIGURE 4-2: Picture added to slide master

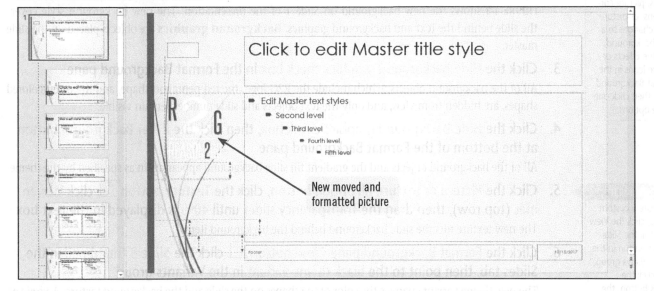

Create custom slide layouts

As you work with PowerPoint, you may find that you need to develop a customized slide layout. For example, you may need to create a presentation for a client that has a slide that displays four pictures with a caption underneath each picture. To make everyone's job easier, you can create a custom slide layout that includes only the placeholders you need. To create a custom slide layout, open Slide Master view, and then click the Insert Layout button in the Edit Master group. A new slide layout appears below the last layout for the selected master in the Master Thumbnails pane.

You can choose to add several different placeholders including Content, Text, Picture, Chart, Table, SmartArt, Media, and Online Image. Click the Insert Placeholder list arrow in the Master Layout group, click the placeholder you want to add, drag ✛ to create the placeholder, then position the placeholder on the slide. In Slide Master view, you can add or delete placeholders in any of the slide layouts. You can rename a custom slide layout by clicking the Rename button in the Edit Master group and entering a descriptive name to better identify the layout.

Customize the Background and Theme

Learning Outcomes
- Apply a slide background and change the style
- Modify presentation theme

Every slide in a PowerPoint presentation has a **background**, the area behind the text and graphics. You modify the background to enhance the slides using images and color. You can quickly change the background appearance by applying a background style, which is a set of color variations derived from the theme colors. Theme colors determine the colors for all slide elements in your presentation, including slide background, text and lines, shadows, fills, accents, and hyperlinks. Every PowerPoint theme has its own set of theme colors. See **TABLE 4-1** for a description of the theme colors. **CASE** *The R2G presentation can be improved with some design enhancements. You decide to modify the background of the slides by changing the theme colors and fonts.*

STEPS

1. **Click the** Design tab **on the Ribbon, then click the** Format Background button **in the Customize group**
   The Format Background pane opens displaying the Fill options. The gradient option button is selected indicating the slide has a gradient background.

QUICK TIP
To add artistic effects, picture corrections, or picture color changes to a slide background, click the Effects or Picture icons in the Format Background pane, then click one of the options.

2. **Click the** Solid fill option button, **review the slide, click the** Pattern fill option button, **then click the** Dotted diamond **pattern (seventh row)**
   FIGURE 4-3 shows the new background on Slide 1 of the presentation. The new background style covers the slide behind the text and background graphics. **Background graphics** are objects placed on the slide master.

3. **Click the** Hide background graphics check box **in the Format Background pane**
   All of the background objects, which include the R2G logo, the red pentagon shape, and the other colored shapes, are hidden from view, and only the text objects and slide number remain visible.

4. **Click the** Hide background graphics check box, **then click the** Reset Background button **at the bottom of the Format Background pane**
   All of the background objects and the gradient fill slide background appear again as specified by the theme.

QUICK TIP
To create a custom theme, click the View tab, click the Slide Master button in the Master Views group, then click the Colors button, the Fonts button, or the Effects button in the Background group.

5. **Click the** Picture or texture fill option button, **click the** Texture button ⊞, **click** Woven mat **(top row), then drag the** Transparency slider **until 40% is displayed in the text box**
   The new texture fills the slide background behind the background items.

6. **Click the** Format Background pane Close button ⊠, **click the** Slide 3 thumbnail **in the Slides tab, then point to the** black theme variant **in the Variants group**
   The new theme variant changes the color of the shapes on the slide and the background texture. A **variant** is a custom variation of the applied theme, in this case the Wisp theme. Theme variants are similar to the original theme, but they are made up of different complementary colors, slide backgrounds, such as textures and patterns, and background elements, such as shapes and pictures.

7. **Point to the other** variants **in the Variants group, click the** second variant **from the left, then save your work**
   The new variant is applied to the slide master and to all the slides in the presentation. Compare your screen to **FIGURE 4-4**.

FIGURE 4-3: New background style applied

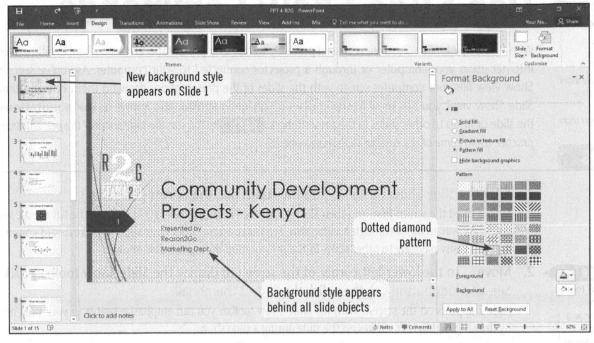

FIGURE 4-4: New theme variant

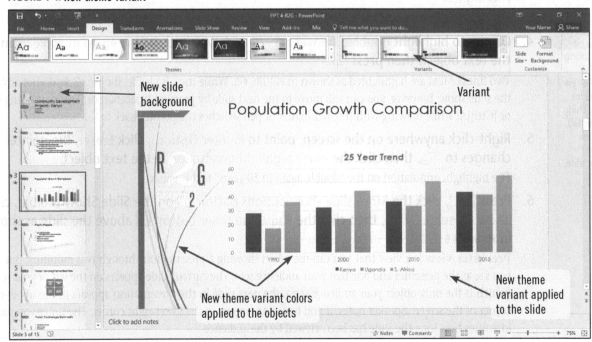

TABLE 4-1: Theme colors

color element	description
Text/Background colors	Contrasting colors for typed characters and the slide background
Accent colors	There are six accent colors used for shapes, drawn lines, and text; the shadow color for text and objects and the fill and outline color for shapes are all accent colors; all of these colors contrast appropriately with background and text colors
Hyperlink color	Colors used for hyperlinks you insert
Followed Hyperlink color	Color used for hyperlinks after they have been clicked

Use Slide Show Commands

Learning
Outcomes
• Preview a slide show
• Navigate a slide show
• Use slide show tools

With PowerPoint, Slide Show view is used primarily to deliver a presentation to an audience, either over the Internet using your computer or through a projector connected to your computer. As you've seen, Slide Show view fills your computer screen with the slides of the presentation, showing them one at a time. In Slide Show view, you can draw freehand pen or highlighter strokes, also known as **ink annotations**, on the slide or jump to other slides in the presentation. **CASE** *You run the slide show of the presentation and practice using some of the custom slide show options.*

STEPS

1. **Click the** Slide Show button 🖵 **on the status bar, then press** [Spacebar]

   Slide 3 filled the screen first, and then Slide 4 appears. Pressing [Spacebar] or clicking the left mouse button is an easy way to move through a slide show. See **TABLE 4-2** for other basic slide show keyboard commands. You can easily navigate to other slides in the presentation during the slide show.

2. **Move** 🔓 **to the lower-left corner of the screen to display the Slide Show toolbar, click the** See all slides button ⭕, **then click the** Slide 2 thumbnail

   Slide 2 appears on the screen. With the Slide Show toolbar you can emphasize points in your presentation by drawing highlighter strokes on the slide during a slide show.

3. **Click the** Pen and laser pointer tools button ⭕, **on the Slide Show toolbar, then click** Highlighter

   The pointer changes to the highlighter pointer ▮. You can use the highlighter anywhere on the slide.

4. **Drag** ▮, **to highlight** doubled between 1970 and 2015 **and** double again in 50 years **in the text object, then press** [Esc]

   Two lines of text are highlighted as shown in **FIGURE 4-5**. While the ▮ is visible, mouse clicks do not advance the slide show; however, you can still move to the next slide by pressing [Spacebar] or [Enter]. Pressing [Esc] or [Ctrl][A] while drawing with the highlighter or pen switches the pointer back to 🔓.

5. **Right-click anywhere on the screen, point to** Pointer Options, **click** Eraser, **the pointer changes to** ✎⃥, **then click the** lower highlight annotation **in the text object**

   The highlight annotation on the "double again in 50 years" text is erased.

6. **Press** [Esc], **click the** More slide show options button ⭕ **on the Slide Show toolbar, click** Show Presenter View, **then click the** Pause the timer button ⏸ **above the slide as shown in FIGURE 4-6**

   Presenter view is a view that you can use when showing a presentation through two monitors; one that you see as the presenter and one that your audience sees. The current slide appears on the left of your screen (which is the only object your audience sees), the next slide in the presentation appears in the upper-right corner of the screen. Speaker notes, if you have any, appear in the lower-right corner. The timer you paused identifies how long the slide has been viewed by the audience.

7. **Click** ⭕, **click** Hide Presenter View, **then click the** Advance to the next slide button ⊙ **on the Slide Show toolbar**

   Slide 3 appears.

8. **Press** [Enter] **to advance through the entire slide show until you see a black slide, then press** [Spacebar]

   If there are ink annotations on your slides, you have the option of saving them when you quit the slide show. Saved ink annotations appear as drawn objects in Normal view.

9. **Click** Discard, **then save the presentation**

   The highlight ink annotation is deleted on Slide 2, and Slide 3 appears in Normal view.

Finishing a Presentation

FIGURE 4-5: Slide 2 in Slide Show view with highlighter drawings

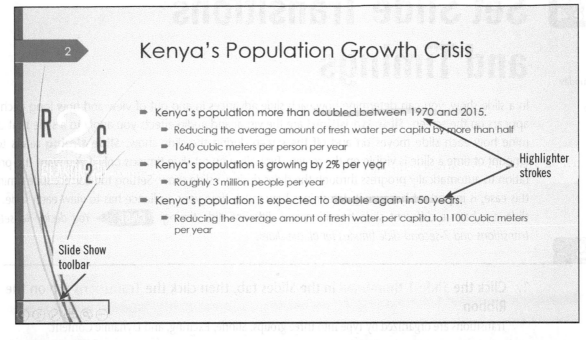

FIGURE 4-6: Slide 2 in Presenter view

TABLE 4-2: Basic Slide Show view keyboard commands

keyboard commands	description
[Enter], [Spacebar], [PgDn], [N], [down arrow], or [right arrow]	Advances to the next slide
[E]	Erases the ink annotation drawing
[Home], [End]	Moves to the first or last slide in the slide show
[up arrow], [PgUp], or [left arrow]	Returns to the previous slide
[S]	Pauses the slide show when using automatic timings; press again to continue
[B]	Changes the screen to black; press again to return
[Esc]	Stops the slide show

Set Slide Transitions and Timings

Learning Outcomes
- Apply and modify a transition
- Modify slide timings

In a slide show, you can determine how each slide advances in and out of view and how long each slide appears on the screen. **Slide transitions** are the visual and audio effects you apply to a slide that determine how each slide moves on and off the screen during the slide show. **Slide timing** refers to the amount of time a slide is visible on the screen. Typically, you set slide timings only if you want the presentation to automatically progress through the slides during a slide show. Setting the correct slide timing, in this case, is important because it determines how much time your audience has to view each slide. Each slide can have a different slide transition and different slide timing. **CASE** *You decide to set slide transitions and 7-second slide timings for all the slides.*

STEPS

1. **Click the** Slide 1 thumbnail **in the Slides tab, then click the** Transitions tab **on the Ribbon**

   Transitions are organized by type into three groups: Subtle, Exciting, and Dynamic Content.

2. **Click the** More button ⟱ **in the Transition to This Slide group, then click** Drape **in the Exciting section**

   The new slide transition plays on the slide, and a transition icon ★ appears next to the slide thumbnail in the Slides tab as shown in **FIGURE 4-7**. You can customize the slide transition by changing its direction and speed.

> **QUICK TIP**
> You can add a sound that plays with the transition from the Sound list arrow in the Timing group.

3. **Click the** Effect Options button **in the Transition to This Slide group, click** Right, **click the** Duration up arrow **in the Timing group until** 3.00 **appears, then click the** Preview button **in the Preview group**

   The Drape slide transition now plays from the right on the slide for 3.00 seconds. You can apply this transition with the custom settings to all of the slides in the presentation.

4. **Click the** Apply To All button **in the Timing group, then click the** Slide Sorter button ▦ **on the status bar**

   All of the slides now have the customized Drape transition applied to them as identified by the transition icons located below each slide. You also have the ability to determine how slides progress during a slide show—either manually by mouse click or automatically by slide timing.

5. **Click the** On Mouse Click check box **under Advance Slide in the Timing group to clear the check mark**

   When this option is selected, you would have to click to manually advance slides during a slide show. Now, with this option disabled, you can set the slides to advance automatically after a specified amount of time.

> **QUICK TIP**
> Click the transition icon under any slide in Slide Sorter view to see its transition play.

6. **Click the** After up arrow **in the Timing group, until** 00:07.00 **appears in the text box, then click the** Apply To All button

   The timing between slides is 7 seconds as indicated by the time under each slide thumbnail in **FIGURE 4-8**. When you run the slide show, each slide will remain on the screen for 7 seconds. You can override a slide's timing and speed up the slide show by using any of the manual advance slide commands.

7. **Click the** Slide Show button 🖵 **on the status bar**

   The slide show advances automatically. A new slide appears every 7 seconds using the Drape transition.

8. **When you see the black slide, press** [Spacebar], **then save your changes**

   The slide show ends and returns to Slide Sorter view with Slide 1 selected.

FIGURE 4-7: Applied slide transition

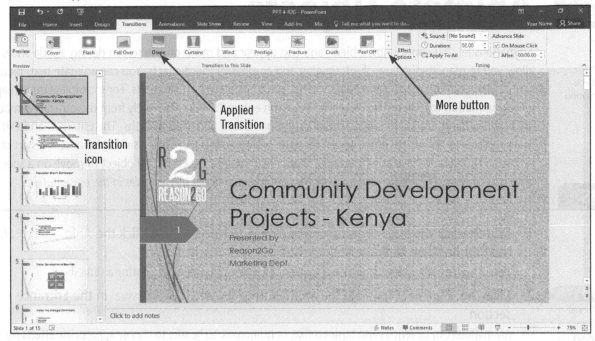

FIGURE 4-8: Slide sorter view showing applied transition and timing

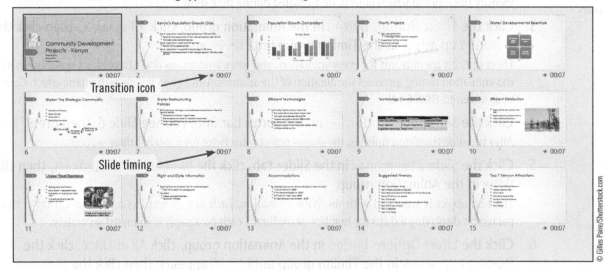

Rehearsing slide show timings

You can set different slide timings for each slide; for example, the title slide can appear for 20 seconds and the second slide for 1 minute. To set timings click the Rehearse Timings button in the Set Up group on the Slide Show tab. Slide Show view opens and the Recording toolbar shown in **FIGURE 4-9** opens. It contains buttons to pause between slides and to advance to the next slide. After opening the Recording toolbar, you can practice giving your presentation by manually advancing each slide in the presentation. When you are finished, PowerPoint displays the total recorded time for the presentation and you have the option to save the recorded timings. The next time you run the slide show, you can use the timings you rehearsed.

FIGURE 4-9: Recording toolbar

PowerPoint 2016

Animate Objects

Animations let you control how objects and text appear and move on the screen during a slide show and allow you to manage the flow of information and emphasize specific facts. You can animate text, pictures, sounds, hyperlinks, SmartArt diagrams, charts, and individual chart elements. For example, you can apply a Fade animation to bulleted text so each paragraph enters the slide separately from the others. Animations are organized into four categories, Entrance, Emphasis, Exit, and Motion Paths. The Entrance and Exit animations cause an object to enter or exit the slide with an effect. An Emphasis animation causes an object visible on the slide to have an effect and a Motion Path animation causes an object to move on a specified path on the slide. **CASE** *You animate the text and graphics of several slides in the presentation.*

STEPS

1. **Double-click the** Slide 5 thumbnail **to return to Normal view, click the** Animations tab **on the Ribbon, then click the** SmartArt object

   Text as well as other objects, such as a shape or picture, can be animated during a slide show.

2. **Click the** More button ▼ **in the Animation group, then click** Swivel **in the Entrance section**

   Animations can be serious and business-like, or humorous, so be sure to choose appropriate effects for your presentation. A small numeral 1, called an animation tag ⬚, appears near the object. **Animation tags** identify the order in which objects are animated during slide show.

3. **Click the** Effect Options button **in the Animation group, click** All at Once, **then click the** Duration up arrow **in the Timing group until** 03.00 **appears**

   Effect options are different for every animation, and some animations don't have effect options. Changing the animation timing increases the duration of the animation and gives it a more dramatic effect. Compare your screen to **FIGURE 4-10**.

4. **Click the** Slide Show button ▭ **on the status bar until you see Slide 6, then press** [Esc]

   After the slide transition finishes, the shapes object spins twice for a total of three seconds.

5. **Click the** Slide 2 thumbnail **in the Slides tab, click the** bulleted list text object, **then click** Wipe **in the Animation group**

   The text object is animated with the Wipe animation. Each line of text has an animation tag with each paragraph displaying a different number. Accordingly, each paragraph is animated separately.

6. **Click the** Effect Options button **in the Animation group, click** All at Once, **click the** Duration up arrow **in the Timing group until** 02.00 **appears, then click the** Preview **button in the Preview group**

   Notice the animation tags for each line of text in the text object now have the same numeral (1), indicating that each line of text animates at the same time.

7. **Click** Population **in the title text object, click** ▼ **in the Animation group, scroll down, then click** Shapes **in the Motion Paths section**

   A motion path object appears over the shapes object and identifies the direction and shape, or path, of the animation. When needed, you can move, resize, and change the direction of the motion path. Notice the numeral 2 animation tag next to the title text object indicating that it is animated *after* the bulleted list text object. Compare your screen to **FIGURE 4-11**.

8. **Click the** Move Earlier button **in the Timing group, click the** Slide Show tab **on the Ribbon, then click the** From Beginning button **in the Start Slide Show group**

   The slide show begins from Slide 1. The animations make the presentation more interesting to view.

9. **When you see the black slide, press** [Enter], **then save your changes**

FIGURE 4-10: Animation applied to SmartArt object

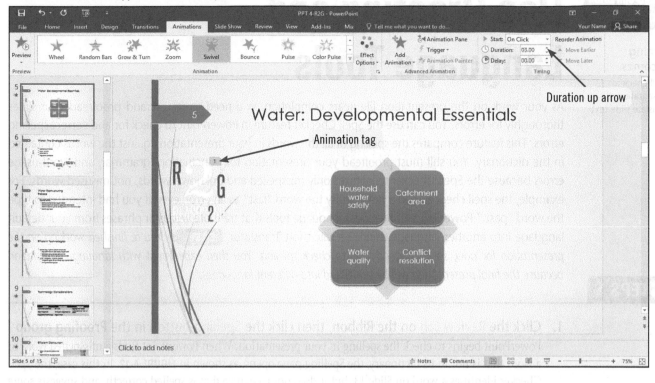

FIGURE 4-11: Motion path applied to title text object

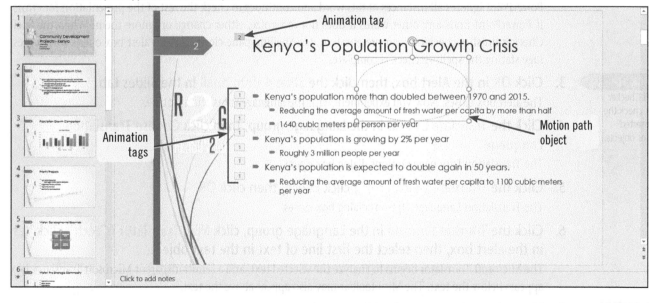

Attaching a sound to an animation

Text or objects that have animation applied can be customized further by attaching a sound for extra emphasis. First, select the animated object, then on the Animations tab, click the Animation Pane button in the Advanced Animation group. In the Animation Pane, click the animation you want to apply the sound to, click the Animation list arrow, then click Effect Options to open the animation effect's dialog box. In the Enhancements section, click the Sound list arrow, then choose a sound. Click OK when you are finished. Now, when you run the slide show, the sound you applied will play with the animation.

Use Proofing and Language Tools

Learning Outcomes
• Spell check a presentation
• Translate slide text

As your work on the presentation file nears completion, you need to review and proofread your slides thoroughly for errors. You can use the Spell Checker feature in PowerPoint to check for and correct spelling errors. This feature compares the spelling of all the words in your presentation against the words contained in the dictionary. You still must proofread your presentation for punctuation, grammar, and word-usage errors because the Spell Checker recognizes only misspelled and unknown words, not misused words. For example, the spell checker would not identify the word "last" as an error, even if you had intended to type the word "past." PowerPoint also includes language tools that translate words or phrases from your default language into another language using the Microsoft Translator. **CASE** ▶ *You're finished working on the presentation for now, so it's a good time to check spelling. You then experiment with language translation because the final presentation will be translated into different languages.*

STEPS

1. **Click the** Review tab **on the Ribbon, then click the** Spelling button **in the Proofing group**

   PowerPoint begins to check the spelling in your presentation. When PowerPoint finds a misspelled word or a word that is not in its dictionary, the Spelling pane opens, as shown in **FIGURE 4-12**. In this case, the Spell Checker identifies a word on Slide 13, but it does not recognize that is spelled correctly and suggests some replacement words.

2. **Click** Ignore All **in the Spelling pane**

   PowerPoint ignores all instances of this word and continues to check the rest of the presentation for errors. If PowerPoint finds any other words it does not recognize, either change or ignore them. When the Spell Checker finishes checking your presentation, the Spelling pane closes, and an alert box opens with a message stating the spelling check is complete.

QUICK TIP
The Spell Checker does not check the text in inserted pictures or objects.

3. **Click** OK **in the Alert box, then click the** Slide 4 thumbnail **in the Slides tab**

   The alert box closes. Now you experiment with the language translation feature.

4. **Click the** Translate button **in the Language group, then click** Choose Translation Language

   The Translation Language Options dialog box opens.

5. **Click the** Translate to list arrow, **click** Czech, **then click** OK

   The Translation Language Options dialog box closes.

6. **Click the** Translate button **in the Language group, click** Mini Translator [Czech], **click** Yes **in the alert box, then select the first line of text in the text object**

   The Microsoft Translator begins to analyze the selected text, and a semitransparent Microsoft Translator box appears below the text. The Mini toolbar may also appear above the text.

QUICK TIP
To copy the translated text to a slide, click the Copy button at the bottom of the Microsoft Translator box, right-click the slide, then click a Paste option.

7. **Move the pointer over the** Microsoft Translator box

   A Czech translation of the text appears as shown in **FIGURE 4-13**. The translation language setting remains in effect until you reset it.

8. **Click the** Translate button **in the Language group, click** Choose Translation Language, **click the** Translate to list arrow, **click** English (United States), **click** OK, **click the** Translate button **again, then click** Mini Translator [English (United States)]

   The Mini Translator is turned off, and the translation language is restored to the default setting.

FIGURE 4-12: Spelling pane

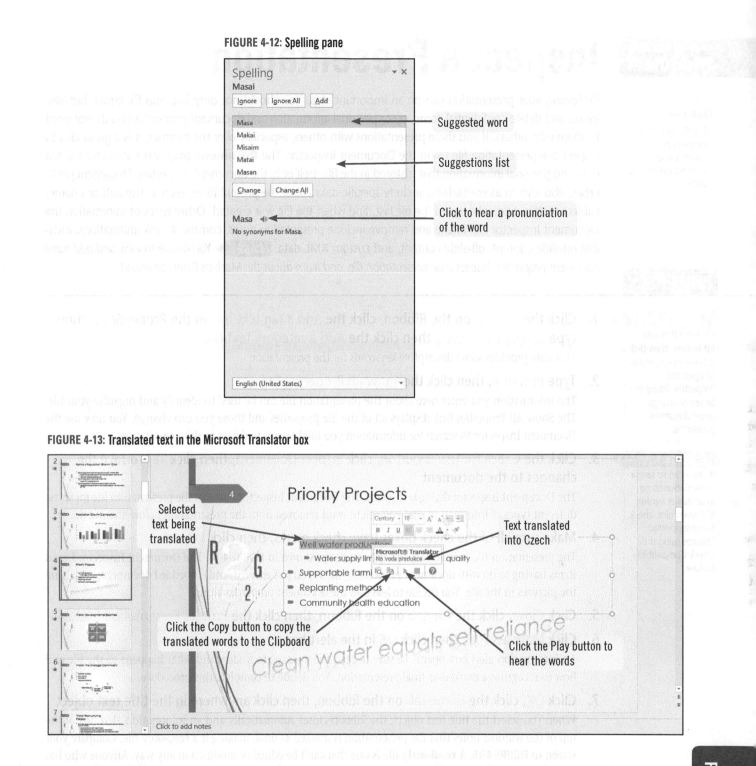

FIGURE 4-13: Translated text in the Microsoft Translator box

Checking spelling as you type

By default, PowerPoint checks your spelling as you type. If you type a word that is not in the dictionary, a wavy red line appears under it. To correct an error, right-click the misspelled word, then review the suggestions, which appear in the shortcut menu. You can select a suggestion, add the word you typed to your custom dictionary, or ignore it. To turn off automatic spell checking, click the File tab, then click Options to open the PowerPoint Options dialog box. Click Proofing in the left column, then click the Check spelling as

you type check box to deselect it. To temporarily hide the wavy red lines, click the Hide spelling and grammar errors check box to select it. Contextual spelling in PowerPoint identifies common grammatically misused words, for example, if you type the word "their" and the correct word is "there," PowerPoint will identify the mistake and place a wavy red line under the word. To turn contextual spelling on or off, click Proofing in the PowerPoint Options dialog box, then click the Check grammar with spelling check box.

Inspect a Presentation

Learning Outcomes
• Modify document properties
• Inspect and remove unwanted data

Reviewing your presentation can be an important step. You should not only find and fix errors, but also locate and delete confidential company or personal information and document properties you do not want to share with others. If you share presentations with others, especially over the Internet, it is a good idea to inspect the presentation file using the Document Inspector. The **Document Inspector** looks for hidden data and personal information that is stored in the file itself or in the document properties. Document properties, also known as **metadata**, include specific data about the presentation, such as the author's name, subject matter, title, who saved the file last, and when the file was created. Other types of information the Document Inspector can locate and remove include presentation notes, comments, ink annotations, invisible on-slide content, off-slide content, and custom XML data. **CASE** ▶ *You decide to view and add some document properties, inspect your presentation file, and learn about the Mark as Final command.*

STEPS

QUICK TIP
Click the Properties list button, then click Advanced Properties to open the Properties dialog box to see or change more document properties.

1. **Click the** File tab **on the Ribbon, click the** Add a tag text box **in the Properties section, type** Kenya, water well, **then click the** Add a category text box
   This data provides some descriptive keywords for the presentation.

2. **Type** Proposal, **then click the** Show All Properties link
   The information you enter here about the presentation file can be used to identify and organize your file. The Show All Properties link displays all of the file properties and those you can change. You now use the Document Inspector to search for information you might want to delete in the presentation.

QUICK TIP
If you need to save a presentation to run in an earlier version of PowerPoint, check for unsupported features using the Check Compatibility feature.

3. **Click the** Check for Issues button, **click** Inspect Document, **then click** Yes **to save the changes to the document**
   The Document Inspector dialog box opens. The Document Inspector searches the presentation file for seven different types of information that you might want removed from the presentation before sharing it.

4. **Make sure all of the check boxes have check marks, then click** Inspect
   The presentation file is reviewed, and the results are shown in **FIGURE 4-14**. The Document Inspector found items having to do with document properties, which you just entered, and embedded documents which are the pictures in the file. You decide to leave all the document properties alone.

5. **Click** Close, **click the** File tab **on the Ribbon, then click the** Protect Presentation button

6. **Click** Mark as Final, **then click** OK **in the alert box**
   An information alert box opens. Be sure to read the message to understand what happens to the file and how to recognize a marked-as-final presentation. You decide to complete this procedure.

7. **Click** OK, **click the** Home tab **on the Ribbon, then click anywhere in the title text object**
   When you select the title text object, the Ribbon closes automatically and an information alert box at the top of the window notes that the presentation is marked as final, making it a read-only file. Compare your screen to **FIGURE 4-15**. A **read-only** file is one that can't be edited or modified in any way. Anyone who has received a read-only presentation can only edit the presentation by changing its marked-as-final status. You still want to work on the presentation, so you remove the marked-as-final status.

8. **Click the** Edit Anyway button **in the information alert box, then save your changes**
   The Ribbon and all commands are active again, and the file can now be modified.

FIGURE 4-14: Document Inspector dialog box

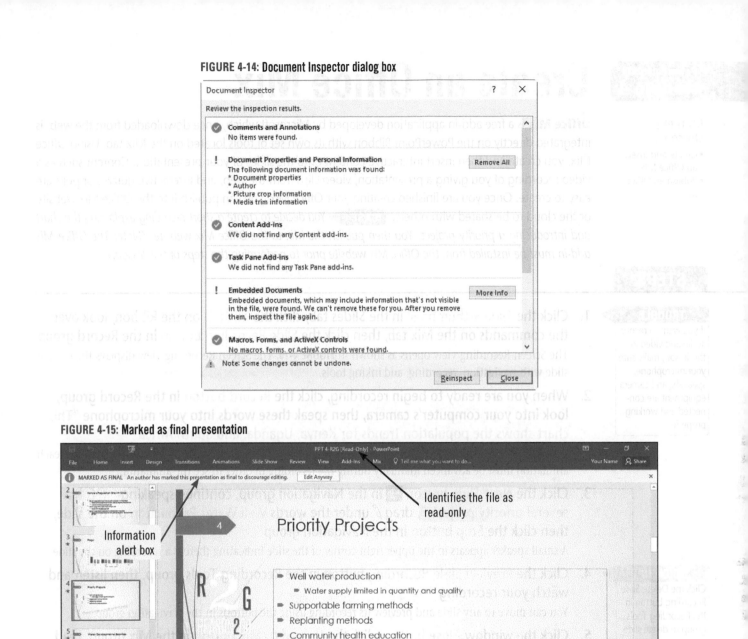

FIGURE 4-15: Marked as final presentation

Digitally sign a presentation

What is a digital signature, and why would you want to use one in PowerPoint? A **digital signature** is similar to a handwritten signature in that it authenticates your document; however, a digital signature, unlike a handwritten signature, is created using computer cryptography and is not visible within the presentation itself. There are three primary reasons you would add a digital signature to a presentation: one, to authenticate the signer of the document; two, to ensure that the content of the presentation has not been changed since it was signed; and three, to assure the reader of the origin of the signed document. To add a digital signature, click the File tab on the Ribbon, click the Protect Presentation button, click Add a Digital Signature, then follow the dialog boxes.

Create an Office Mix

Office Mix is a free add-in application developed by Microsoft which, once downloaded from the web, is integrated directly on the PowerPoint Ribbon with its own set of tools located on the Mix tab. Using Office Mix, you create and then insert interactive content onto the slides of your presentation. Content such as a video recording of you giving a presentation, video clips from the web, and interactive quizzes or polls are easy to create. Once you are finished creating your Office Mix, you can publish it to the Office Mix website or the cloud to be shared with others. **CASE** ▸ *You decide to create a short recording explaining the chart and introducing a priority project. You then publish the Mix to the Office Mix website. (Note: The Office Mix add-in must be installed from the Office Mix website prior to performing the steps of this lesson.)*

STEPS

TROUBLE
If you want to record audio and video in this lesson, make sure your microphone, speakers, and camera equipment are connected and working properly.

1. **Click the** Slide 3 thumbnail **in the Slides tab, click the** Mix tab **on the Ribbon, look over the commands on the Mix tab, then click the** Slide Recording button **in the Record group**
   The Screen Recording view opens as shown in **FIGURE 4-16**. The Screen Recording view displays the current slide with navigation, recording, and inking tools.

2. **When you are ready to begin recording, click the** Record button **in the Record group, look into your computer's camera, then speak these words into your microphone** "This chart shows the population trends for Kenya, Uganda, and South Africa"
   Your Office Mix recording begins as soon as you click the Record button. If a slide has animations, each animation must be advanced manually during the recording in order to see the animation.

3. **Click the** Next Slide button ➡ **in the Navigation group, continue speaking** "R2G has several priority projects", **drag** 🖊 **under the words** Well Water Production **on the slide, then click the** Stop button **in the Navigation group**
   A small speaker appears in the upper right corner of the slide indicating there is a recording on the slide.

QUICK TIP
Click the Delete Slide Recording button in the Recording Tools group to delete slide recordings.

4. **Click the** Preview Slide Recording **button in the Recording Tools group, then listen and watch your recording**
   You can move to any slide and preview its recording using the buttons in the Navigation group.

5. **Click the window** Close button, **click the** Upload to Mix button **in the Mix group, read the information, then click the** Next button **in the Upload to Mix pane**
   The Upload to Mix pane displays sign in account methods.

TROUBLE
If you are not sure which account login option to use, check with your instructor.

6. **Click your** account button **in the Upload to Mix pane, enter your sign in information, click the** Sign in **button, then click the** Next button
   The new Office Mix is uploaded and published to the Office Mix website. There is a percentage counter showing you the upload and publishing progress.

7. **Click the** Show me my Mix button **in the Upload to Mix pane, then, if necessary, click the** Sign in button **on the webpage that appears**
   The Office Mix webpage appears with the new Office Mix you just created as shown in **FIGURE 4-17**. On this page you can provide a content description, a category, or a tag, as well as set permissions.

8. **Click** My Mixes **at the top of the window, click the** PPT 4-R2G Play button, **then follow the directions on the screen to watch the Office Mix**
   Each slide in the presentation, including the Office Mix recordings you made on Slide 3 and 4, appears.

9. **Click** Your Name **at the top of the window, click** sign out, **click your** web browser Close button, **click the** Close button **in the Upload to Mix pane, save your changes, submit your presentation to your instructor, then exit PowerPoint**

FIGURE 4-16: Office Mix screen recording view

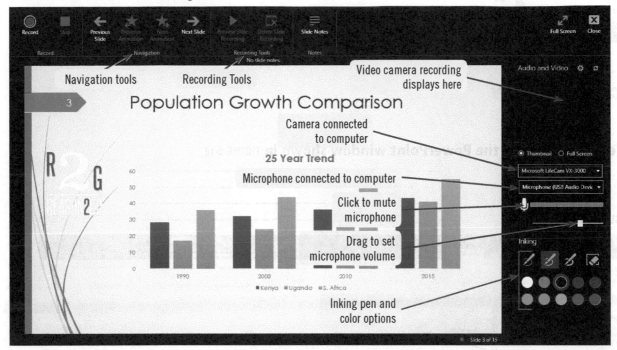

FIGURE 4-17: Office Mix webpage

Inserting a multiple choice interactive quiz

Using the Mix tab, you can create a custom interactive quiz that can be presented in Slide Show view or uploaded to the Office Mix website to share with others. On the Mix tab, click the Quizzes Videos Apps button in the Insert group. In the Lab Office Add-ins dialog box, click Multiple Choice Quiz, then click Trust It. A multiple choice quiz object appears on your slide with blank text boxes that you fill out with a quiz question and answers. Be sure to enter the correct answer in the light green answer text box, then add as many other possible answers as you like. You can customize your question by shuffling the answer every time the question is opened, limiting the number of answer attempts, and allowing more than one right answer.

Practice

Concepts Review

Label each element of the PowerPoint window shown in FIGURE 4-18.

FIGURE 4-18

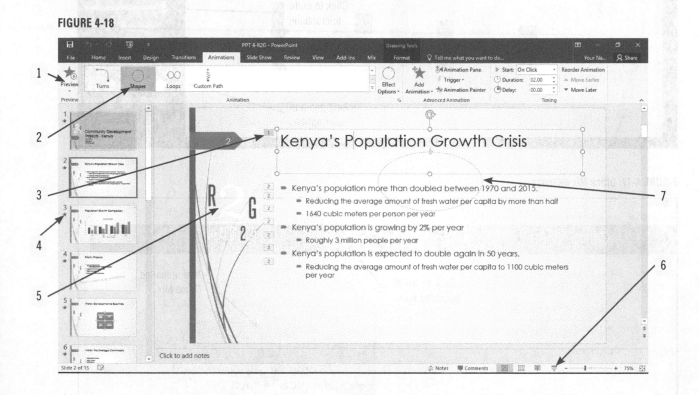

Match each term with the statement that best describes it.

8. Masters

9. Background

10. Presenter view

11. Slide timing

12. Office Mix

13. Ink annotations

   a. The area behind the text and graphics

   b. Drawings on slide created during slide show

   c. A special view that you use when showing a presentation on two monitors

   d. Add-in application you use to create interactive content

   e. Determines how long slide is visible on screen

   f. Slides that store theme and placeholder information

Select the best answer from the list of choices.

14. What determines the position and size of text and content placeholders and the slide background of a presentation?

    a. Home tab   **c.** Master

    b. Background   **d.** Normal view

15. Apply this to your presentation to quickly modify the applied theme.

    a. Office Mix   **c.** Animation

    b. Background   **d.** Variant

16. Freehand pen and highlighter strokes are also known as _____.

    a. ink annotations   **c.** markings

    b. pictures   **d.** scribbles

17. A slide _____ is a special visual effect that determines how a slide moves during a slide show.

    a. annotation   **c.** background

    b. view   **d.** transition

18. Set slide _____ to make your presentation automatically progress through the slides during a slide show.

    a. animations   **c.** hyperlinks

    b. timings   **d.** recordings

19. Animation _____ identify the order in which objects are animated during a slide show.

    a. tags   **c.** thumbnails

    b. paths   **d.** schemes

20. A _____ file is one that can't be edited or modified in any way.

    a. signed   **c.** read-only

    b. final   **d.** saved

Skills Review

1. **Modify masters.**

    a. Open the presentation PPT 4-3.pptx from the location where you store your Data Files, then save the presentation as **PPT 4-Dual Arm**.

    b. Open Slide Master view using the View tab, then click the Circuit Slide Master thumbnail.

    c. Insert the picture PPT 4-4.jpg, then set the background color to transparent.

    d. Resize the picture so it is 1.0" wide.

    e. Drag the picture to the upper-right corner of the slide to align with the top of the Title text object, then deselect the picture.

    f. Switch to Normal view, then save your changes.

2. **Customize the background and theme.**

    a. Click the Design tab, then click the second variant from the left.

    b. Go to Slide 4, then open the Format Background pane.

    c. Click the Solid fill option button, then click Gold, Accent 1, Darker 25%.

    d. Set the Transparency to 30%, close the Format Background pane then save your changes.

Skills Review (continued)

3. Use slide show commands.

  a. Open Slide Show view, then go to Slide 1 using the See all slides button on the Slide Show toolbar.

  b. Use the Pen ink annotation tool to circle the slide title.

  c. Go to Slide 2, then use the Highlighter to highlight four points in the bulleted text on the slide.

  d. Erase two highlight annotations on the bulleted text, then press [Esc].

  e. Open Presenter view, then stop the timer.

  f. Advance the slides to Slide 5, then click the Zoom into the slide button (now called the Zoom out button) on the Slide Show toolbar, then click in the center of the graph.

  g. Click the Zoom into the slide button, then return to Slide 1.

  h. Hide Presenter view, advance through the slide show, save your ink and highlight annotations, then save your work.

4. Set slide transitions and timings.

  a. Go to Slide Sorter view, click the Slide 1 thumbnail, then apply the Fall Over transition to the slide.

  b. Change the effect option to Right, change the duration to 2.50, then apply to all the slides.

  c. Change the slide timing to 5 seconds, then apply to all of the slides.

  d. Switch to Normal view, view the slide show, then save your work.

5. Animate objects.

  a. Go to Slide 3, click the Animations tab, then select both arrows on the slide. (*Hint*: Use SHIFT to select both arrows.)

  b. Apply the Wipe effect to the objects, click the Effect Options button, then apply the From Top effect.

  c. Select the lower two box shapes, apply the Random Bars animation, then preview the animations.

  d. Change the effect options to Vertical, then preview the animations.

  e. Select the top two box shapes, apply the Shape animation, click the Effect Options button, then click Box.

  f. Click the Move Earlier button in the Timing group until the two top box shape animation tags display 1.

  g. Preview the animations, then save your work.

6. Use proofing and language tools.

  a. Check the spelling of the document, and change any misspelled words. Ignore any words that are correctly spelled but that the spell checker doesn't recognize. There is one misspelled word in the presentation.

  b. Go to Slide 6, then set the Mini Translator language to Thai.

  c. View the Thai translation of text on Slide 6.

  d. Choose one other language (or as many as you want), translate words or phrases on the slide, reset the default language to English (United States), turn off the Mini Translator, then save your changes.

7. Inspect a presentation.

  a. On the File tab in the Properties section, type information of your choosing in the Tags and Categories text fields.

  b. Open the Document Inspector dialog box.

  c. Make sure the Off-Slide Content check box is selected, then inspect the presentation.

  d. Delete the off-slide content, then close the dialog box. Save your changes.

8. Create an Office Mix.

  a. Go to Slide 2, open the Mix tab, then click the Slide Recording button.

  b. Click the Record button, speak these words into your microphone, "Here you see the typical applications for the new R2G series dual robotic arm," use your pen to underline the slide title, then click the Stop button.

  c. Preview your slide recording, then close the window.

  d. Click the Upload to Mix button, sign in to your account, then upload your new mix to the Office Mix website.

  e. Watch the Office Mix, sign out of your account, then close the webpage window.

  f. Close the Upload to Mix pane, then save your work.

Skills Review (continued)

g. Switch to Slide Sorter view, then compare your presentation to **FIGURE 4-19**.

h. Submit your presentation to your instructor, then close the presentation.

FIGURE 4-19

Independent Challenge 1

You work for World International Studies Program (WISP) as a study consultant. You have been working on a presentation that describes a new study program developed in Russia. You need to finish up what you have been working on by adding transitions, timings, and animation effects to the presentation.

a. Open the file PPT 4-5.pptx from the location where you store your Data Files, and save the presentation as **PPT 4-WISP**.

b. Add the slide number and your name as the footer on all slides, except the title slide.

c. Open Slide Master view, click the Celestial Slide Master thumbnail, insert the picture PPT 4-6.jpg, then resize the picture so it is 1.5" wide.

d. Click the Color button, then click the Purple, Accent color 1 Dark in the Recolor section.

e. Move the picture to the top left corner of the slide, then close Slide Master view.

f. Apply the Shape animation to the title text on each slide.

g. Apply the Float In animation to the bulleted text objects on each slide.

h. Apply the Shape animation to the picture on Slide 3, then change the effect option to Box.

i. Apply the Vortex slide transition, apply a 5-second slide timing, then apply to all of the slides.

j. Check the spelling of the presentation, save your changes, then view the presentation in Slide Show view.

k. Submit your presentation to your instructor, close the presentation, then exit PowerPoint.

Independent Challenge 2

You are a development engineer at Adtec Global Systems, Inc., a manufacturer of civilian drone technology located in Phoenix, Arizona. Adtec designs and manufactures personal drone systems largely used in the movie industry and in commercial agricultural business. You need to finish the work on a quarterly presentation that outlines the progress of the company's newest technologies by adding animations, customizing the background, and using the Document Inspector.

a. Open the file PPT 4-7.pptx from the location where you store your Data Files, and save the presentation as **PPT 4-Adtec**.

Independent Challenge 2 (continued)

b. Apply an appropriate design theme, then apply a gradient fill slide background to the title slide using the Format Background pane.

c. Apply the Airplane slide transition to all slides, apply the Shape animation to the following objects: the bulleted text on Slide 2 and the table on Slide 4, then change the Effect options on the table to a box shape with an out direction.

d. Use the Microsoft Translator to translate the bulleted text on Slide 2 using two different languages.

e. Run the Document Inspector with all options selected, identify what items the Document Inspector finds, close the Document Inspector dialog box, then review the slides to find the items.

f. Add a slide at the end of the presentation that identifies the items the Document Inspector found.

g. Run the Document Inspector again, and remove all items except the document properties.

h. View the slide show, and make ink annotations to the slides. Save the annotations at the end of the slide show.

i. Add your name as a footer to all slides, check the spelling, fix any misspellings, then save your work.

j. Submit your presentation to your instructor, then close the presentation and exit PowerPoint.

Independent Challenge 3

You work for Buffington, Genung, O'Lynn & Associates, a full-service investment and pension firm. Your manager wants you to create a presentation on pension plan options. You completed adding the information to the presentation, now you need to add a design theme, format information to highlight important facts, add animation effects, and add slide timings.

a. Open the file PPT 4-8.pptx from the location where you store your Data Files, and save the presentation as **PPT 4-Invest**.

b. Apply an appropriate design theme, then apply a theme variant.

c. Apply animation effects to the following objects: the shapes on Slide 3 and the bulleted text on Slide 4. View the slide show to evaluate the effects you added, and make adjustments as necessary.

d. Convert the text on Slide 5 to a Circle Relationship SmartArt graphic (found in the Relationship category).

e. Apply the Inset SmartArt style to the SmartArt graphic, then change its color to Dark 2 Fill.

f. Go to Slide 3, align the Sector and Quality arrow shapes to their bottoms, then align the Allocation and Maturity arrow shapes to their right edges.

g. On Slides 6 and 7, change the table style format to Themed Style 1 - Accent 2, and adjust the tables.

h. Apply a 7-second timing to Slides 3–7 and a 5-second timing to Slides 1 and 2.

i. Add your name as a footer to the slides, check the spelling, then save your work. An example of a finished presentation is shown in **FIGURE 4-20**.

j. Submit your presentation to your instructor, then close the presentation and exit PowerPoint.

FIGURE 4-20

Independent Challenge 4: Explore

You work for the Office of Veterans Affairs at your college. Create a basic presentation that you can publish to the Office Mix website that describes the basic services offered by the school to service members. (*Note: To complete this Independent Challenge, you may need to be connected to the Internet.*)

a. Plan and create the slide presentation that describes the veteran services provided by the college. To help create content, use your school's website or use the Internet to locate information at another college. The presentation should contain at least six slides.

b. Use an appropriate design theme then change the theme variant.

c. Add one or more photographs to the presentation, then style and customize at least one photo.

d. Save the presentation as **PPT 4-Vet** to the location where you store your Data Files.

e. Add slide transitions and animation effects to the presentation. View the slide show to evaluate the effects you added.

f. Go to Slide 5, translate the last line of text in the bulleted text box into Greek, then click the Copy button on the Microsoft Translator box.

g. Insert a new text box on Slide 5, paste the Greek text into the text box, then drag the Greek text box below the bulleted text box.

h. Change the language in the Microsoft translator back to English, then turn off the Microsoft Translator.

i. Add the slide number and your name as a footer to the slides, check the spelling, inspect the presentation, then save your work.

j. Make an Office Mix of this presentation, then upload it to the Office Mix website. Make sure to include information in your recording on at least 2 slides and use the pen to make ink annotations on your slides.

k. Submit your presentation to your instructor, then exit PowerPoint. An example of a finished presentation is shown in **FIGURE 4-21**.

FIGURE 4-21

© Ruth Choi/Shutterstock.com

Visual Workshop

Create a presentation that looks like **FIGURE 4-22**, and **FIGURE 4-23**, which shows two slides with a specific slide layout, slide background, theme, and theme variant. Insert pictures **PPT 4-9** and **PPT 4-10** to the slides, then insert the picture **PPT 4-6** to the presentation slide master. (*Hint*: the slide master picture background is transparent.) Add your name as footer text to the slide, save the presentation as **PPT 4-Corp** to the location where you store your Data Files, then submit your presentation to your instructor.

FIGURE 4-22

© Prasit Rodphan/Shutterstock.com

FIGURE 4-23

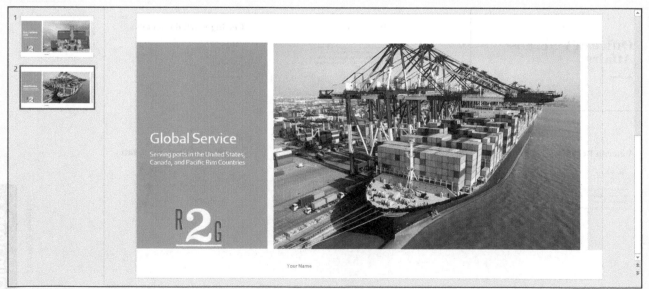

© tcly/Shutterstock.com

Working with Advanced Tools and Masters

CASE As a marketing representative for Reason2Go (R2G), you have been working on a presentation that details specific information on proposed community projects for Kenya. After receiving some initial feedback, you revise the presentation by enhancing shapes, adding animations, and customizing the master views.

Module Objectives

After completing this module, you will be able to:

- Draw and format connectors
- Use advanced formatting tools
- Customize animation effects
- Create custom slide layouts

- Format master text
- Change master text indents
- Adjust text objects
- Use templates and add comments

Files You Will Need

PPT 5-1.pptx	PPT 5-4.pptx
PPT 5-2.pptx	PPT 5-5.pptx
PPT 5-3.pptx	PPT 5-6.pptx

Draw and Format Connectors

Learning Outcomes
• Add and modify connectors

PowerPoint has a number of connector tools that enable you to create three different types of connector lines or arrows—straight, elbow (bent), or curved. For example, you would use the connector tools to connect shapes with a line or arrow. Once you have drawn a line or connector, you can format it using Quick Styles, outline color, or effects. **CASE** *Drawing and formatting connecting lines between the shapes on Slide 15 will enhance the look of the shapes.*

STEPS

1. **Start PowerPoint, open the presentation** PPT 5-1.pptx **from the location where you store your Data Files, save the presentation as** PPT 5-R2G, **click the** Slide 15 thumbnail **in the Slides tab, then click the** More button ⬇ **in the Drawing group**

   Slide 15 of the presentation appears in Normal view, and the Shapes gallery is open.

2. **Right-click the** Elbow Connector button �🔲 **in the Lines section, click** Lock Drawing Mode **on the shortcut menu, then position** ╋ **on the top connection site** ◉ **on the** Nairobi Nat. Park diamond shape

   Notice the shape has four possible connection sites to anchor a line or arrow. Locking the drawing mode allows you to draw the same shape multiple times without having to reselect the tool in the Shapes Gallery. See **FIGURE 5-1**.

TROUBLE
If you accidentally release the mouse before you reach a ◉, a white endpoint is created at the end of the connector. Drag the connector endpoint to the correct connection site.

3. **Press and hold the** left mouse button **on the** ◉, **then drag** ╋ **up to connect to the** bottom ◉ **on the** Mt. Kenya diamond shape

   Green handles (circles) appear at each end of the elbow connector line, indicating that it is attached to the two shapes. The line has one adjustment handle (yellow circle) in the middle of the elbow connector that allows you to alter the path of the line.

4. **Position** ╋ **on the top** ◉ **on the** Mt. Kenya diamond shape, **drag** ╋ **to the right** ◉ **on the** Hells Gate Nat. Park shape, **then press** [Esc]

   A second connector line now flows from the top of the Mt. Kenya diamond shape to the right of the Hells Gate Nat. Park diamond shape. Pressing [Esc] unlocks the drawing mode.

QUICK TIP
If you rearrange shapes that are joined with connector lines, the connector lines remain attached and move with the shapes.

5. **Click the** Mt. Kenya to Hells Gate Nat. Park connector line, **position** ⬈ **over the** green handle **on the** Hells Gate Nat. Park diamond, **then drag the** green handle **to the bottom** ◉ **on the** Hells Gate Nat. Park diamond shape

   The connector line now flows from the top of the Mt. Kenya diamond shape to the bottom of the Hells Gate Nat. Park diamond shape as shown in **FIGURE 5-2**.

6. **Click the** Nairobi Nat. Park to Mt. Kenya connector line, **click the** Drawing Tools Format tab **on the Ribbon, click** ⬇ **in the Shape Styles group, then click** Intense Line – Accent 2 **(third row)**

   The style of the line becomes more distinct.

7. **Click the** Shape Outline list arrow **in the Shape Styles group, point to** Weight, **then click** 3pt

   The line is wider and easier to see.

QUICK TIP
To reroute a connector to the closest points between shapes, right-click the connector, then click Reroute Connectors on the shortcut menu.

8. **Right-click the** Nairobi Nat. Park to Mt. Kenya connector line, **point to** Connector Types **on the shortcut menu, click** Straight Connector, **click a blank area of the slide, then save your presentation**

   The connector line is now straight. Compare your screen to **FIGURE 5-3**.

FIGURE 5-1: Shape with connection sites displayed

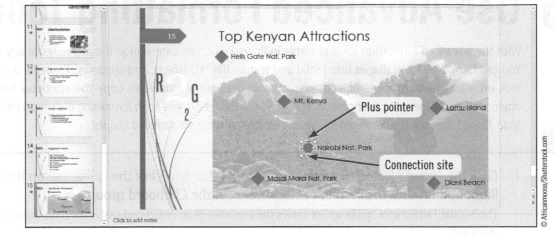

FIGURE 5-2: Moved connector line

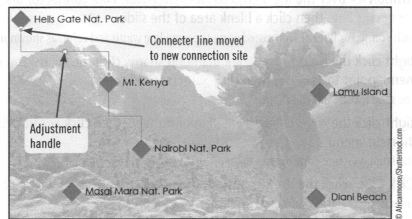

FIGURE 5-3: Formatted connector line

Changing page setup and slide orientation

When you need to customize the size and orientation of the slides in your presentation, you can do so using the Slide Size command in the Customize group on the Design tab. Click the Slide Size button to change the slide size to Widescreen (16:9) or Standard (4:3), or click Custom Slide Size to open the Slide Size dialog box. In the Slide Size dialog box, you can change the width and height of the slides to 13 different settings, including On-screen Show,

Letter Paper, 35mm Slides, and Banner. You can also set a custom slide size by specifying the height and width of the slides. If the presentation would work better in Portrait rather than Landscape mode, you can set the slide orientation by clicking either the Portrait or Landscape option button in the Slides section. The orientation setting for the slides is separate from the orientation setting for the notes, handouts, and outline.

PowerPoint 2016

Use Advanced Formatting Tools

With the advanced formatting tools available in PowerPoint, you can change the attributes of any object. You can format text and shapes using solid and texture fills, 3D effects, and shadows. To create a cohesive look on a slide with multiple objects, you can use the Format Painter to copy the attributes from one object and apply them to other objects. **CASE** ▶ *In this lesson, you finish formatting the connector lines on Slide 15 and then use the advanced formatting tools to enhance the diamond shapes.*

STEPS

1. **Click the** Nairobi Nat. Park to Mt. Kenya connector line, **click the** Home tab **on the Ribbon, then click the** Format Painter button **in the Clipboard group**

   The Format Painter tool "picks up" or copies the attributes of an object and pastes them on the next object you select.

2. **Position** ⬚ **over the** Mt. Kenya to Hells Gate Nat. Park connector line, **click the** connector line, **then click a blank area of the slide**

   Both connector lines are formatted using the same line width and color, as shown in **FIGURE 5-4**.

QUICK TIP
To fill a shape with a picture, right-click the shape, click the Fill button, then click Picture to open the Insert Pictures dialog box.

3. **Right-click the** Nairobi Nat. Park diamond shape, **click the** Fill button **on the shortcut menu, point to** Texture, **then click** Sand **(second row)**

   The sand texture fills the shape.

4. **Right-click the** Nairobi Nat. Park diamond shape, **then click** Format Picture **on the shortcut menu**

   The Format Picture pane opens.

5. **Click** Glow, **click the** Presets button, **then click** Orange, 8 pt glow, Accent color 1

   An orange color band surrounds the shape.

6. **Click** 3-D Format, **click the** Top bevel button, **click the** Angle icon, **scroll down the Format Picture pane, click the** Lighting button, **then click the** Balance icon **in the Neutral section**

   The lighting effect defines the bevel effect better.

7. **Click** Artistic Effects, **scroll down the Format Picture pane, click the** Artistic Effects button 🖼, **click** Pencil Grayscale **(1st row), then click the** Close button ✕ **in the Format Picture pane**

   Changing the artistic effect changes the 3D effect already applied to the shape.

QUICK TIP
You can also press [Esc] to turn off the Format Painter.

8. **Double-click the** Format Painter button **in the Clipboard group, click each of the five remaining** diamond shapes, **then click** Format Painter button **again to turn off the Format Painter**

   Double-clicking the Format Painter button locks the Format Painter allowing you to apply the same formatting to multiple objects on the slide without having to reselect the tool. Now the six diamond shapes on the slide have the same fill and 3D effects.

9. **Click a blank area of the slide, then save your changes**

   Compare your screen with **FIGURE 5-5**.

FIGURE 5-4: Formatted connector lines

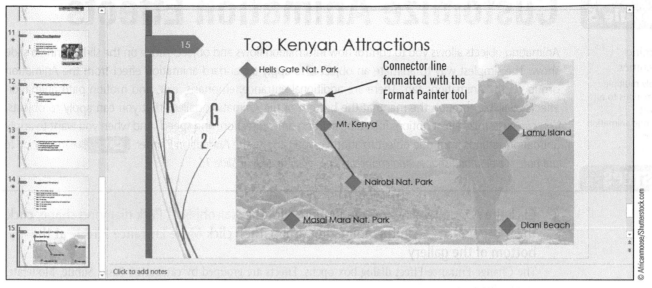

FIGURE 5-5: Formatted shapes

© Africanmoose/Shutterstock.com

Creating columns in a text box

When the information you are working with fits better in a column format, you have the ability to create columns within text objects. Select the text object, click the Add or Remove Columns button in the Paragraph group on the Home tab, then click either One Column, Two Columns, Three Columns, or More Columns.

The More Columns option allows you to set up to 16 columns and customize the spacing between columns. You can display the ruler to set specific widths for the columns and further customize the columns.

Customize Animation Effects

Learning Outcomes
- Apply multiple animations to an object
- Change animation order

Animating objects allows you to control how information flows and objects move on the slide during a slide show. The simplest way to animate an object is to apply a standard animation effect from the Animation group on the Animations tab. There are additional entrance, emphasis, exit, and motion path animation effects available through the menu at the bottom of the Animation gallery that you can apply to objects. You can customize effect options including starting time, direction, and speed. And when you want to apply animation settings from one object to another, you can use the Animation Painter. **CASE** *You decide to animate the diamond shapes and connector lines you created on Slide 15.*

STEPS

1. **Click the** Animations tab **on the Ribbon, click the** Nairobi Nat. Park diamond shape, **click the** More button ⤓ **in the Animation group, then click** More Entrance Effects **at the bottom of the gallery**

   The Change Entrance Effect dialog box opens. Effects are grouped by categories: Basic, Subtle, Moderate, and Exciting.

2. **Click** Basic Zoom **in the Moderate section, click** OK, **click the** Duration up arrow **in the Timing group until** 01.00 **appears in the text box, then click the** Preview button **in the Preview group**

   An animation tag ☐1☐ appears next to the diamond shape.

3. **Click the** Nairobi Nat. Park to Mt. Kenya connector line, **click** Wipe **in the Animation group, click the** Nairobi Nat. Park diamond shape, **click the** Add Animation button **in the Advanced Animation group, click** Fill Color **in the Emphasis group, then click the** Preview button

   The Add Animation feature allows you to apply multiple animations to the same object. Notice another animation tag appears beside Animation tag 1, which indicates the diamond shape now has two animations applied to it. You want both animations to run consecutively.

4. **Click the** Animation tag 2 ☐2☐ **on the slide, click the** Move Later button **in the Timing group, then click the** Preview button

   The animations for the diamond shape now run consecutively before the animation for the connector line. Compare your screen to **FIGURE 5-6**.

5. **Click the** Nairobi Nat. Park diamond shape, **click the** Animation Painter button **in the Advanced Animation group, then click the** Mt. Kenya diamond shape

   When you use the Animation Painter all the animations and animation settings from the first shape are applied to the second shape. The Nairobi Nat. Park to Mt. Kenya connector line animation would look better if it was delayed.

6. **Click the** Nairobi Nat. Park to Mt. Kenya connector line, **click the** Delay up arrow **in the Timing group until** 00.50 **appears, then click the** Preview button

   The delay between the diamond shape and the connector line animations defines each animation effect.

7. **Click the** Animation Painter button **in the Advanced Animation group, click the** Mt. Kenya to Hells Gate Nat. Park connector line, **then click the** Preview button

   Now both connector lines have the same animation and animation settings. The Mt. Kenya to Hells Gate Nat. Park connector line would look a little better if animated from the right.

8. **Click the** Effect Options button **in the Animation group, click** From Right, **click the** Preview button, **then save your changes**

   Compare your screen to **FIGURE 5-7**.

FIGURE 5-6: Animation effects applied to the objects

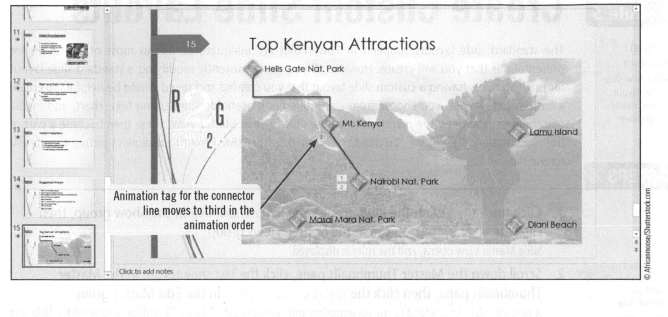

Animation tag for the connector line moves to third in the animation order

FIGURE 5-7: Completed animation effects

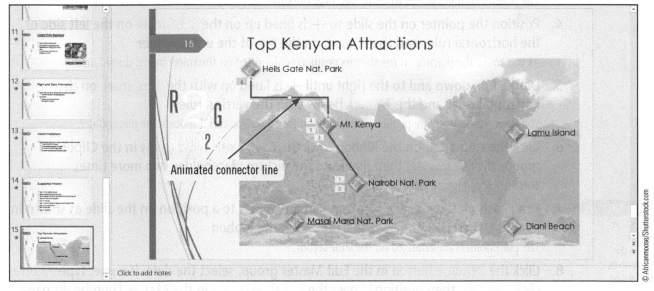

Animated connector line

Understanding animation timings

Each animated object on a slide has a starting time in relation to the other animated objects. There are three different starting time options: Start On Click, Start With Previous, and Start After Previous. The Start On Click timing option starts the animation effect when you click the mouse. The Start With Previous timing option begins the animation effect at the same time as the previous effect in the animation list, so two or more animation effects play at once. The Start After Previous timing option begins the animation immediately after the previous animation without clicking the mouse.

Working with Advanced Tools and Masters

© Africanmoose/Shutterstock.com

Create Custom Slide Layouts

Learning
Outcomes
• Add a new slide
  master layout
• Create master
  placeholders

The standard slide layouts supplied in PowerPoint are adequate to design most of the slides for presentations that you will create. However, if you are consistently modifying a standard slide layout for presentations, having a custom slide layout that you created and saved would be helpful. To create a custom slide layout, you choose from eight different placeholders, including text, chart, and media placeholders. You draw the placeholder on the slide in Slide Master view; these then become a part of the presentation. **CASE** *You decide to create a custom slide layout that displays picture thumbnails on the slide.*

STEPS

1. **Click the View tab on the Ribbon, click the Ruler check box in the Show group, then click the Slide Master button in the Master Views group**

   Slide Master view opens, and the ruler is displayed.

QUICK TIP
To insert an additional slide master to use in your presentation, click the Insert Slide Master button in the Edit Master group.

2. **Scroll down the Master Thumbnails pane, click the last slide layout in the Master Thumbnails pane, then click the Insert Layout button in the Edit Master group**

   A new slide layout is added to the presentation and appears in the Master Thumbnails pane with a title text placeholder and footer placeholders as shown in **FIGURE 5-8**. The new slide layout contains all of the slide background elements associated with the current theme.

3. **Click the Insert Placeholder list arrow in the Master Layout group, then click Picture**

   The pointer changes to ┼ when moved over the slide.

4. **Position the pointer on the slide so ┼ is lined up on the 3 ½" mark on the left side of the horizontal ruler and the 1" mark on the top of the vertical ruler**

   As you move the pointer on the slide its position is identified on the rulers by red dotted lines.

5. **Drag a box down and to the right until ┼ is lined up with the 1 ½" mark on the horizontal ruler and the 1" mark below 0 on the vertical ruler**

   You drew a 2" x 2" square picture placeholder on the slide. You can duplicate the placeholder.

6. **Click the Home tab on the Ribbon, click the Copy button list arrow in the Clipboard group, click Duplicate, then duplicate the picture placeholder two more times**

   There are four picture placeholders on the slide.

QUICK TIP
To help position placeholders precisely on the slide as shown in **FIGURE 5-9**, you can also display the guides and use the Align and Distribute commands.

7. **Drag each picture placeholder using Smart Guides to a position on the slide as shown in FIGURE 5-9, then click the Slide Master tab on the Ribbon**

   The placeholders are arranged on the slide layout.

8. **Click the Rename button in the Edit Master group, select the default name, type Picture, click Rename, then position ⥢ over the last slide layout in the Master Thumbnails pane**

   The new name of the custom slide layout appears in the ScreenTip. The new Picture layout now appears when you click the Layout button or the New Slide list button in the Slides group on the Home tab.

9. **Right-click a blank area of the slide, click Ruler, click the Close Master View button in the Close group, then save your changes**

   The rulers close, and Slide 15 appears in Normal view.

FIGURE 5-8: New custom slide layout

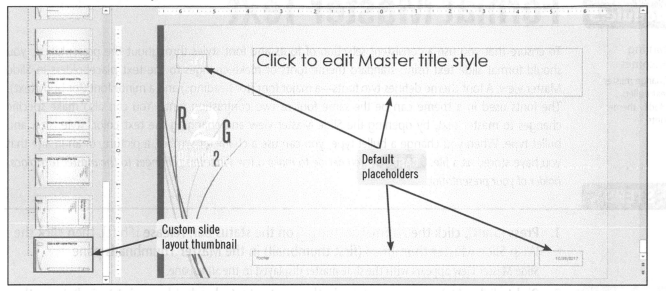

FIGURE 5-9: Custom slide layout with new placeholders

Restoring the slide master layout

If the slide master is missing a placeholder, open Slide Master view, then click the Master Layout button in the Master Layout group to reapply the placeholder. Clicking the Master Layout button opens the Master Layout dialog box, as shown in **FIGURE 5-10**. Click the placeholder check box to reapply the placeholder. To quickly apply or remove the title or footer placeholders on a slide master, click the Title or Footers check boxes in the Master Layout group.

FIGURE 5-10: Master Layout dialog box

Master Layout   ?   ×

Placeholders

☐ Title
☑ Text
☑ Date
☐ Slide number
☑ Footer

OK   Cancel

Format Master Text

To ensure that you use a consistent selection of fonts and font styles throughout the presentation, you should format slide text using standard theme fonts or make changes to the text placeholders in Slide Master view. A font theme defines two fonts—a major font (for headings) and a minor font (for body text). The fonts used in a theme can be the same font or two contrasting fonts. You can also make specific changes to master text, by opening the Slide Master view and changing the text color, style, size, and bullet type. When you change a bullet type, you can use a character symbol, a picture, or an image that you have stored as a file. **CASE** *You decide to make a few formatting changes to the master text place-holder of your presentation.*

STEPS

1. **Press [Shift], click the** Normal button 🔲 **on the status bar, release [Shift], then click the Wisp Slide Master thumbnail (first thumbnail) in the Master Thumbnails pane**

   Slide Master view appears with the slide master displayed in the Slide pane.

2. **Right-click** Edit Master text styles **in the master text placeholder, point to** Bullets **on the shortcut menu, then click** Bullets and Numbering

   The Bullets and Numbering dialog box opens. The Bulleted tab is selected; the Numbered tab in this dialog box is used to create sequentially numbered or lettered bullets.

3. **Point to each bullet option, read each ScreenTip, then click the** Arrow Bullets **option shown in FIGURE 5-11**

   A new symbol is selected.

4. **Click the** Color list arrow 🎨▾ **, then click** Red, Accent 2 **in the Theme Colors section**

5. **Click the** Size up arrow 🔼 **until 110 appears, then click** OK

   The symbol and color of the new bullet in the second level of the master text placeholder changes. The size of the bullet is increased to 110% of the size of the second-level text.

6. **Click the** Fonts button **in the Background group, then click** Franklin Gothic

   All of the slide layouts in the Master Thumbnail pane now display the new font theme.

7. **Click the** Preserve button **in the Edit Master group**

   A pushpin icon 📌 appears next to the Wisp Slide Master thumbnail in the Master Thumbnail pane indicating the master is preserved as shown in **FIGURE 5-12**. Preserving a master ensures it remains with the presentation even if you eventually use another master.

8. **Click the** Close Master View button **in the Close group, click the** Slide 14 thumbnail **in the Slides tab, then save your changes**

   You see how the changes affect the fonts and the text bullets in Normal view.

FIGURE 5-11: Bullets and Numbering dialog box

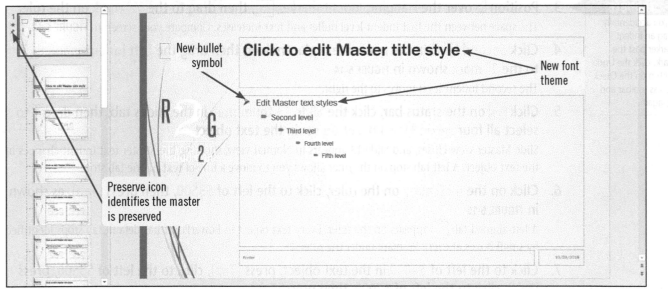

Arrow bullet option

FIGURE 5-12: New bullets and new font theme applied to the slide master

New bullet symbol

Click to edit Master title style

New font theme

> Edit Master text styles
>   • Second level
>   ▸ Third level
>   • Fourth level
>   ▪ Fifth level

Preserve icon identifies the master is preserved

Organizing slides into sections

To help you organize the slides of your presentation into groups, you can create sections. A section of slides can be grouped in different meaningful ways, such as by subject matter. To create a section, click the slide thumbnail in the Slides tab where you want the section to start, then on the Home tab click the Section button in the Slides group. Click Add Section in the drop down menu to create a new section of slides. Each section you create can be customized with a new name. Sections can be collapsed or expanded in the Slides tab depending on how you want to view the slides of a section.

Change Master Text Indents

Learning Outcomes
• Change text indents
• Set tab stops

Master text and content placeholders have five levels of text, called **indent levels**. You can modify indent levels using PowerPoint's ruler. For example, you can change the space between a bullet and text of an indent level or change the position of the whole indent level. The position of each indent level on the ruler is represented by two small triangles and a square called **indent markers**. You can modify an indent level by moving these indent markers on the ruler. You can also set tabs on the horizontal ruler, which identifies where a text indent or a column of text begins. By clicking the **tab selector** located at the far left of the horizontal ruler, you are able to choose which of the four tab options you want to use. **TABLE 5-1** describes PowerPoint's indent and tab markers. **CASE** ▷ *To better emphasize the text in the master text placeholder, you change the first two indent levels.*

STEPS

1. **Press [Shift], click the Normal button 🔲 on the status bar, release [Shift], then click the Wisp Slide Master thumbnail (first thumbnail) in the Master Thumbnails pane**
   Slide Master view opens. The Wisp slide master appears in the Slide pane.

2. **Click Edit Master text styles in the master text placeholder, click the View tab on the Ribbon, then click the Ruler check box in the Show group**
   The horizontal and vertical rulers for the master text placeholder appear. The indent markers, on the horizontal ruler, are set so the first line of text—in this case, the bullet—begins to the left of subsequent lines of text. This is called a **hanging indent**.

TROUBLE
If you accidentally drag an indent marker past the mark, click the Undo button on the Quick Access toolbar and try again.

3. **Position ▷ over the Hanging Indent marker △, then drag to the ½" mark on the ruler**
   The space between the first indent-level bullet and text increases. Compare your screen to **FIGURE 5-13**.

4. **Click Second level in the master text placeholder, then drag the Left indent marker ▢ to the 1" mark shown in FIGURE 5-14**
   The second indent level moves to the right.

5. **Click 🔲 on the status bar, click the Slide 13 thumbnail in the Slides tab, then drag Ⅰ to select all four second level bullet points in the text object**
   Slide Master view closes, and Slide 13 appears in Normal view, showing the Master text indent changes in the text object. A left tab stop on the ruler allows you to move a line of text in one tab stop.

6. **Click on the 4 ½" mark on the ruler, click to the left of $3500, then press [Tab], as shown in FIGURE 5-15**
   A left-aligned tab ⌐ appears on the ruler. Every text object in PowerPoint has default tab stops identified by small boxes at every ½" mark under the ruler.

7. **Click to the left of $4000 in the text object, press [Tab], click to the left of $5500, press [Tab], click to the left of $7000, then press [Tab]**
   All of the accommodation prices move to the right to the tab stop you placed on the ruler.

8. **Right-click a blank area of the slide, click Ruler in the shortcut menu, then save your changes**
   The rulers close.

FIGURE 5-13: Master level text with moved hanging indent marker

FIGURE 5-14: Second-level indent moved

FIGURE 5-15: Left tab stop added to ruler

TABLE 5-1: Indent and tab markers

symbol	name	function
▽	First line indent marker	Controls the position of the first line of text in an indent level
△	Hanging indent marker	Controls the position of the hanging indent
▢	Left indent marker	Controls the position of subsequent lines of text in an indent level
∟	Left-aligned tab	Aligns tab text on the left
⊥	Center-aligned tab	Aligns tab text in the center
⌐	Right-aligned tab	Aligns tab text on the right
⊥	Decimal-aligned tab	Aligns tab text on a decimal point

Working with Advanced Tools and Masters

Adjust Text Objects

Learning Outcomes
• Adjust text line spacing
• Set text object margins

You have complete control over the placement of text on slides in PowerPoint, whether the text is in a shape or in a text object. All text in PowerPoint is created within a text box, which has **margins** that determine the distance between the edge of the text and all four edges of the text box. You can also modify the space between paragraphs, and the space between lines of text within a paragraph. **Paragraph spacing** is the space before and after paragraphs (bullet levels). **Leading**, (rhymes with "wedding") refers to the amount of space between lines of text within the same paragraph (bullet level). Using the text-alignment feature, you can move text within text boxes or shapes. **CASE** *You decide to move the text margin in the text object on Slide 11, change the alignment of text on Slide 10, and then change paragraph spacing of the text object on Slide 12.*

STEPS

1. **Click the** Slide 11 thumbnail **in the Slides tab, click the** Home tab **on the Ribbon, right-click a blank area of the slide, then click** Ruler **on the shortcut menu**
   Slide 11 appears in the slide pane with the rulers showing.

QUICK TIP
When you right-click the text of a grouped object, the individual object is selected within the grouped object and the indent markers for the text appear in the ruler.

2. **Right-click** Exciting **in the text object, click** Format Shape **on the shortcut menu, click the** Size & Properties icon 📷 **in the Format Shape pane, then click** Text Box **in the Format Shape pane**
   The Format Shape pane opens and the text box options are expanded.

3. **Click the** Left margin up arrow **until** 0.3" **appears, then click the** Top margin up arrow **until** 0.7" **appears**
   This adjusts the left, and top text margins and centers the text left to right within the shape as shown in **FIGURE 5-16**.

4. **Click the** Slide 10 thumbnail **in the Slides tab, click** Repair **in the text object, then click** 📷 **in the Format Shape pane**

QUICK TIP
You can also use the Align Text button in the Paragraph group to change how text is aligned within a text box.

5. **Click the** Resize shape to fit text option button **in the Format Shape pane, click the** Vertical alignment list arrow, **click** Middle Centered, **then close the** Format Shape pane
   The text in the text object is aligned in the middle center of the shape. The Format Shape pane closes.

6. **Click the** Slide 12 thumbnail **in the Slides tab, press [Shift], click the** text object, **release [Shift], click the** Line Spacing button 📷 **in the Paragraph group, then click** Line Spacing Options
   The Paragraph dialog box opens.

7. **In the Spacing section, click the** Before up arrow **until** 18 pt **appears, click the** After up arrow **until** 6 pt **appears, then click** OK
   The spacing before and after each bullet on Slide 12 changes. Compare your screen to **FIGURE 5-17**.

8. **Right-click a blank area of the slide, click** Ruler, **add your name and the date to the slide footer then save your changes**
   The Ruler closes.

9. **Submit your work to your instructor, click the** File tab, **then click** Close **to close the presentation but do not exit PowerPoint**

FIGURE 5-16: Changed text margin

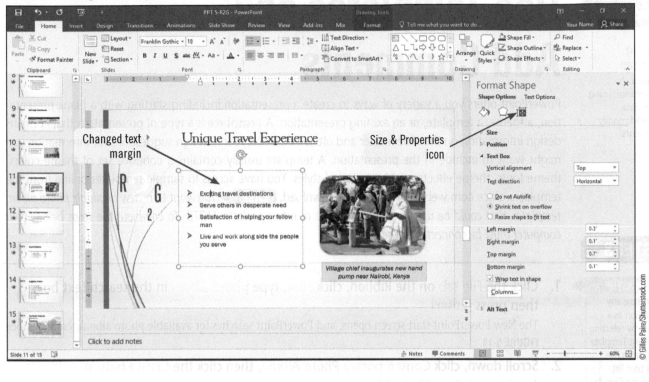

FIGURE 5-17: Changed line spacing

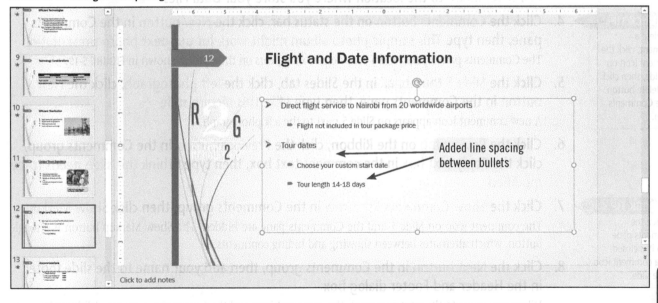

Changing text direction

Using the Text Direction button in the Paragraph group on the Home tab, you can change the direction of text in a text object or shape. There are four text direction options available: Horizontal, Rotate all text 90°, Rotate all text 270°, and Stacked. The Horizontal option is the standard default text direction for all text in PowerPoint.

The Rotate all text 90° text direction rotates text so it faces the right margin of a text object or shape. The Rotate all text 270° text direction rotates text so it faces the left margin of a text object or shape. The Stacked text direction stacks letters vertically on top of one another.

PowerPoint 2016

Use Templates and Add Comments

Learning Outcomes
- Create a presentation using a template
- Add and modify comments

PowerPoint offers you a variety of ways to create a presentation including starting with a blank presentation, a theme, a template, or an existing presentation. A **template** is a type of presentation that contains design information on the slide master and often includes text and design suggestions for information you might want to include in the presentation. A template usually contains a cohesive set of theme colors, theme fonts, theme effects, and background styles. You have access to sample templates online from the templates.office.com website that you can download. **CASE** ▶ *You want to review available photo album templates that could be used to display pictures of future projects. NOTE: To complete the steps below, your computer must be connected to the Internet.*

STEPS

QUICK TIP
You can save any presentation as a template by selecting PowerPoint Template (*.potx) from the Save as type list arrow in the Save As dialog box.

1. **Click the** File tab **on the Ribbon, click** New, **type** photo album **in the search text box, then press** [Enter]

   The New PowerPoint start screen opens, and PowerPoint searches for available photo album templates. See **FIGURE 5-18**.

2. **Scroll down, click** Contemporary Photo Album, **then click the** Create button

   A new presentation with six slides appears.

3. **Click the** Save button 🖫 **on the Quick Access toolbar, then save the file as** PPT 5-Template **to the location where you store your Data Files**

QUICK TIP
To delete a comment, click the comment icon on the slide, then click the Delete button in the Comments group.

4. **Click the** Comments button **on the status bar, click the** New button **in the Comments pane, then type** This sample photo album might work for our next photo presentation

   The Comments pane opens, and a comment icon appears on the slide, as shown in **FIGURE 5-19**.

5. **Click the** Slide 5 thumbnail **in the Slides tab, click the** left photograph, **click the** New button **in the Comments pane, then type** I like this picture style

   A new comment icon appears on Slide 5 next to the left photograph.

6. **Click the** Review tab **on the Ribbon, click the** Previous button **in the Comments group, click the** Reply text box **in the comment text box, then type** I think this slide needs to be modified

QUICK TIP
To open the Comments pane when it is closed, click a comment icon on the slide.

7. **Click the** Show Comments list arrow **in the Comments group, then click** Show Markup

   The comment icon on Slide 1 and the Comments pane are hidden. The Show Markup button is a toggle button, which alternates between showing and hiding comments.

8. **Click the** Next button **in the Comments group, then add your name to the slide footer in the Header and Footer dialog box**

   When you move to the next comment, the comment icon and the Comments pane are visible again.

9. **Click the** Comments button **on the status bar, save your work, submit your presentation to your instructor, close the presentation, then exit PowerPoint**

FIGURE 5-18: Sample photo album templates available

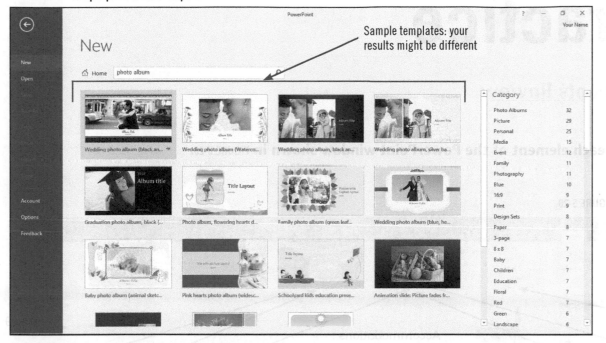

FIGURE 5-19: Applied template and new comment

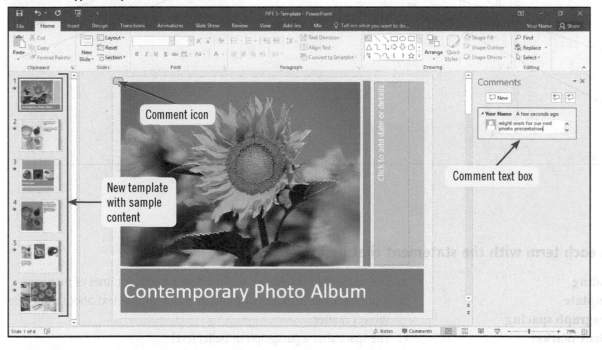

Understanding PowerPoint templates and themes

So what exactly is the difference between a PowerPoint template and a PowerPoint theme? A theme is a coordinated set of colors, fonts, and effects (such as shadows and reflections) that is used to modify the slide design of your presentation. For example, a theme is like the various colors a painter uses to paint the inside of a house where the walls are one color, the ceilings are a second color, and the window and door trim is a third color. A template, on the other hand, is a presentation that contains a theme and includes sample text about a specific subject matter, such as health and fitness. The sample text in a template provides you with the basic information that you can then use to modify the presentation with your own information.

Practice

Concepts Review

Label each element of the PowerPoint window shown in FIGURE 5-20.

FIGURE 5-20

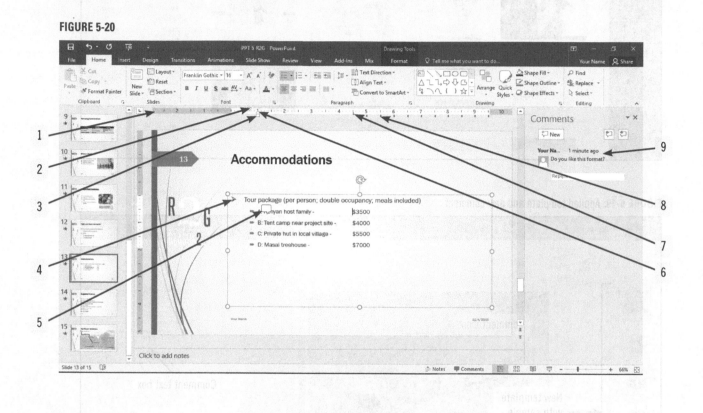

Match each term with the statement that best describes it.

10. Leading
11. Template
12. Paragraph spacing
13. Indent marker
14. Hanging indent
15. Margin

a. The first line of text begins to the left of subsequent lines of text
b. A presentation with a theme and includes sample text about a specific subject matter
c. The space after a paragraph or bullet level
d. The distance between the edge of text and the edge of a text box
e. Identifies where the indent level is on the ruler
f. The space between lines of text

Select the best answer from the list of choices.

16. Objects have _____ sites where you can anchor a line or an arrow.
    - **a.** plug-in
    - **b.** connection
    - **c.** painter
    - **d.** drop

17. Which would you change to increase the spacing between lines of text within a paragraph?
    - **a.** Letter spacing
    - **b.** Paragraph spacing
    - **c.** Leading
    - **d.** Indent spacing

18. Locking the _____ of a shape allows you to draw the same shape multiple times.
    - **a.** Drawing mode
    - **b.** Format painter
    - **c.** Animation painter
    - **d.** Connection site

19. A _____ is a type of presentation that contains custom design information and includes suggestions for sample text.
    - **a.** Theme
    - **b.** Section
    - **c.** Template
    - **d.** Layout

20. What do you use to apply animation settings from one object to another?
    - **a.** Duplicate tool
    - **b.** Animation painter
    - **c.** Format Painter
    - **d.** Animation wand

21. The small triangles and square on the ruler that represent the position of each level in a text placeholder are _____.
    - **a.** Indent markers
    - **b.** Ruler tabs
    - **c.** Indent tabs
    - **d.** Indent levels

Skills Review

1. **Draw and format connectors.**
   a. Start PowerPoint and open the presentation PPT 5-2.pptx, then save it as **PPT 5-Rogatsky** to the location where you store your Data Files.
   b. Go to Slide 4, click the More button in the Drawing group, right-click the Elbow Arrow Connector shape icon, then click Lock Drawing Mode.
   c. Position the pointer over the left connection site on the Plant shape, then drag to the top connection site on the Regional Distribution shape.
   d. Position the pointer over the right connection site on the Plant shape, drag to the top connection site on the Direct Sales shape, then press [Esc].
   e. Click the Line button (top row) in the Drawing group, position the pointer over the right connection site on the Regional Distribution shape, then drag to the left connection site on the Direct Sales shape.
   f. Click the Select button in the Editing group, click Selection Pane, press [Ctrl], click each elbow connector, then release [Ctrl] to select the three connectors.
   g. Right-click one of the connectors, click the Outline button, make the line style for the connectors 3 pt wide and change the line color to a black solid line, then deselect the objects.
   h. Right-click the connector between the Regional Distribution shape and the Direct Sales shape, click the Outline button, point to Dashes, click Long Dash Dot Dot, then deselect the object.
   i. Click the Selection pane Close button, then save the presentation.

Skills Review (continued)

2. Use advanced formatting tools.

   a. Go to Slide 1, right-click the 2017 Fiscal Year shape, then click Format Shape.

   b. In the Format Shape pane, click Fill, click the Gradient fill option button, click the Preset gradients list arrow, then click one of the Accent 5 gradients.

   c. Scroll down the Format Shape pane, click Line, then set the Width to 3 pt.

   d. Click the Color button, click White, Background 1, then click Text Options at the top of the Format Shape pane.

   e. Click the Color button, click Light Yellow, Background 2, then close the Format Shape pane.

   f. On the Home tab, double-click the Format Painter button in the Clipboard group, go to Slide 4, apply the picked up styles to both of the diamond objects, press [Esc], then save your changes.

3. Customize animation effects.

   a. Click the Animations tab, click the Plant shape, click the More button in the Animation group, then click Shape in the Entrance section.

   b. Click the Effect Options button in the Animation group, then click Plus.

   c. Select the left elbow arrow connector, click the More button in the Animation group, click More Entrance Effects, apply the Strips animation, click OK, then click the Duration up arrow until 1.00 appears.

   d. Click the left elbow arrow connector, click the Animation Painter button, then click the right elbow arrow connector.

   e. Click the Effects Options button, click Right Down, then click the Preview button.

   f. Select the Regional Distribution shape, apply the Shape animation, then change the Effect Options to Diamond.

   g. Click the Move Earlier button in the Timing group, then click the Preview button.

   h. Use the Animation Painter to apply the Regional Distribution shape animation to the Direct Sales shape, then click the Preview button.

   i. Select the dotted line, click Split in the Animation group, then click the Duration up arrow until 1.00 appears.

   j. Click the Add Animation button, click Split, change the Effect Options to Vertical Out, then click the Preview button.

   k. Save your changes.

4. Create custom slide layouts.

   a. Switch to Slide Master view, then click the last slide layout in the Master Thumbnails pane.

   b. Insert a new custom slide layout, then display the ruler and the guides.

   c. Add a 3" wide by 6" high Online Image placeholder. Use the guides and rulers to help you create the placeholder.

   d. Add an approximately 4" wide by 3" high Media placeholder, then place the new placeholders appropriately on the slide.

   e. Name the custom slide layout **Online Media**, turn off guides, then save your changes.

5. Format master text.

   a. Click the Frame Slide Master thumbnail in the Master Thumbnails pane, then format the first-level bulleted item in the master text placeholder as bold.

   b. Use the Bullets and Numbering dialog box to change the bullet symbol of the first-level bullet to Star Bullets.

   c. Change the size of the bullet to 110% of the text then change the bullet color to Orange, Accent 6.

   d. Set the size of the second-level bullet symbol to 150% of the text, then change the color to Purple.

   e. Preserve the master, then save your changes.

Skills Review (continued)

6. Change master text indents.

   a. Move the hanging indent marker of the first-level bullet to the ½" mark on the ruler and left indent marker of the second-level bullet to the 1" mark as shown in **FIGURE 5-21**.

   b. Hide the rulers, switch to Normal view, go to Slide 2, then save the presentation.

FIGURE 5-21

7. Adjust text objects.

   a. Press [Shift], right-click anywhere in the left text object on Slide 2, release [Shift], then click Format Shape on the shortcut menu.

   b. Click the Size and Properties icon in the Format Shape pane, then click Text Box.

   c. Change the vertical alignment of the text to Middle Centered, then click the Resize shape to fit text option button.

   d. Close the Format Shape pane, then use the Format Painter to apply the formatting changes to the right text object. **FIGURE 5-22** shows the completed presentation in Slide Sorter view.

   e. Add your name to the slide footer, save your work, then close the presentation but do not exit PowerPoint.

FIGURE 5-22

8. Use templates and add comments.

   a. Click the File tab, click New, click Education in the Suggested searches section, click Academic presentation, pinstripe and ribbon design presentation, then click Create. *Note: If this template is not available, choose another. Internet connection required.*

   b. Save the presentation as **PPT 5-Academic** to the location where you store your Data Files.

   c. Click the Review tab on the Ribbon, click the New Comment button, type **What do you think of this template?**, then go to Slide 8.

   d. Add a new comment, type **I like this title slide also.**, click the Previous button, then click the New button on the Comments pane.

   e. Type **We can use our logo on this slide.**, close the Comments pane, add your name to the slide footer, then save your work.

   f. Submit your presentation to your instructor, close the presentation, then exit PowerPoint.

Independent Challenge 1

You work in marketing at the Leland Winslow Agency in Louisville, Kentucky. The Leland Winslow agency represents all types of commercial businesses and specializes in high-profile and celebrity clients. As a growing company, your business is looking for private investment capital to expand its business markets. It is your responsibility to develop a presentation the owners can present to potential investors. You have been working on the content of the presentation, and now you are ready to add custom animations and customize slide master text.

a. Open the presentation PPT 5-3.pptx from the location where you store your Data Files, then save it as **PPT 5-Winslow**.
b. Open Slide Master view, click the Damask Slide Master thumbnail, then bold the text in the first-level indent.
c. Right-click the first level indent, open the Bullets and Numbering dialog box, click the Customize button, click the Double Dagger bullet (Character code 2021), then click OK.
d. Change the bullet to 115% the size of text, change the bullet color to White, Text 1, then click OK.
e. Adjust the indent markers for the first indent level as shown in **FIGURE 5-23**, then preserve the master.

FIGURE 5-23

f. Go to Slide 5, create at least three shapes connected by connectors, then format all of the objects using advanced formatting techniques you learned in the lesson.
g. Apply animation effects to objects and text on at least three slides, then preview the presentation in Slide Show view.
h. Add comments to two slides, then add your name and slide number to the slides (except the title slide).
i. Check spelling, save the presentation, then submit your presentation to your instructor.
j. Close the presentation and exit PowerPoint.

Independent Challenge 2

You work for Dine To U, a restaurant meal delivery service company in Vancouver, Washington. Using Dine To U, clients can order meals from local major food chain restaurants and have the food delivered in over 20 major U.S. cities. Dine To U wants to expand the variety of restaurant choices it offers its clients and open up in two more cities. Continue working on a presentation you've already started.

a. Open the presentation PPT 5-4.pptx from the location where you store your Data Files, then save it as **PPT 5-Dine**.
b. Open Slide Master view, click the Banded Slide Master thumbnail, click the Fonts button in the Background group, then change the Font theme to Times New Roman-Arial.
c. Change the bullet in the first-level indent level to an arrow bullet 110% of text size, then change the bullet in the second-level indent level to a small filled square, 125% of text size.
d. Adjust the indent marker for the first indent level so there is $1/2$" of space between the arrow bullet and the text.
e. Connect the four shapes on Slide 2 using arrow connectors. Format the arrow shapes weight and color.
f. Change the left margin of the text object on Slide 4 to 1", then click the Resize shape to fit text option button.

Independent Challenge 2 (continued)

g. On Slide 3 change the line spacing to 6 pt Before and 12 pt After in the text object.

h. Create a new custom slide layout using at least two different placeholders, then save the new layout as **Custom1**.

i. View the presentation in Reading view, then add your name and slide number to the slides footer (except the title slide).

j. Check spelling, save the presentation, then submit your presentation to your instructor.

k. Close the presentation and exit PowerPoint.

Independent Challenge 3

You are a computer game designer for FLASH Games, an Internet interactive game developer. One of your responsibilities is to develop new interactive game concepts and present the information at a company meeting. Complete the presentation provided, which promotes two new interactive Internet game concepts you've developed. Use the following game ideas in your presentation or create two game ideas of your own.

- *Spy Network* is an interactive game where you play a CIA member fighting foreign spies during the 1980's. You have the option to play with and against others online.
- *Galactic World Wars* is an interactive science fiction game where you play an aircraft pilot defending Earth against alien invaders.

a. Open the presentation PPT 5-5.pptx from the location where you store your Data Files, then save it as **PPT 5-Flash**. If you develop your own material, open a new presentation, storyboard the ideas for the presentation, then create at least five slides. What do you want your audience to know about the product idea?

b. Apply a theme, and then change the theme variant. Modify the theme as necessary, such as changing background objects, font theme, color theme, or effect theme.

c. Edit existing text, and add additional information you think is appropriate to create a professional presentation.

d. Format the master text and title placeholders on the slide master to fit the subject matter.

e. Change the bullet for the first and second indent levels in the master text placeholder, then format the bullets.

f. Create a custom slide layout, name it **Concept**, then apply it to at least one slide in the presentation.

g. Add your name and the slide number to the slides footer, then save the presentation.

h. View the presentation in Slide Show view, check spelling, save the presentation, then submit your presentation to your instructor.

i. Close the presentation, and exit PowerPoint.

Independent Challenge 4: Explore

You work at the Lincoln College Student Activities Center. You have been working on a presentation that you eventually will publish to the college website that describes all of the services offered at the Student Activities Center. Complete work on the presentation by working with masters and animation effects.

a. Open the presentation PPT 5-6.pptx from the location where you store your Data Files, save it as **PPT 5-Lincoln**, then apply a theme.

b. Apply animation effects to at least four objects in the presentation. Customize the animation settings as necessary.

c. Create a custom slide layout, and apply it to a slide.

d. Format the bullet and text in the master text and title placeholders on the slide master to fit the subject matter.

e. Modify master text indents on the slide master, then create shapes and connector lines on at least one slide.

f. Adjust the alignment, line spacing, and margins of at least one text object.

g. Create and name a section between Slides 5 and 6.

h. Add your name to the slides footer, check spelling, view the final slide show, then submit your presentation to your instructor.

i. Close the presentation and exit PowerPoint.

Visual Workshop

Create a slide that looks like the example in **FIGURE 5-24**. Be sure to use connector lines. Use the features on the Drawing Tools Format tab to customize the connector lines. (Hint: the shapes are formatted with the Preset 2 shape effect) Add your name to the slide footer, then save the presentation as **PPT 5-Training**. Submit your presentation to your instructor, then exit PowerPoint.

FIGURE 5-24

Working with Advanced Tools and Masters

Enhancing Charts

In this module, you continue to work on the Reason2Go (R2G) Kenya project presentation. You will focus on the slides that include charts. You customize the chart layout, format chart elements, and animate the chart. To present the work done by the finance team, you embed an Excel chart, and then you link an Excel worksheet to the presentation so the presentation will always have the most recent data.

Module Objectives

After completing this module, you will be able to:

- Work with charts in PowerPoint
- Change chart design and style
- Customize a chart
- Format chart elements
- Animate a chart
- Embed an Excel chart
- Link an Excel worksheet
- Update a linked Excel worksheet

Files You Will Need

PPT 6-1.pptx	PPT 6-8.pptx
PPT 6-2.xlsx	PPT 6-9.pptx
PPT 6-3.xlsx	PPT 6-10.xlsx
PPT 6-4.pptx	PPT 6-11.xlsx
PPT 6-5.xlsx	PPT 6-12.pptx
PPT 6-6.xlsx	PPT 6-13.xlsx
PPT 6-7.pptx	PPT 6-14.xlsx

PowerPoint 2016
Module 6

Learning
Outcomes
• Explain
  PowerPoint charts

Work with Charts in PowerPoint

One of the best ways to enhance a presentation is to insert graphic elements such as a chart. When you have numerical data that you want to compare, a chart helps the audience visualize and understand the information. Because Excel is integrated with PowerPoint, you can easily create informative charts on any slides in your presentation. **CASE** ▸ *As you continue to develop the R2G Kenya presentation, you plan to include charts on several slides. You review the features, benefits, and methods of charting in PowerPoint.*

DETAILS

- **Create PowerPoint charts**

  If you have Microsoft Office installed on your computer, PowerPoint integrates with Excel to create charts. When you create a chart in PowerPoint using the Chart button on the Insert tab or the Insert Chart icon in a content placeholder, a chart is placed on the slide and a separate worksheet window opens displaying the chart's data. See **FIGURE 6-1**. Using the worksheet window you can perform basic functions such as adding or editing chart data. If you want to manipulate the data in the worksheet using advanced commands, filters, or formulas, you can open the worksheet directly in Excel without exiting PowerPoint.

- **Embed or link a chart**

  You have two options when inserting an Excel chart to your presentation: you can embed it or link it. Embedded and linked charts are objects created in another program, such as Excel, and inserted in a slide. An embedded chart becomes a part of the presentation like a picture. The embedded chart's data is stored in the worksheet that is included with the presentation file. You can embed a chart in PowerPoint using the Object button on the Insert tab or by copying a chart from Excel and pasting it on a slide. A linked chart displays a picture of the chart on the slide that is linked or a connected to the original file in Excel. The chart is saved in a separate file, not with the presentation. If you want to make changes to a linked Excel chart, you must open the saved Excel file that contains the chart. You can open embedded or linked charts through PowerPoint or Excel.

- **Modify charts using styles and layouts**

  Because themes and theme effects are alike for all Office programs, you can apply a specific theme or effect to a chart in Excel, and PowerPoint will recognize the theme or effect. Using themes gives your chart a consistent look with other objects in your presentation; in addition, there are a number of chart layouts that you can apply to your chart. A chart layout specifies where chart elements, such as axes titles, data labels, and the legend, are displayed within the chart area. To easily format a chart you can select one of the three formatting buttons on the right side of the chart as shown in **FIGURE 6-2**: the Chart Elements button ⊞, the Chart Styles button ✎, and the Chart Filters button ▼. The Chart Elements button allows you to show, hide, or format specific elements such as axis, labels, and gridlines. The Chart Styles button provides chart styles and color themes you can apply to a chart. The Chart Filters button allows you to show or hide specific data in a chart, such as a data series or category.

- **Apply advanced formatting to charts**

  If the basic predefined chart styles do not provide you with the formatting options you want, you can choose to modify individual elements. For example, you may want to alter the way data labels look or how axes are displayed. You can specify the axes scales and adjust the interval between the values or categories. You can fine-tune individual elements, such as the data series or legend of your chart. You can also add trendlines and error bars to a chart to provide more information about the data. A **trendline** is a graphical representation of an upward or downward trend in a data series, also used to predict future trends. **Error bars** identify potential error amounts relative to each data marker in a data series.

FIGURE 6-1: Embedded chart and worksheet

FIGURE 6-2: Formatted chart

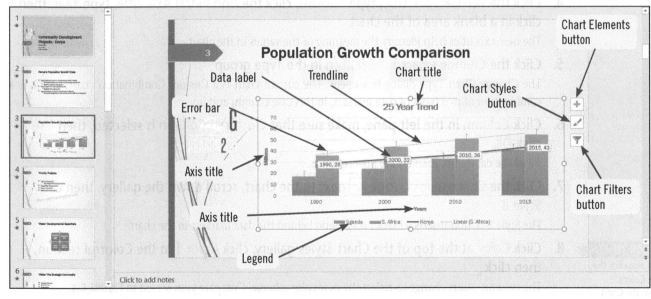

Using Paste Special

Paste Special is used to paste text or objects into PowerPoint using a specific format. For example, you may want to paste text as a picture or as plain text without formatting. Copy the text, or object, then in PowerPoint click the Home tab, click the Paste list arrow, click Paste Special, then select the appropriate format option. You can keep source formatting or apply the destination theme. You can also choose whether to embed or link an object

or selected information from another program to PowerPoint using the Paste Special command. This technique is useful when you want to link part of an Excel worksheet or a chart from a workbook that contains both a worksheet and a chart. To link just the chart, open the Excel worksheet, then copy the chart. Leaving the Excel source file open, click the Paste list arrow, click Paste Special, click one of the Paste link options, then click OK.

Change Chart Design and Style

Learning Outcomes
- Modify a chart layout
- Change the chart type

Being able to use Excel to create and modify charts in PowerPoint offers you many advantages, including the ability to use Excel Chart tools to customize chart design, layout, and formatting. After you create a chart, you can immediately alter the way it looks by changing individual chart elements or by applying a predefined chart layout or style. For example, you can select a chart layout that adds a chart title and moves the legend to the bottom of the chart. You can also easily change the color and effects of chart elements by applying one of the styles found in the Chart Styles gallery. **CASE** ▸ *You change the chart layout, style, and type of chart on Slide 3.*

STEPS

QUICK TIP

To quickly move to the beginning or the end of the presentation press [Home] to jump to the first slide or press [End] to jump to the last slide.

1. **Start PowerPoint, open the presentation** PPT 6-1.pptx **from the location where you store your Data Files, save the presentation as** PPT 6-R2G, **then click the** Slide 3 **thumbnail in the Slides tab**

   Slide 3 appears in the Slide pane.

2. **Click the** chart, **then click the** Chart Tools Design **tab on the Ribbon**

   The chart is selected and ready to edit.

3. **Click the** Quick Layout button **in the Chart Layouts group, then click** Layout 7 **in the Layout gallery**

   This particular layout option adds value and category axis titles to the chart, moves the legend to the right side of the chart, removes the chart title, and removes the data labels as shown in **FIGURE 6-3**.

4. **Click the** Vertical Axis Title, **type** Millions, **click the** Horizontal Axis Title, **type** Year, **then click in a blank area of the chart**

   The new axis titles help identify the meaning of the values in the chart.

5. **Click the** Change Chart Type button **in the Type group**

   The Change Chart Type dialog box opens. The current chart is a Custom Combination chart, which is a combination of two types of data markers, in this case column and line.

6. **Click** Column **in the left pane, make sure that** Clustered Column **is selected, then click** OK

   All of the data series markers are now columns.

7. **Click the** Chart Styles button ▨ **next to the chart, scroll down the gallery, then click** Style 8

   The Style 8 option inserts a black background behind the data markers in the chart.

QUICK TIP

You can also click the Change Colors button in the Chart Styles group to change the chart colors.

8. **Click** Color **at the top of the Chart Styles gallery, click** Color 1 **in the Colorful section, then click** ▨

   The column colors change to reflect the new color scheme. Compare your screen to **FIGURE 6-4**.

9. **Click a blank area of the slide, then save your presentation**

FIGURE 6-3: New layout applied to the chart

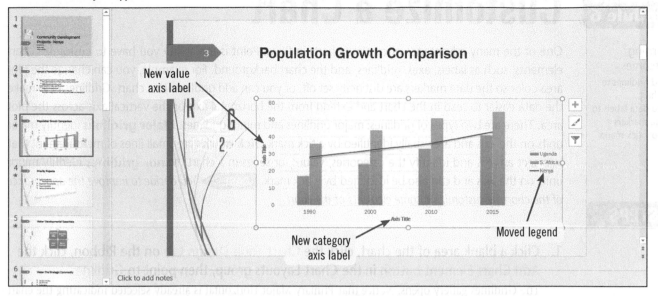

FIGURE 6-4: Chart with new chart type and colors applied

Using AutoFit Options to divide and fit body text

If the AutoFit Options button ![icon] appears while you are entering text in a body text object on a slide with either the Title and Content or the Content with Caption layout, you can click the button and choose from one of three options for dividing up the text in the object. The first option is to split text between two slides. If you choose this option, PowerPoint creates a second slide with the same title and then automatically divides the text between the two slides. The second option is to continue the text on a new slide. Here again, PowerPoint creates a second slide with the same title, but instead of splitting the text between the slides, you are given a blank body text object on the new slide to insert more text. The final option on the AutoFit Options button for splitting text in a body text object is to change the body text object from one column to two columns.

Customize a Chart

Learning Outcomes
- Add gridlines to a chart
- Add data labels to data markers
- Apply tick marks

One of the many advantages of creating charts in PowerPoint is the ability you have to customize chart elements, such as labels, axes, gridlines, and the chart background. For example, you can change the plot area color so the data markers are distinctly set off, or you can add gridlines to a chart. Gridlines help make the data easier to read in the chart and extend from the horizontal axis or the vertical axis across the plot area. There are two types of gridlines: major gridlines and minor gridlines. **Major gridlines** identify major units on the axis and are usually identified by a tick mark. **Tick marks** are small lines of measurement that intersect an axis and identify the categories, values, or series in a chart. **Minor gridlines** identify minor units on the axis and can also be identified by a tick mark. **CASE** *You decide to improve the appearance of the chart by customizing some elements of the chart.*

STEPS

1. **Click a blank area of the chart, click the** Chart Tools Design tab **on the Ribbon, click the** Add Chart Element button **in the Chart Layouts group, then point to** Gridlines

   The Gridlines gallery opens. Notice that Primary Major Horizontal is already selected indicating the chart already has major gridlines on the horizontal axis.

2. **Move ⬦ over each gridline option to see how the gridlines change on the chart, then click** Primary Minor Horizontal

   Minor horizontal gridlines appear on the chart as shown in **FIGURE 6-5**. Notice that the major gridlines are wider and darker in color than the minor gridlines.

3. **Click the** Add Chart Element button, **point to** Data Table, **move ⬦ over each data table option to see how the chart changes, then click** None

   You like seeing the data displayed in the chart because it helps define the data markers. However, using the data table takes up too much room on the slide and makes the chart difficult to read.

4. **Click the** Chart Elements button ⊞, **then click the** Data Labels checkbox

   Data labels, the actual value for each data series marker, appear just above each data marker. You like the data labels, but you want to move them to the inside of the data markers.

5. **Click the** Data Labels list arrow, **click** Center, **then click** ⊞

   The data labels are placed to the inside center of each of the data series markers.

6. **Right-click** 50 **on the vertical axis, click** Format Axis, **click** Tick Marks **in the Format Axis pane, then scroll down**

   The Format Axis pane opens with options for changing the axes, tick marks, labels, and numbers.

7. **In the Tick Marks section, click the** Major type list arrow, **click** Outside, **click the** Fill & Line icon ⬧ **at the top of the pane, click** Line, **click the** Color button list arrow ⬥, **then click** White, Background 1

   The tick marks on the chart's vertical axis change to white and are easier to see. The value axis title would also look better with a border around it.

8. **Click** Millions **in the chart, click the** Solid line option button **in the Border section of the** Format Axis Title **pane, click the** Color button list arrow ⬥, **then click** Yellow

   A yellow border appears around the value axis title. The category axis title would also look better with a border around it.

9. **Click** Year **in the chart, press** [F4], **close the** Format Axis Title **pane, click a blank area of the slide, then save your presentation**

   Pressing [F4] repeats the last formatting action. Compare your screen to **FIGURE 6-6**.

FIGURE 6-5: Minor gridlines applied to the chart

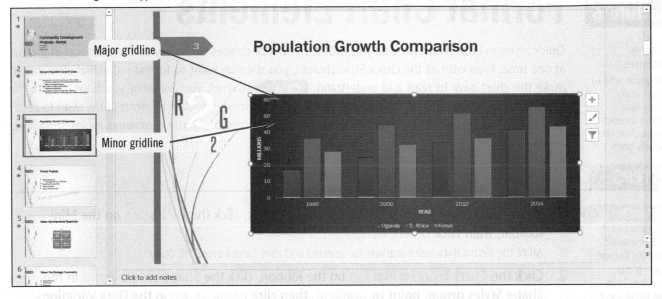

FIGURE 6-6: Chart with additional formatted elements

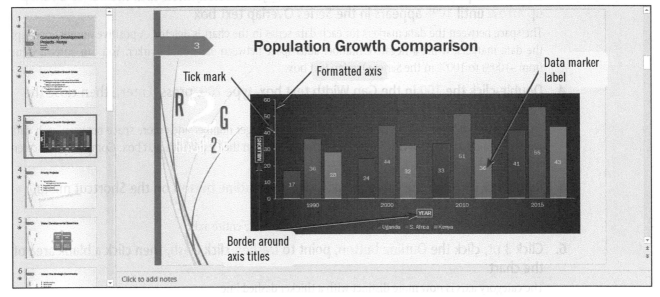

Using the Insights task pane

Sometimes when you are developing a presentation, you need help formulating your ideas or researching a particular subject. Using the Insights task pane, you can find information on a selected word or phrase, such as definitions, Wiki articles, images, and other related information. To open the Insights task pane, select a word or small phrase on a slide, then click the Smart Lookup button in the Insights group on the Review tab. The Insights task pane has an Explore section, which displays articles and images, and a Define section, which provides a definition of the word or phrase. The information that appears in the Insights task pane is generated by the Microsoft Bing search engine.

Format Chart Elements

Learning Outcomes
- Add gradient fill to data markers
- Modify data markers overlap
- Format chart title and axis labels

Quick Styles in PowerPoint provide you with a number of choices to modify all the elements in a chart at one time. Even with all the Quick Style choices, you still may want to format individual elements to make the chart easy to read and understand. **CASE** ▶ *Overall, you like what you have done to the population comparison chart so far, but you decide to format some individual elements of the chart to better fit the R2G presentation design. You also consider using the copy and paste commands for inserting other charts on a slide.*

STEPS

1. **Right-click one of the** orange Kenya data markers, **click the** Fill button **on the Mini toolbar, then click** Green, Accent 6

   All of the Kenya data series markers are selected and now have a green fill color.

2. **Click the** Chart Tools Format tab **on the Ribbon, click the** Shape Fill list arrow **in the Shape Styles group, point to** Gradient, **then click** Linear Down **in the Dark Variations section (top row)**

   A gradient effect is added to the Kenya data series markers.

3. **Click the** Format Selection button **in the Current Selection group to open the Format Data Series pane, make sure** Series Options 📊 **is selected, then click the** Series Overlap up arrow **until** 10% **appears in the Series Overlap text box**

   The space between the data markers for each data series in the chart is deleted. A positive number overlaps the data markers, while a negative number adds space between each data marker. You can enter a value from –100% to 100% in the Series Overlap text box.

4. **Double-click the** 100 **in the Gap Width text box, type** 200, **press [Enter], then close the Format Data Series pane**

   Space is added between each of the three data series. A larger number adds more space between each data series in the chart. You can enter a value from 0% to 500% in the Gap Width text box. Compare your screen to **FIGURE 6-7**.

5. **Right-click** 1990 **on the category axis, click the** Outline button **on the Shortcut menu, then point to** Weight

   Clicking any of the numbers on the category axis selects the entire axis.

6. **Click** 3 pt, **click the** Outline button, **point to** Dashes, **click** Dash, **then click a blank area of the chart**

   The category axis is now more distinct with a thicker dashed line.

7. **Click the** chart legend, **click the** Chart Tools Format tab **on the Ribbon, then click the** More button ▾ **in the Shape Styles group**

   The Theme Styles gallery opens.

8. **Click** Colored Outline - Red, Accent 2 **(first row), right-click the** chart legend, **click the** Outline button, **point to** Weight, **then click** 3 pt

   A solid red 3 pt border line appears around a white filled legend.

9. **Click a blank area of the slide, then save the presentation**

   Compare your screen to **FIGURE 6-8**.

FIGURE 6-7: Modified data markers

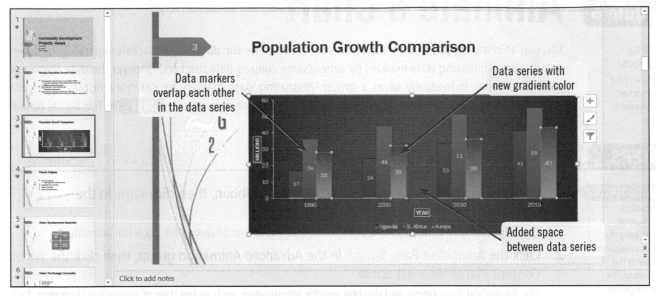

Data markers overlap each other in the data series

Data series with new gradient color

Added space between data series

FIGURE 6-8: Completed chart

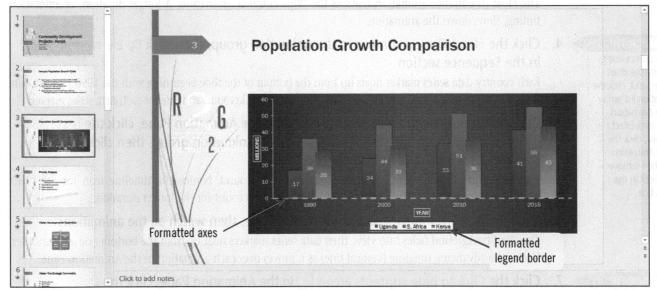

Formatted axes

Formatted legend border

Changing PowerPoint options

You can customize your installation of PowerPoint by changing various settings and preferences. To change PowerPoint settings, click the File tab on the Ribbon, then click Options to open the PowerPoint Options dialog box. Nine sections identified in the left pane offer you ways to customize PowerPoint.

For example, the General area includes options for viewing the Mini toolbar, enabling Live Preview, and personalizing your copy of Office. You can also set Language options for editing and proofing as well as which language appears on buttons and ScreenTips.

Animate a Chart

Learning Outcomes
• Animate chart data markers
• Set animation effects

You can animate a chart as one object, or you can animate the data series markers separately by series or category. Animating data markers by series (same colored data markers) displays the data marker of each data series individually or as a group. Animating data markers by category displays the data marker of each specific category in the chart individually or as a group. **CASE** *You decide to animate the data series markers of the chart.*

STEPS

QUICK TIP
Exit animation effects cause an object to leave the slide. Exit animation effects are in the Exit section of the Animation gallery.

1. **Click the chart, click the Animations tab on the Ribbon, then click Wipe in the Animation group**

   The Wipe entrance animation is applied to the entire chart, and PowerPoint plays the animation.

2. **Click the Animation Pane button in the Advanced Animation group, then click the Wipe: Content Placeholder list arrow**

   The Animation Pane opens and displays specific information, such as the type of animation (Entrance, Exit, Emphasis, or Motion Path), the sequence and timeline of the animation, and the name of the animated object. Clicking an animation's list arrow provides access to other custom options. Compare your screen to **FIGURE 6-9**.

3. **Click Float In in the Animation group, then click the Duration up arrow in the Timing group until 1.50 appears**

   The Float In entrance animation replaces the Wipe entrance animation. A longer duration, or animation timing, slows down the animation.

QUICK TIP
If you don't want to animate the chart background, click the animation list arrow in the Animation Pane, click Effect Options, click the Chart Animation tab, then remove the check in the check box.

4. **Click the Effect Options button in the Animation group, then click By Element in Series in the Sequence section**

   Each country data series marker floats up from the bottom of the slide beginning with the 1990 Uganda data series. There are now 13 animation tags, one for the chart background and one for each data series marker.

5. **Click the Click to expand contents arrow ⥥ in the Animation Pane, click the first animation tag ▢ on the slide, click Fade in the Animation group, then click the Duration up arrow until 1.50 appears**

   The Fade animation is now applied to the chart background. Notice the timeline icon for the chart background animation in the Animation Pane is wider to account for the longer duration.

6. **Click the Play From button in the Animation Pane, then watch all the animations**

   The chart background fades into view, then data series markers float up from the bottom one after another. Notice the advancing timeline (vertical line) as it moves over each animation in the Animation Pane.

QUICK TIP
Though there are many animation options available with charts and other objects, limit how many objects you animate on one slide.

7. **Click the Click to hide contents arrow ⥣ in the Animation Pane, click the Delay up arrow until 00.50 appears, then click the Play Selected button in the Animation Pane**

   A half-second delay is applied between each animation. Watch closely at how the changed settings affect the progression of the animated data series markers.

8. **Click the Start list arrow in the Timing group, click After Previous, click the Trigger button in the Advanced Animation group, point to On Click of, then click Title 1**

   Now when Slide 3 appears in Slide Show view, you can click the slide title to play the chart animations. The animation tags combine into one lightning bolt tag indicating the animation has a trigger.

9. **Click the Slide Show button ▣ on the status bar, click the slide title, watch the animation, press [Esc], close the Animation Pane, then save the presentation**

   Compare your screen to **FIGURE 6-10**.

FIGURE 6-9: Chart with added animation effect

FIGURE 6-10: Finished chart

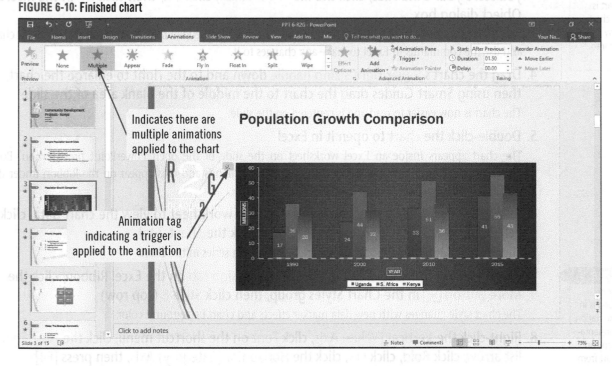

Inserting a picture as a slide background

As you have seen, using digital pictures in a presentation can really enhance the look of the presentation and make it more appealing. Most often pictures are inserted as objects on slides, but you can also use a picture as the slide background for one or more slides. To insert a picture as the slide background on an individual slide, click the slide in the Thumbnails pane in Normal view, click the Design tab on the Ribbon, then click the Format Background button in the Customize group. Click the Picture or texture fill option button, click the File button to locate a picture stored on your computer or click the Online button to search for a picture on the Internet, then click Insert. To insert a picture as the slide background for multiple slides, open Slide Master view, then use the same procedure to insert a picture on the slide master.

Embed an Excel Chart

When a chart is the best way to present information on a slide, you can either create one within PowerPoint or you can embed an existing Excel chart directly to the slide. When you use another program to create an object, the program, Excel in this case, is known as the **source program**. The object you create with the source program is saved to a file called the **source file**. When you embed a chart into a presentation, the presentation file in which the chart is embedded becomes the **destination file**. **CASE** > *You want to include last year's sales numbers in your presentation, so you embed an Excel chart in a new slide.*

STEPS

1. **Click the** Slide 13 thumbnail **in the Slides tab, click the** Home tab **on the Ribbon, click the** New Slide list arrow **in the Slides group, then click** Title Only

   A new slide with the Title Only layout is added to the presentation as slide 14.

2. **Click the** slide title placeholder, **type** R2G Sales by Region, **click the** Insert tab **on the Ribbon, then click the** Object button **in the Text group**

   The Insert Object dialog box opens. Using this dialog box, you can create a new chart or locate an existing one to insert on a slide.

3. **Click the** Create from file option button, **click** Browse, **navigate to the location where you store your Data Files, click the file** PPT 6-2.xlsx, **click** OK, **then click** OK **in the Insert Object dialog box**

   The chart from the Excel data file containing sales figures is embedded in the slide. You can open the chart and use the commands in Excel to make any changes to it.

4. **Drag the chart's** lower-right sizing handle **down and to the right to enlarge the chart, then using Smart Guides drag the chart to the middle of the blank area of the slide**

   The chart is now easier to read and is centered on the slide.

5. **Double-click the** chart **to open it in Excel**

   The chart appears inside an Excel worksheet on the slide of the open PowerPoint presentation. Both PowerPoint and Excel are open together, and Excel commands and tabs appear on the Ribbon under the PowerPoint title bar as shown in **FIGURE 6-11**.

6. **Click the** Sheet 1 tab **at the bottom of the Excel worksheet to view the chart data, click cell** C6, **type** 123,673.11, **press** [Enter], **then click the** Sheet 2 tab

   The changed value is reflected for the Quarter 2 India data series in the chart.

7. **Click the** chart **in Excel, click the** Chart Tools Design tab **on the Excel Ribbon, click the** More button ⊟ **in the Chart Styles group, then click** Style 8 **(top row)**

   The chart style changes with new data marker effects and chart background color.

8. **Right-click the** Vertical (Value) Axis, **click** Font **on the shortcut menu, click the** Font Style list arrow, **click** Bold, **click** OK, **click the** Horizontal (Category) Axis, **then press** [F4]

   Both the value and category axes labels are bold and now easier to read.

9. **Right-click the** legend, **click** Format Legend **on the shortcut menu, click the** Top option button, **then click** OK

   The legend moves to the top of the chart.

10. **Click outside the chart to exit Excel, click a blank area of the slide, then save the presentation**

    Compare your screen to **FIGURE 6-12**.

FIGURE 6-11: Embedded Excel chart

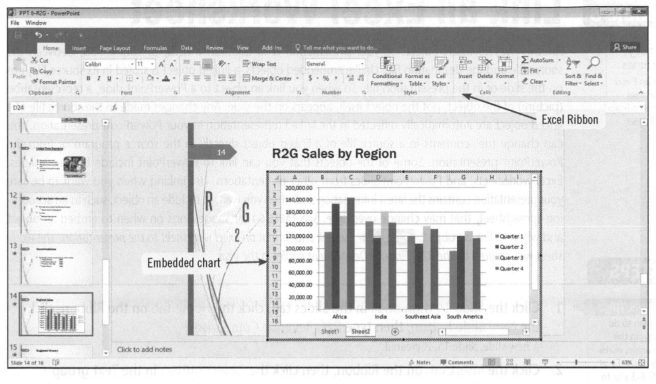

FIGURE 6-12: Formatted Excel chart

Embedding a worksheet

You can embed all or part of an Excel worksheet in a PowerPoint slide. To embed an entire worksheet, go to the slide where you want to place the worksheet. Click the Insert tab on the Ribbon, then click the Object button in the Text group. The Insert Object dialog box opens. Click the Create from file option button, click Browse, locate and double-click the worksheet filename, then click OK. The worksheet is embedded in the slide. Double-click it to edit it using Excel commands as needed to work with the worksheet. To insert only a portion of a worksheet, open the Excel workbook and copy the cells you want to include in your presentation.

Link an Excel Worksheet

Learning Outcomes
- Link an Excel worksheet
- Format a linked worksheet

Another way to insert objects to your presentation is to establish a **link**, or connection, between the source file and the destination file. Unlike embedded objects, a linked object is stored in its source file, not on the slide or in the presentation file. So when you link an object to a PowerPoint slide, a representation (picture) of the object, not the object itself, appears on the slide. Any changes made to the source file of a linked object are automatically reflected in the linked representation in your PowerPoint presentation. You can change the contents in a source file of a linked object directly in the source program or from the PowerPoint presentation. Some of the objects that you can link to PowerPoint include bitmap images, Excel worksheets, and PowerPoint slides from other presentations. Use linking when you want to be sure your presentation contains the latest information and when you want to include an object, such as an accounting spreadsheet, that may change over time. See **TABLE 6-1** for suggestions on when to embed an object and when to link an object. **CASE** ▶ *You link and format an Excel worksheet to the presentation. The worksheet was created by the R2G Finance Department earlier in the year.*

STEPS

QUICK TIP
If you plan to do the steps in this lesson again, make a copy of the Excel file PPT 6-3.xlsx to keep the original data intact.

1. **Click the** Slide 14 thumbnail **in the Slides tab, click the** Home tab **on the Ribbon, click the** New Slide button, **then type** R2G Revenue Comparison
   A new slide, Slide 15, is created.

2. **Click the** Insert tab **on the Ribbon, then click the** Object button **in the Text group**
   The Insert Object dialog box opens.

3. **Click the** Create from file option button, **click** Browse, **navigate to the location where you store your Data Files, click the file** PPT 6-3.xlsx, **click** OK, **click the** Link check box, **then click** OK
   The Excel worksheet appears on the slide. The worksheet would be easier to read if it were larger.

4. **Drag the** lower-right sizing handle **down and to the right, then position the worksheet in the middle of the blank area of the slide as shown in** FIGURE 6-13
   If the worksheet had a background fill color, it would help to emphasize the data and direct the audience's attention.

5. **Right-click the** worksheet, **then click** Format Object **on the shortcut menu**
   The Format Object pane opens.

6. **Click the** Fill & Line icon ⬧ **in the Format Object pane, then click the** Solid fill option button
   A background color is applied to the worksheet.

QUICK TIP
To create custom theme colors, click the View tab, click the Slide Master button, click the Colors button in the Background group, then click Customize Colors.

7. **Click the** Color list arrow ⬧▾, **click** Red, Accent 2, Lighter 60% **(3rd row), then click** Line **in the Format Object pane**
   The background color changes to a 60% transparent red.

8. **Click the** Solid line option button, **click** ⬧▾, **click** Black, Text 1, **click the** Width up arrow **until** 2 pt **appears in the Width text box, then click a blank area of the slide**
   The worksheet appears with a new border color and width.

9. **Close the Format Background pane, then save the presentation**
   Compare your screen to **FIGURE 6-14**.

FIGURE 6-13: Linked Excel worksheet

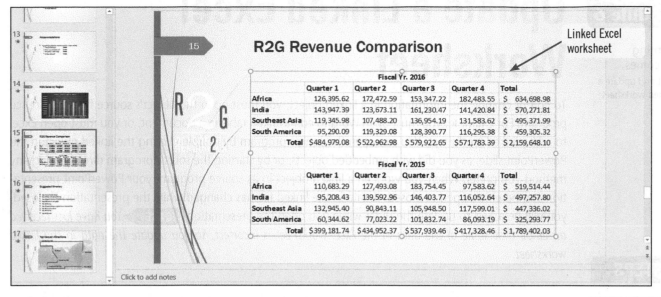

FIGURE 6-14: Formatted linked worksheet

TABLE 6-1: Embedding vs. linking

situation	action
When you are the only user of an object and you want the object to be a part of your presentation	Embed
When you want to access the object in its source program, even if the original file is not available	Embed
When you want to update the object manually while working in PowerPoint	Embed
When you always want the latest information in your object	Link
When the object's source file is shared on a network for other users to access and change	Link
When you want to keep your presentation file size small	Link

Learning Outcomes
- Edit and update a linked worksheet

Update a Linked Excel Worksheet

To edit or change the information in a linked object, you must open the object's source file in its source program. For example, you must open Word to edit a linked table in a document, or you must open Excel to edit a linked worksheet. You can open the source program by double-clicking the linked object in the PowerPoint slide, as you did with embedded objects, or by starting the source program directly using any method you prefer. When you work on a linked object in its source program, your PowerPoint presentation can be either open or closed. If data in the linked file has changed while the presentation is closed, you will be asked to update the slides when you open the presentation. **CASE** ➤ *You have just received an email that some of the data in the Excel worksheet is incorrect, so you update the data in the linked worksheet.*

STEPS

QUICK TIP
You can also double-click the linked worksheet to open it in Excel.

1. **Right-click the Excel worksheet on Slide 15, point to Linked Worksheet Object, then click Edit**
   The worksheet PPT 6-3.xlsx opens in the Excel window.

2. **Drag the edge of the Excel window to see all the data if necessary, click cell B6, type 97,839.59, click cell D11, type 177,903.83, then press Enter**
   The Fiscal Yr. 2016 Quarter 1 value for South America and the Fiscal Yr. 2015 Quarter 3 value for Africa change. All totals that include these values in the Total cells are updated accordingly. Compare your screen to **FIGURE 6-15.**

QUICK TIP
To edit or open a linked object in your presentation, the object's source program and source file must be available on your computer or network.

3. **Click cell B3, press and hold [Shift], click cell E6, release [Shift], right-click in the selected cell area, then click the Accounting Number Format button $ on the Mini toolbar**
   All of the selected cells now have the accounting format and display the dollar symbol.

4. **Click cell B11, drag to cell E14, then press [F4]**
   The same accounting number format is applied to these cells.

5. **Click cell F7, press [Ctrl], click cell F15, release [Ctrl], then click the Bold button B in the Font group**
   The bold font attribute is added to cells F7 and F15.

QUICK TIP
If your presentation is closed when you update a linked object, a security dialog box opens the next time you open your presentation. Click Update Links in the dialog box to update the linked object.

6. **Click the Bottom Border list arrow ⊞ ⌄ in the Font group, click Thick Outside Borders, then click a blank cell in the worksheet**
   A black border is added to cells F7 and F15 to highlight the overall totals.

7. **Click the Excel window Close button ✕, click Save to save your changes, then click a blank area of the slide**
   The Excel window closes. The Excel worksheet in the PPT 6-R2G.pptx presentation file is now updated with the new data and shows the formatting changes you made. PowerPoint automatically makes all of the changes to the linked object. Compare your screen to **FIGURE 6-16.**

8. **Check the spelling, add your name as the footer to the slides and to the handouts, save the presentation, then submit your presentation to your instructor**
   If your instructor requires you to print your presentation, then use the print layout setting 6 Slides Horizontal.

9. **Close the presentation, then exit PowerPoint**

FIGURE 6-15: Modified Excel worksheet

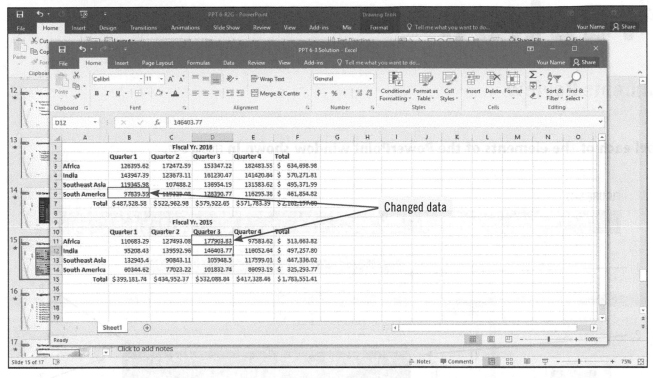

FIGURE 6-16: Updated Excel worksheet

Editing links

Once you link an object to your presentation, you have the ability to edit its link. Using the Links dialog box, you can update a link, open or change a linked object's source file, break a link, and determine if a linked object is updated manually or automatically. The Links dialog box is the only place where you can change a linked object's source file, break a link, and change the link updating method. To open the Links dialog box, click the File tab on the Ribbon, then click Edit Links to Files button under Related Documents in the pane.

Practice

Concepts Review

Label each of the elements of the PowerPoint window shown in FIGURE 6-17.

FIGURE 6-17

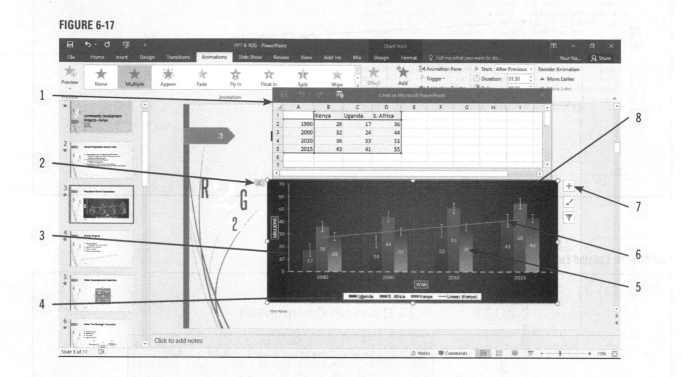

Match each of the terms with the statement that describes its function.

9. **Source file**
10. **Error bar**
11. **Trendline**
12. **Tick marks**
13. **Destination file**

a. The file that an embedded object is inserted into
b. Used to predict future tendencies
c. Identifies possible mistakes relative to each data series marker
d. Small lines that intersect an axis and identify a category or value
e. An object saved in a separate file that can be embedded into a presentation

Select the best answer from the list of choices.

14. You have two options when inserting an Excel chart into a presentation: you can embed it or _____ it.
    - **a.** autofit
    - **b.** link
    - **c.** adapt
    - **d.** integrate

15. _____ identify potential mistake amounts relative to each data marker in a data series.
    - **a.** Trendlines
    - **b.** Tick marks
    - **c.** Major gridlines
    - **d.** Error bars

16. A(n) _____ program is used to create an object that can be embedded into a presentation.
    - **a.** destination
    - **b.** source
    - **c.** linked
    - **d.** object

17. _____ identify minor and major units on the value axis of a chart.
    - **a.** Gridlines
    - **b.** Bars
    - **c.** Guides
    - **d.** Labels

18. A _____ is applied to an animation tag when it displays a lightning bolt.
    - **a.** delay
    - **b.** duration
    - **c.** trigger
    - **d.** timing

19. What does a positive number in the Overlap text box do?
    - **a.** Adds space between data markers
    - **b.** Adjusts the space between gridlines
    - **c.** Overlaps data markers
    - **d.** Removes space between data markers

20. To edit a linked object, you must open the object's _____ file.
    - **a.** source
    - **b.** network
    - **c.** embedded
    - **d.** destination

Skills Review

1. **Change chart design and style.**
   a. Start PowerPoint, open the presentation PPT 6-4.pptx, then save it as **PPT 6-Solomon** to the location where you store your Data Files.
   b. Go to Slide 2, then select the chart.
   c. Open the Chart Tools Design tab, click the Quick Layout button, then apply Layout 9.
   d. Change the Vertical (Value) Axis title to **Millions**, then change the Horizontal (Category) Axis title to **Divisions**.
   e. Apply Style 14 from the Chart Styles group, then change the chart type to Clustered Bar.
   f. Type **Fiscal Year** as the chart title, then save your changes.

2. **Customize a chart.**
   a. Click the Add Chart Elements button, then add primary minor vertical gridlines, primary major horizontal gridlines, and outside end data labels.
   b. In the Chart Element gallery, point to Error Bars, click Standard Error then close the Chart Elements gallery.
   c. Right-click the value axis label, click the Outline button on the Mini toolbar, then click Black, Text 1.
   d. Select the category axis label, then press [F4].
   e. Right-click 10 on the value axis, click Format Axis, click Tick Marks in the Format Axis pane, click the Major type list arrow, then click Cross.

    f. Click the Minor type list arrow, click Outside, then close the Format Axis pane.

    g. Click a blank area of the chart, then save your changes.

3. Format chart elements.

    a. Open the Chart Tools Format tab, click the Chart Area list arrow in the Current Selection group, then click Series "1st Qtr."

    b. Click the Format Selection button in the Current Selection group, change the Gap Width to 150%, then change the Series Overlap to –20%.

    c. Click the Fill & Line icon at the top of the pane, then change the fill to a gradient fill, click the Preset gradients list arrow, then click Bottom Spotlight - Accent 1.

    d. Click the Effects icon at the top of the pane, then click Glow.

    e. Click the Presets list arrow, click Blue-Gray, 11 pt glow, Accent color 1, then close the pane.

    f. Right-click the legend, click Format Legend, then click the Right option button.

    g. Click the Fill & Line icon, click Fill, click the Solid fill option button, set the Transparency to 75%, then close the pane.

4. Animate a chart.

    a. Select the Animations tab, then apply the Wipe Entrance animation to the chart.

    b. Click the Effect Options button, click From Left, click the Effect Options button again, then change the animation to By Element in Series.

    c. Click the Animation Pane button, click the Object 4 list arrow in the Animation Pane, click Effect Options, then click the Chart Animation tab in the Wipe dialog box.

    d. Click the Start animation by drawing the chart background check box to deselect it, then click OK.

    e. Change the duration to 1.50 and the delay to .75 for all the animations, then click the Play Selected button in the Animation Pane.

    f. Close the Animation Pane, then save your changes.

5. Embed an Excel chart.

    a. Go to Slide 3, click the Insert tab, then click the Object button in the Text group.

    b. Click the Create from file option button, click Browse, then locate and embed the file PPT 6-5.xlsx from the location where you store your Data Files.

    c. Drag the lower-right sizing handle to increase the size of the chart, then move to the blank area of the slide.

    d. Double-click the chart, click the Sheet1 tab in the worksheet that opens, change the value in cell D6 to **35,590.20**, change the value in cell D7 to **67,429.00**, then click the Sheet2 tab.

    e. Right-click the value axis, click the Outline button on the Mini toolbar, click Automatic, click the category axis, then press [F4].

    f. Right-click the legend, click the Outline button on the Mini toolbar, then click Blue, Accent 1.

    g. Right-click the legend again, then change the legend outline to a 2 ¼pt square dot dash.

    h. Click a blank area of the slide, then save your changes.

6. Link an Excel worksheet.

    a. Insert a new slide after slide 3 with the Title Only layout.

    b. Type **Credit Balance**, click the Insert tab, then click the Object button in the Text group.

    c. Click the Create from file option button, click Browse, locate the file PPT 6-6.xlsx from the location where you store your Data Files, then link it to the slide. (*Hint*: make a copy of the Excel file PPT 6-6.xlsx to keep the original data intact.)

    d. Resize the worksheet object by dragging its sizing handles, then center it in the blank area of the slide.

    e. Right-click the worksheet, click Format Object, click the Solid fill option button, click the Color list arrow, then click Green, Accent 6.

    f. Change the fill transparency to 20%, close the pane, then save your changes.

Skills Review (continued)

7. Update a linked Excel worksheet.

   a. Double-click the worksheet.

   b. Select cells B4 to E7, click the Number Format list arrow in the Number group, then click Currency.

   c. Click cell F8, then click the Bold button in the Font group.

   d. Click cell D5, type **31,596.54**, click cell B6, then type **74,992.21**.

   e. Close the Excel window, then click Save to save your changes. The changes appear in the linked worksheet. **FIGURE 6-18** shows the completed presentation.

   f. Add your name to the slide footer, save your work, submit your presentation to your instructor, close the presentation, and exit PowerPoint.

FIGURE 6-18

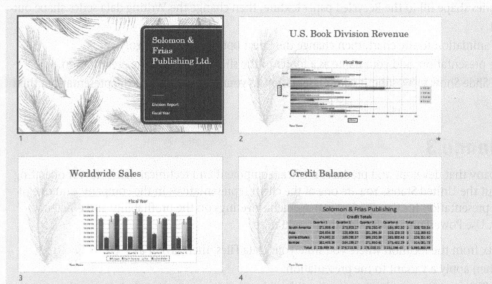

Independent Challenge 1

You work for Vortec Systems, a business consulting company that helps businesses organize or restructure themselves to be more efficient and profitable. You are one of four consultants who work directly with clients. To prepare for an upcoming meeting with executives at a local Internet communications company, you create a brief presentation outlining typical investigative and reporting techniques, past results versus the competition's, and the company's business philosophy. Use PowerPoint to customize a chart on Slide 3 of the presentation.

   a. Start PowerPoint, open the presentation PPT 6-7.pptx from the location where you store your Data Files, then save it as **PPT 6-Vortec**.

   b. Select the chart on Slide 3, then apply Layout 3 from the Quick Layout gallery.

   c. Type **I.S. Rating Scale** in the chart title text box.

   d. Change the chart type to Clustered Bar, then add primary minor vertical gridlines to the chart.

   e. Right-click the value axis, click Format Axis, click Tick Marks, add outside major tick marks, then close the pane.

   f. Click the Chart Elements button, add Inside End data labels, then add percentage error bars.

   g. Add your name as a footer to the slides, check the spelling of the presentation, then view the presentation in Reading View.

   h. Save the presentation, submit your presentation to your instructor, close the presentation, then exit PowerPoint.

Independent Challenge 2

One of your responsibilities working in the Indiana State schools system is to provide program performance data for educational programs designed for ESL and special needs IP children in the state. You need to develop and give a presentation describing the program's results at an upcoming national education forum. You have been working on the presentation, and now you need to use PowerPoint to put the finishing touches on a chart.

a. Start PowerPoint, open the presentation PPT 6-8.pptx from the location where you store your Data Files, then save it as **PPT 6-Indiana**.

b. Select the chart on Slide 6, then change the chart type to Clustered Column.

c. Add primary major vertical gridlines, move the legend to the top of the chart then change the data series overlap to –25% and the gap width to 200%.

d. Open the Chart Tools Format tab, click the Reading data series, then change the shape fill to a dark Linear Down gradient.

e. Change the Math data series shape fill to the Recycled paper texture, then change the Writing data series shape outline to a blue 3 pt weight.

f. Apply the Split Entrance animation to the chart, then change the Effect options to By Category.

g. Check the spelling in the presentation, add your name as a footer to the slides, then save the presentation.

h. View the presentation in Slide Show view, submit your presentation to your instructor, close the presentation, then exit PowerPoint.

Independent Challenge 3

Jendos Industries is a large company that develops and produces medical equipment and technical machines for operating and emergency rooms throughout the United States. You are one of the client representatives in the company, and one of your assignments is to prepare a presentation for the division management meetings on the profitability and efficiency of each division in the company. Use PowerPoint to develop the presentation.

a. Open the file PPT 6-9.pptx from the location where you store your Data Files, then save it as **PPT 6-Jendos**.

b. Apply the Crop theme, then apply a variant to the presentation.

c. Add a new slide with the Title and Content layout after the title slide titled **Company Divisions**, then create a SmartArt graphic that identifies the company's five divisions: **Administration**, **Accounting**, **Sales and Marketing**, **Research and Development**, and **Manufacturing**.

d. Format the new SmartArt graphic using SmartArt Styles and colors.

e. Go to the Division Performance slide, then embed the chart in the Excel file PPT 6-10.xlsx from the location where you store your Data Files.

f. Drag the corner sizing handles of the chart so it fills the blank area of the slide, double-click the chart, click the chart in Excel, then click the Chart Tools Design tab.

g. Apply the Style 5 chart style to the chart, right-click Last Yr. in the chart, click Format Axis, scroll down, click Labels, click the Label Position list arrow, click Low, click OK, then click a blank area of the slide.

h. Go to the Division Budgets slide, then link the worksheet in the Excel file PPT 6-11.xlsx from the location where you store your Data Files.

i. Open the linked worksheet in Excel, select cells B4 through F10, click the Accounting Number Format button in the Number group, save the changes to the worksheet, then close Excel.

j. Right-click the linked worksheet, click Format Object, click the Solid fill option button, change the fill color to an accent color at 30% transparency.

k. Close the pane, resize the worksheet to fill the slide, add your name as a footer to the slides and handouts, check the spelling, then view your presentation in Slide Show view.

l. Submit your presentation to your instructor, close the presentation, then exit PowerPoint.

Independent Challenge 4: Explore

You are on staff at your college newspaper. One of your jobs is to review online computer games and post a presentation on the paper's website. The presentation identifies the top online computer games based on student testing and other reviews. Use PowerPoint to create a presentation that includes research and your own information. Use the basic information in the presentation provided as a basis to develop your presentation. *NOTE: To complete the Independent Challenge, your computer must be connected to the Internet. (Before you complete this step make a copy of the Data File PPT 6-13.xlsx.)*

As you create this presentation, research online game descriptions and reviews to help you develop information for your presentation. Assume the top three gaming categories are Sci Fi, Superhero, and Mythology.

a. Connect to the Internet, then use a search engine to locate websites that have information on online PC computer games. Review at least two websites that contain information about computer games. Print the home pages of the websites you use to gather data for your presentation.

b. Open the presentation PPT 6-12.pptx from the location where you store your Data Files, then save it as **PPT 6-Review**.

c. Add the slide number and your name as the footer on all slides, apply the Vapor Trail design theme then apply a variant to the presentation.

d. Go to the Game Reviews slide, locate and link the Excel chart PPT 6-13.xlsx from the location where you store your Data Files.

e. Resize the chart to fit on the slide, then open the linked chart in Excel.

f. Click the Sheet 1 tab at the bottom of the Excel window, provide a name for each game, click the Sheet 2 tab, then save your changes.

g. Right-click the chart legend, click Delete on the shortcut menu, click the Chart Styles button, click Color, then click Color 3, save your changes, then exit Excel.

h. Click the File tab, click Edit Links to Files under Related Documents to open the Links dialog box, then click the Automatic Update check box to deselect it.

i. Click the Open Source button, click Sheet1 at the bottom of the Excel window, click cell B3, type **10.2**, click Sheet2 tab, save your work, then exit Excel.

j. Click the Back button to return to your presentation, right-click the Excel chart, then click Update Link.

k. Check the spelling in the presentation, save the presentation, then view the presentation in Slide Show view. An example of a finished presentation is shown in **FIGURE 6-19**.

l. Submit your presentation to your instructor, close the presentation, then exit PowerPoint.

FIGURE 6-19

Visual Workshop

Create a slide that looks like the example in **FIGURE 6-20**. Start a new presentation, then embed the Excel worksheet PPT 6-14.xlsx from the location where you store your Data Files. (*Hint*: The worksheet is formatted with a gradient fill.) Save the presentation as **PPT 6-Capital**. Add your name and the slide number as a footer to the slide, then submit your presentation to your instructor.

FIGURE 6-20

Capital Micro Systems

	Quarter 1	Quarter 2	Quarter 3	Quarter 4	Total
Division 1	$ 82,403.56	$ 68,534.49	$ 84,295.27	$ 75,432.29	$ 310,665.61
Division 2	$ 95,167.59	$ 109,356.88	$ 62,954.08	$ 65,938.43	$ 333,416.98
Division 3	$ 26,654.38	$ 41,321.77	$ 28,909.52	$ 25,103.18	$ 121,988.85
Division 4	$ 71,939.40	$ 94,777.23	$ 56,432.88	$ 84,592.50	$ 307,742.01
Total	$ 276,164.93	$ 313,990.37	$ 232,591.75	$ 251,066.40	$1,073,813.45

Inserting Graphics, Media, and Objects

CASE ▶ In this module, you work on a short presentation that describes side tours to Egypt that clients can take while on their Kenyan vacation. You then link it to your primary Kenyan project presentation. You use the advanced features in PowerPoint to customize a table, a picture, and a SmartArt graphic. You also insert a video and sound that complements the information as well as action buttons and hyperlinks for better navigation.

Module Objectives

After completing this module, you will be able to:

- Create a custom table
- Design a SmartArt graphic
- Enhance a SmartArt graphic
- Insert and edit digital video
- Insert and trim audio
- Edit and adjust a picture
- Add action buttons
- Insert hyperlinks

Files You Will Need

PPT 7-1.pptx	PPT 7-12.jpg
PPT 7-2.jpg	PPT 7-13.mp4
PPT 7-3.jpg	PPT 7-14.m4a
PPT 7-4.jpg	PPT 7-15.jpg
PPT 7-5.jpg	PPT 7-16.docx
PPT 7-6.wmv	PPT 7-17.pptx
PPT 7-7.m4a	PPT 7-18.pptx
PPT 7-8.jpg	PPT 7-19.pptx
PPT 7-9.pptx	PPT 7-20.pptx
PPT 7-10.docx	PPT 7-21.jpg
PPT 7-11.pptx	

Create a Custom Table

Learning Outcomes
- Customize table line style
- Insert table rows
- Split table cells

In PowerPoint, you have the ability to create dynamic tables. Tables you create in PowerPoint automatically display the style as determined by the theme assigned to the slide, including color combinations and shading, line styles and colors, and other effects. It is easy to customize the layout of a table or change how data is organized. You can delete and insert rows or columns, merge two or more cells together, or split one cell into more cells.   **CASE**   *You open a short presentation on Egyptian side tours that you have been working on and finish customizing a table.*

STEPS

1. **Start PowerPoint, open the presentation** PPT 7-1.pptx **from the location where you store your Data Files, save the presentation as** PPT 7-R2G, **click the** Slide 3 thumbnail **in the Slides tab, then click the** table
   Slide 3 appears in the Slide pane with the table selected.

2. **Click the** Table Tools Design tab **on the Ribbon, click the** Pen Style button **in the Draw Borders group, click the** dot style **(3rd style), click the** Pen Weight button **in the Draw Borders group, click** 3 pt, **click the** Pen Color button **in the Draw Borders group, then click** Green **in the Standard Colors section**
   The pointer changes to ✐, which indicates that you are in drawing mode.

3. **Click the** white vertical column line **that divides the Attraction and Hotel/Transportation columns in the first row in the table, then click the** vertical column line **for each row in that column**
   Compare your screen to **FIGURE 7-1**.

4. **Click the** Draw Table button **in the Draw Borders group, click the** Table Tools Layout tab **on the Ribbon, click the** Valley of Kings cell **in the table, click the** Insert Above button **in the Rows & Columns group, then enter the information below in the new row**

Colossi of Memnon	Camel	2 Meals/day

   Clicking the Draw Table button turned the drawing mode off. A new row is added to the table.

5. **Click the** Valley of Kings cell, **then click the** Split Cells button **in the Merge group**
   The Split Cells dialog box opens. The default table is 2 columns and 1 row.

6. **Click the** Number of columns down arrow **once, click the** Number of rows up arrow **once, then click** OK
   You split the cell to create a new row in that cell.

7. **Drag to select all the text below Valley of Kings in that cell, right-click the** selected text, **click** Cut **on the shortcut menu, right-click the** new row, **click the** Keep Source Formatting Paste Options button 📋 **on the shortcut menu, then press** [Backspace]
   The text for the optional tour is in a separate row. See **TABLE 7-1** for Paste button options.

8. **Click the** Distribute Rows button **in the Cell Size group**
   All the rows distributed proportionally as shown in **FIGURE 7-2**.

9. **Click outside the table, then save your presentation**

FIGURE 7-1: Table with new column line style

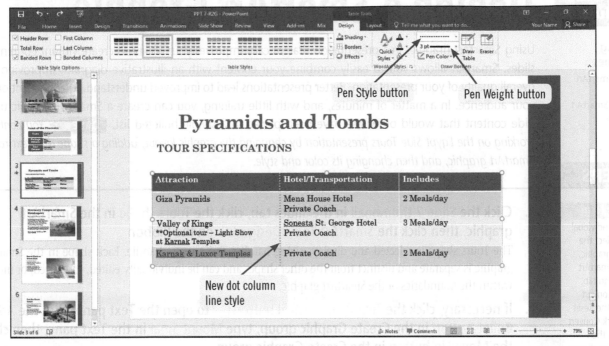

Pen Style button

Pen Weight button

Pyramids and Tombs

TOUR SPECIFICATIONS

Attraction	Hotel/Transportation	Includes
Giza Pyramids	Mena House Hotel Private Coach	2 Meals/day
Valley of Kings **Optional tour – Light Show at Karnak Temples	Sonesta St. George Hotel Private Coach	3 Meals/day
Karnak & Luxor Temples	Private Coach	2 Meals/day

New dot column line style

FIGURE 7-2: Modified table

Pyramids and Tombs

TOUR SPECIFICATIONS

Attraction	Hotel/Transportation	Includes
Giza Pyramids	Mena House Hotel Private Coach	2 Meals/day
Colossi of Memnon	Camel	2 Meals/day
Valley of Kings	Sonesta St. George Hotel Private Coach	3 Meals/day
**Optional tour – Light Show at Karnak Temples		
Karnak & Luxor Temples	Private Coach	2 Meals/day

New cell with moved data

TABLE 7-1: Understanding common Paste button options

button	button name	result
	Use Destination Theme	Use the current theme of the presentation
	Keep Source Formatting	Use the formatting characteristics from the object's source file
	Picture	Insert the object as a picture
	Keep Text Only	Insert the object as text only with no formatting
	Embed	Insert the object as an embedded object

Design a SmartArt Graphic

Using SmartArt graphics in a presentation dramatically improves your ability to create vibrant content on slides. SmartArt allows you to easily combine your content with an illustrative diagram, improving the overall quality of your presentation. Better presentations lead to improved understanding and retention by your audience. In a matter of minutes, and with little training, you can create a SmartArt graphic using slide content that would otherwise have been placed in a simple bulleted list. **CASE** *You continue working on the Egypt Side Tours presentation by changing the graphic layout, adding a shape and text to the SmartArt graphic, and then changing its color and style.*

STEPS

QUICK TIP

To create individual shapes, select the SmartArt graphic, click the SmartArt Tools Design tab, click the Convert button in the Reset group, click Convert to Shapes, then ungroup the shapes.

1. **Click the** Slide 2 thumbnail **in the Slides tab, click the** Tours shape **in the SmartArt graphic, then click the** SmartArt Tools Design tab **on the Ribbon**

   The Tours shape is selected and displays sizing handles and a rotate handle. Each shape in the SmartArt graphic is separate and distinct from the other shapes and can be individually edited, formatted, or moved within the boundaries of the SmartArt graphic.

2. **If necessary, click the** Text Pane control button ⬧ **to open the Text pane, click the** Add Bullet button **in the Create Graphic group, type** Mount Sinai **in the Text pane, then click the** Move Up button **in the Create Graphic group**

   A new bullet appears in the Text pane and in the graphic. Compare your screen with **FIGURE 7-3**.

3. **Click the** More button ⬧ **in the Layouts group, click** Horizontal Picture List **(4th row), then click the** Package Details shape

   Live Preview shows you how each layout changes the SmartArt graphic. The SmartArt graphic layout is now a Horizontal Picture List.

QUICK TIP

While the Text pane is open, use the Promote and Demote buttons to increase or decrease the level of the bullet or shape in the graphic.

4. **Click the** Add Shape list arrow **in the Create Graphic group, click** Add Shape After, **then click the** Move Down button **once in the Create Graphic group**

   A new shape in the same style appears with a new bullet in the Text pane and then is moved to the end of the Text pane.

5. **Type** Upgrades, **press [Enter], press [Tab], type** Valley of the Queens, **press [Enter], type** Cairo, **press [Enter], then type** Personal guide

6. **Click** ⬧ **in the SmartArt Styles group, then click** Moderate Effect **in the Best Match for Document section**

   The style of the SmartArt graphic changes.

7. **Click the** Change Colors button **in the SmartArt Styles group, then click** Colorful Range - Accent Colors 4 to 5 **in the Colorful section**

   Each shape now has a different color that follows the Theme colors of the presentation.

8. **Click the** Text Pane button **in the Create Graphic group to close the Text pane, then click the** Right to Left button **in the Create Graphic group**

   The graphic flips and appears as a mirror image. You prefer the original arrangement of the graphic.

9. **Click the** Right to Left button, **click a blank area of the slide, then save your changes**

   Compare your screen to **FIGURE 7-4**.

FIGURE 7-3: SmartArt graphic with added text

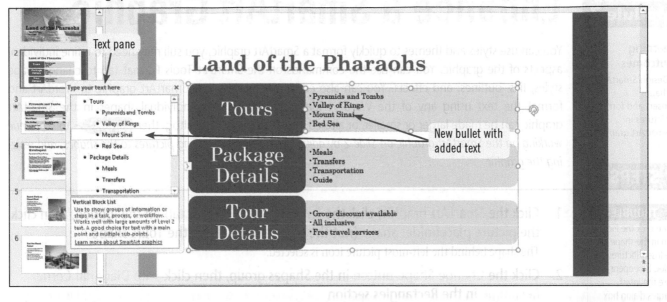

FIGURE 7-4: SmartArt graphic with new design

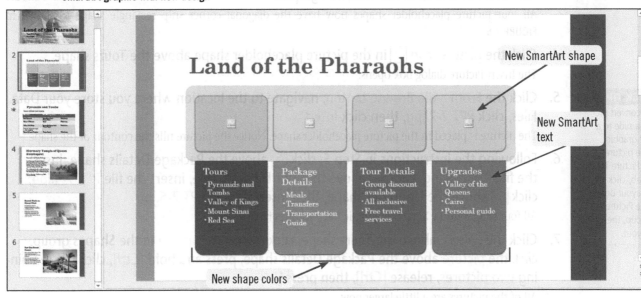

Creating mathematical equations

You can insert or create mathematical equations using the Equation button in the Symbols group on the Insert tab. Click the Equation button list arrow to access nine common equations, which include the area of a circle, the Pythagorean Theorem (my personal favorite), and the Quadratic Formula (my editor's favorite). To create your own equations click the Equation button to open the Equation Tools Design tab. On this tab you can use the Ink Equation button to insert an equation using your own handwriting or you can create an equation using eight different types of mathematical symbols including basic math, geometry, operators, and scripts. You also have the ability to create mathematical structures such as integrals and functions.

Enhance a SmartArt Graphic

Learning Outcomes
• Design SmartArt shapes
• Insert and format pictures in SmartArt graphics

You can use styles and themes to quickly format a SmartArt graphic, you still may need to refine individual aspects of the graphic. You can use the commands on the SmartArt Tools Format tab to change shape styles, fills, outlines, and effects. You can also convert text within the SmartArt graphic to WordArt and format the text using any of the WordArt formatting commands. Individual shapes in the SmartArt graphic can be made larger or smaller, or altered into a different shape altogether. **CASE** *You continue working on the SmartArt graphic on Slide 2 by adjusting four shapes, adding pictures to the shapes, and resizing the graphic.*

STEPS

TROUBLE
If you click the Picture icon in the shape and the Insert Pictures dialog box opens, close the Insert Pictures dialog box.

1. **Click the** SmartArt graphic, **click the** SmartArt Tools Format tab **on the Ribbon, then click the** picture placeholder shape **(not the picture icon) above the Tours shape**
   The shape behind the left-most picture icon is selected.

2. **Click the** Change Shape button **in the Shapes group, then click** Snip Diagonal Corner Rectangle **in the Rectangles section**
   The form of the shape changes.

3. **Click the** picture placeholder shape **above the Package Details shape, press and hold** [Ctrl], **click the remaining** two picture placeholder shapes, **release** [Ctrl], **press** [F4], **then click in a blank area of the SmartArt graphic**
   All four picture placeholder shapes now have the diagonal corner snip rectangle shape as shown in **FIGURE 7-5**.

4. **Click the** picture icon 🖼 **in the picture placeholder shape above the Tours shape**
   The Insert Picture dialog box opens.

QUICK TIP
You can convert pictures on a slide to a SmartArt graphic. Select the pictures, click the Picture Tools Format tab, click the Picture Layout button in the Picture Styles group, then click a layout.

5. **Click the** From a file Browse button, **navigate to the location where you store your Data Files, click** PPT 7-2.jpg, **then click** Insert
   The picture is placed in the picture placeholder shape. Notice the picture fills the contour of the shape.

6. **Following the instructions in Step 5, click** 🖼 **above the Package Details shape, insert the file** PPT 7-3.jpg, **click** 🖼 **above the Tour Details shape, insert the file** PPT 7-4.jpg, **click** 🖼 **above the Upgrades shape, then insert the file** PPT 7-5.jpg
   All four shapes in the SmartArt graphic have pictures in them.

7. **Click the** picture **above the Tours shape, click the** Larger button **in the Shapes group, click the** picture **above the Package Details shape, press and hold** [Ctrl], **click the remaining** two pictures, **release** [Ctrl], **then press** [F4]
   All of the pictures are a little larger now.

8. **Click a blank area inside the SmartArt graphic, then drag the SmartArt graphic's** sizing handles **to enlarge the graphic**
   The SmartArt graphic fills the white area on the slide as shown in **FIGURE 7-6**.

9. **Click a blank area of the slide, then save your work**

FIGURE 7-5: New shapes in SmartArt graphic

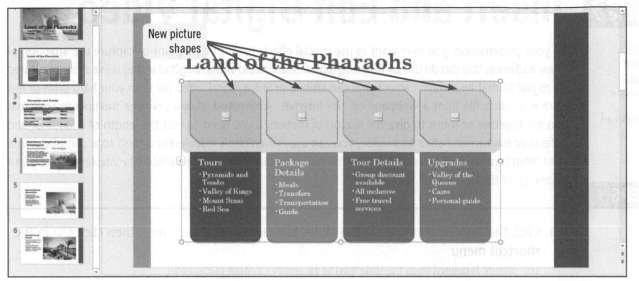

New picture shapes

Land of the Pharaohs

FIGURE 7-6: Completed SmartArt graphic

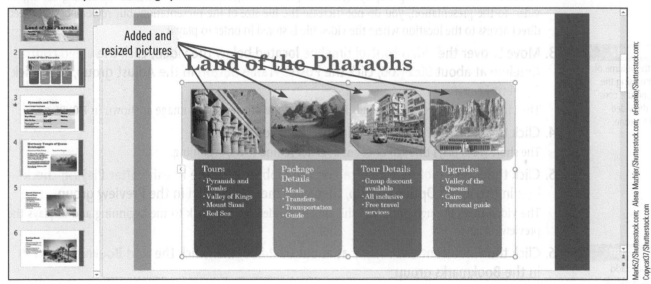

Added and resized pictures

Land of the Pharaohs

Saving a presentation in PDF, XPS, or other fixed file formats

In certain situations, such as when sharing sensitive or legal materials with others, you may find it necessary to save your presentation file in a fixed layout format. A **fixed layout format** is a specific file format that "locks" the file from future change and allows others only the ability to view or print the presentation. To save a presentation in one of these fixed formats, click the File tab on the Ribbon, click Export, click Create PDF/XPS Document, then click the Create PDF/XPS button. The Publish as PDF or XPS dialog box opens. Select the appropriate file type in the Save as type list box, choose other options (optimization), then publish your presentation in a fixed layout format. To view a fixed layout format presentation, you need appropriate viewer software that you can download from the Internet. Other common file formats supported in PowerPoint include PowerPoint Template (.potx), PowerPoint Show (.ppsx), OpenDocument Presentation (.odp), and PowerPoint Picture Presentation (.pptx). On the File tab click Export, then click Change File Type to save a file in another file format and to view descriptions of these and other supported file formats.

Insert and Edit Digital Video

Learning Outcomes
• Link a video
• Apply a poster frame
• Add a bookmark

In your presentation, you may want to use special effects to illustrate a point or capture the attention of your audience. You can do this by inserting digital or animated video. **Digital video** is live action captured in digital format by a video camera. You can embed or link a digital video file from your hard drive or link a digital video file from a webpage on the Internet. **Animated video** contains multiple images that stream together or move to give the illusion of motion. If you need to edit the length of a video or add effects or background color to a video, you can use PowerPoint's video-editing tools to accomplish those and other basic editing tasks. **CASE** ▶ *You continue to develop your presentation by inserting and editing a video clip of the Mount Sinai Sacred Pools.*

STEPS

1. **Click the** Slide 5 thumbnail **in the Slides tab, right-click the** picture, **then click** Cut **in the shortcut menu**
   The picture is deleted from the slide leaving an empty Content placeholder.

2. **Click the** Insert Video icon 🎞 **in the Content placeholder, click the** From a file Browse button, **navigate to the location where you store your Data Files, click** PPT 7-6.wmv, **click the** Insert list arrow, **then click** Link to File
   The PPT 7-6.wmv video clip displaying a black preview image is linked to the slide. By linking the digital video to the presentation, you do not increase the file size of the presentation, but remember, you need direct access to the location where the video file is stored in order to play it.

QUICK TIP
Adjust the volume of the video using the Mute/Unmute control on the video control timeline.

3. **Move** ⬚ **over the** video control timeline **located below the video, click the** video control timeline **at about** 00:21.00, **click the** Poster Frame button **in the Adjust group, then click** Current Frame
   The video frame at about 21 seconds is now set as the preview video image as shown in **FIGURE 7-7**.

4. **Click the** Play/Pause button ▶ **in the video control bar**
   The short video plays through once but does not rewind to the beginning.

5. **Click the** Video Tools Playback tab **on the Ribbon, click the** Rewind after Playing check box **in the Video Options group, then click the** Play button **in the Preview group**
   The video plays through once, and this time the video rewinds back to the beginning and displays the preview image.

QUICK TIP
You can also add fade effects to the beginning and end of a video using the Fade Duration commands in the Editing group.

6. **Click the** video control timeline **at about** 00:24.00, **then click the** Add Bookmark button **in the Bookmarks group**
   A yellow circle appears in the video control timeline, indicating the video has a bookmark. A **bookmark** can indicate a point of interest in a video; it can also be used to jump to a specific point in a video.

7. **Click the** Slide Show button 🖵 **on the status bar, move** ⬚ **over the video, the pointer changes to** 🖑, **then click the bookmark as shown in** FIGURE 7-8
   The video moves to the bookmarked frame.

8. **Click the** Play/Pause button ▶ **on the video**
   The video plays from the bookmarked frame to the end of the video and then rewinds to the beginning.

QUICK TIP
Click the Reset Design button in the Adjust group to remove all formatting changes you made to the video.

9. **Press** [Esc], **click the** video, **click the** Video Tools Format tab **on the Ribbon, click the** More button ▼ **in the Video Styles group, then click** Moderate Beveled Rectangle **in the Moderate section**
   A bevel effect is added to the video.

10. **Click a blank area of the slide, then save your work**

FIGURE 7-7: Video clip inserted on the slide

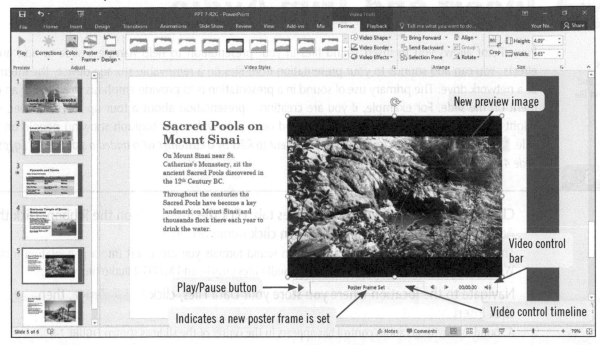

FIGURE 7-8: Video in Slide Show view with selected bookmark

Trimming a video

After you watch a video clip, you may determine certain portions of the video are not relevant to your slide show. From PowerPoint, a video clip can be trimmed only from the beginning or the end of the clip; you can't use PowerPoint to trim out the middle of a clip. To trim a video clip, select the video, click the Video Tools Playback tab, then click the Trim Video button in the Editing group. The Trim Video dialog box opens. To trim the beginning of the video clip, drag the start point (green marker) to the right until you reach a new starting point. To trim the end of a video clip, drag the end point (red marker) to the left until you reach a new ending point. If you want to precisely choose a new beginning or ending point for the video clip, you can click the up or down arrows on the Start Time and End Time text boxes.

Insert and Trim Audio

PowerPoint allows you to insert sound files in your presentation to help narrate a slide or add audio effects. You can add sounds to your presentation from files on a removable storage device, the Internet, or a network drive. The primary use of sound in a presentation is to provide emphasis to a slide or an element on the slide. For example, if you are creating a presentation about a tour up the Nile River, you might consider inserting a rushing water sound on a slide with a photograph showing people on the Nile. **CASE** *You insert a recorded sound file sent to R2G by a customer who added a side tour to Egypt on Slide 4 of the presentation.*

STEPS

1. **Click the Slide 4 thumbnail in the Slides tab, click the Insert tab on the Ribbon, click the Audio button in the Media group, then click Audio on My PC**

   The Insert Audio dialog box opens. Common sound formats you can insert into a presentation include Windows audio files (waveform) (.wav), MP4 audio files (.mp4), and MPEG 4 audio files (.m4a).

2. **Navigate to the location where you store your Data Files, click PPT 7-7.m4a, then click Insert**

   A sound icon with an audio control bar appears in the center of the slide as shown **FIGURE 7-9**.

3. **Drag the sound icon ◀ beneath the slide text, then click the Play/Pause button ▶ in the audio control bar**

   The sound icon moves off the picture and plays one time through. After hearing the audio play, you decide to trim the end point to cut out the end of the audio clip.

4. **Click the Trim Audio button in the Editing group on the Audio Tools Playback tab**

   The Trim Audio dialog box opens as shown in **FIGURE 7-10**. Notice on the audio timeline there is a start point (green marker) and an end point (red marker), which identify the beginning and end of the audio. The audio is 14.953 seconds long.

5. **Click the Play button ▶ in the Trim Audio dialog box, watch the sound on the audio timeline, then drag the end point ▌ to the left to about 00:12.000**

   The audio will now end at this point when played. The beginning of the audio can also be adjusted.

6. **Click the Start Time up arrow until 00:01.200 appears as shown in FIGURE 7-11, click OK, then click ▶ on the audio control bar**

   The audio now plays between the new start and end points. By default, the audio plays when you click the sound icon during a slide show.

7. **Click the Start button in the Audio Options group, then click Automatically**

   The audio will now run automatically as soon as the slide appears in Slide Show view.

8. **Click the Slide Show button 🖵 on the status bar, then listen to the audio**

   Notice that the sound icon appears during the slide show.

9. **Press [Esc], click a blank area of the slide, then save your changes**

FIGURE 7-9: Sound clip inserted on the slide

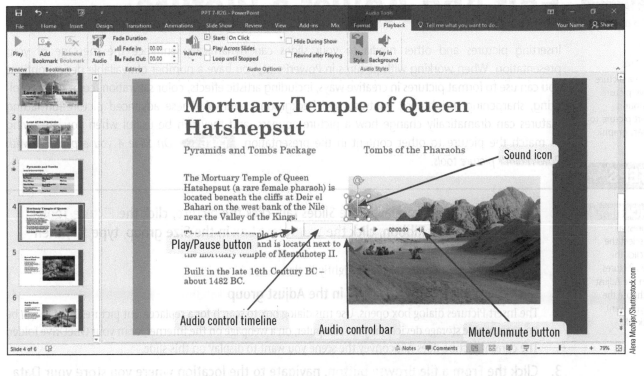

FIGURE 7-10: Trim Audio dialog box

FIGURE 7-11: Trim Audio dialog box with trimmed audio

Recording a narration on a slide

If your computer has speakers, a sound card, and a microphone, you can record a voice narration and then play it during a slide show. To record a narration, click the Insert tab on the Ribbon, click the Audio button in the Media group, then click Record Audio. The Record Sound dialog box opens. To start recording, click the Record button in the dialog box, then click the Stop button when you are finished. A sound icon appears on the slide. Narration recordings and other sounds are embedded in the presentation and will increase the PowerPoint file size. You can preview a narration in Normal view by pointing to the sound icon on the slide, then clicking the Play/Pause button in the audio control bar.

Edit and Adjust a Picture

Learning Outcomes
• Replace a picture
• Remove picture background
• Convert picture to SmartArt graphic

Inserting pictures and other media to your slides can dynamically enhance the message of your presentation. When working with pictures in PowerPoint, you have a number of available design options you can use to format pictures in creative ways, including artistic effects, color saturation, color tone, recoloring, sharpening, brightness, contrast, and background removal. These advanced picture-formatting features can dramatically change how a picture appears, and they can be useful when you are trying to match the picture to other content in the presentation. **CASE** ▸ *On Slide 4 you experiment with PowerPoint's picture tools.*

STEPS

QUICK TIP
To compress a picture, select the picture, click the Compress Pictures button in the Adjust group, choose the options you want, then click OK.

1. **Click the** Slide 4 thumbnail **in the Slides tab, click the** picture, **click the** Picture Tools Format tab **on the Ribbon, click the** Width text box **in the Size group, type** 5.5, **then press** [Enter]

   The picture proportionally decreases slightly in size.

2. **Click the** Change Picture button **in the Adjust group**

   The Insert Pictures dialog box opens. Use this dialog box to search for a replacement picture. The file can be on a removable storage device, on your computer, on a webpage on the Internet, or in your OneDrive folder. The current picture does not convey the scene you want to display on this slide.

3. **Click the** From a file Browse button, **navigate to the location where you store your Data Files, click** PPT 7-8.jpg, **then click** Insert

   A new picture takes the place of the original picture at the same size. Eliminating the background of a picture can highlight the subject or remove distracting aspects of the picture.

4. **Click the** Remove Background button **in the Adjust group**

   The Background Removal tab opens on the Ribbon. The suggested background is highlighted in pink. The picture displays a removal marquee box with sizing handles that surrounds the subject of the picture you might want to keep, as shown in **FIGURE 7-12.**

5. **Drag the** removal marquee sizing handles **to match** FIGURE 7-13, **then click the** Keep Changes button **in the Close group**

   The entire blue sky portion of the picture is removed from the picture.

QUICK TIP
To make one color in a picture transparent, select the picture, click the Color button in the Adjust group, click Set Transparent Color, then click the color on the picture you want to make transparent.

6. **Click the** Color button **in the Adjust group, click** Saturation: 0% **in the Color Saturation section, click the** Corrections button **in the Adjust group, then click** Brightness: –20% Contrast: +40% **in the Brightness/Contrast section (5th row)**

   The picture color, saturation, brightness, and contrast change. You like the adjusted picture formatting, but you want to compare it to the original.

7. **Click the** Reset Picture button **in the Adjust group, view the** picture, **then click the** Undo button 🔄 **on the Quick Access**

   After looking at the picture in its original condition, you decide to keep all of the formatting you have applied to the picture.

8. **Click the** Picture Layout button **in the Picture Styles group, click** Bending Picture Semi-Transparent Text **(2nd row), click the** text box, **then type** Temple

   The picture is converted to a SmartArt graphic with a stylistic text box.

9. **Drag the** SmartArt graphic corner sizing handles **until the SmartArt graphic looks similar to** FIGURE 7-14, **click a blank area of the slide, then save your work**

FIGURE 7-12: Picture with background area to be removed

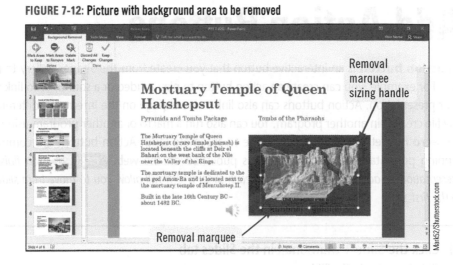

Mark52/Shutterstock.com

FIGURE 7-13: Adjusted removal marquee

Mark52/Shutterstock.com

FIGURE 7-14: Picture converted to SmartArt graphic

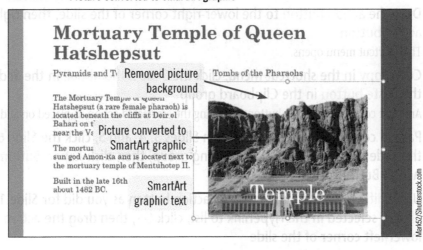

Mark52/Shutterstock.com

Compressing pictures

It's important to know that when you compress a picture you change the amount of detail in the picture, so it might look different than it did before the compression. Compressing a picture changes the amount of color used in the picture with no loss of quality. By default, all inserted pictures in PowerPoint are automatically compressed using the settings in the PowerPoint Options dialog box. To locate the compression settings, click the File tab, click Options, then click Advanced in the left pane. In the Image Size and Quality section, you can change picture compression settings or stop the automatic compression of pictures. If you want to apply an effect from the Artistic Effects gallery to a compressed picture, compress the picture first to maintain the best picture quality possible.

Inserting Graphics, Media, and Objects

Add Action Buttons

Learning Outcomes
• Create action button
• Duplicate action buttons

An **action button** is an interactive button that you create from the Shapes gallery to perform a specific task. For example, you can create an action button to play a video or a sound, or to link to another slide in your presentation. Action buttons can also link to a webpage on the Internet, a different presentation, or any file created in another program. You can also run a macro or another program using an action button. A **macro** is a set of actions that you use to automate tasks. Action buttons are commonly used in self-running presentations and presentations published on the web. **CASE** *You finish working on this presentation by adding action buttons to each slide, which will allow you to move from slide to slide and back to the first slide.*

STEPS

1. **Click the** Slide 1 thumbnail **in the Slides tab**
   Slide 1 appears in the Slide pane.

QUICK TIP
Any shape in the Shapes gallery as well as most objects can be an action button. Click the shape or object, click the Insert tab, click the Action button in the Links group, then select an action.

2. **Click the** More button ⤓ **in the Drawing group to open the Shapes gallery, click** Action Button: Forward or Next ▷ **in the Action Buttons section, press and hold [Shift], drag to create a button as shown in** FIGURE 7-15, **then release [Shift]**
   A small action button appears on the slide, and the Action Settings dialog box opens. Pressing [Shift] while you create a shape maintains the shape's proportions as you change its size.

3. **Make sure** Next Slide **is selected in the Hyperlink to list, then click** OK
   The dialog box closes. The action button now has an action, in this case, linking to the next slide.

4. **Click the** Drawing Tools Format tab **on the Ribbon, click** ⤓ **in the Shape Styles group, point to** Other Theme Fills, **then click** Style 6
   The new theme fill makes the action button easier to see on the slide.

QUICK TIP
Use the arrow keys on your keyboard or press [Alt] while dragging the action button to nudge the action button into place.

5. **Drag the** action button **to the lower-right corner of the slide, then right-click the** action button
   The shortcut menu opens.

6. **Click** Copy **in the shortcut menu, click the** Slide 2 thumbnail **in the Slides tab, then click the** Paste button **in the Clipboard group**
   An exact copy of the action button, including the associated action, is placed on Slide 2.

7. **Paste a copy of the** action button **on Slides 3, 4, and 5, click the** Slide 6 thumbnail **in the Slides tab, click** ⤓ **in the Drawing group, then click** Action Button: Home 🏠 **in the Action Buttons section**

8. **Use [Shift] to create a similar-sized action button as you did for Slide 1, make sure** First Slide **is selected in the Hyperlink to list, click** OK, **then drag the** action button **to the lower-left corner of the slide**
   Compare your screen to FIGURE 7-16.

9. **Click the** Slide Show button 🖵 **on the status bar, click the** Home action button, **click the** action buttons **to move from Slide 2 to Slide 6, then press [Esc] to end the slide show**
   The pointer changes to 👆 when you click each action button.

10. **Add your name to the slide footer, save your changes, submit your presentation to your instructor, click the** File tab **on the Ribbon, then click** Close **to close the presentation, but do not exit PowerPoint**

FIGURE 7-15: Inserted action button

Action button

FIGURE 7-16: Home action button on last slide

Home action button

Changing the transparency of a picture

Pictures in PowerPoint are commonly used as slide backgrounds, individual objects on a slide, or inserted in another object, such as a SmartArt graphic. To change the transparency of a picture used as a slide background, insert the picture as a slide background using the Format Background button on the Design tab, then adjust the Transparency slider in the Format Background pane. To change the transparency of a picture you want to insert on a slide, first draw a shape from the Shapes gallery, such as a rectangle the size you want the picture to be, then right-click the shape. Click Format Shape on the shortcut menu, click Fill, click the Picture or texture fill option button, click the File button, locate and insert the picture, then move the Transparency slider in the Format Picture pane.

Inserting Graphics, Media, and Objects

Insert Hyperlinks

While creating a presentation, there might be a circumstance where you want to view a document that either won't fit on the slide or is too detailed for your presentation. In these cases, you can insert a **hyperlink**, a specially formatted word, phrase, graphic, or drawn object that you click during a slide show to "jump to," or display, another slide or PowerPoint presentation in your current presentation; a document from another program, like Word; or a webpage. A hyperlinked object is similar to a linked object because you can modify the object in its source program from within PowerPoint. **CASE** *You add two hyperlinks to the primary presentation you have been working on that provide more detail on the 5-day Egypt side tours.*

STEPS

1. **Open the presentation** PPT 7-9.pptx **from the location where you store your Data Files, then save the presentation as** PPT 7-Final.pptx

2. **Click the** Slide 12 thumbnail **in the Slides tab, select** Egypt Side Tour **in the text object, click the** Insert tab **on the Ribbon, click the** Hyperlink button **in the Links group, then click** Existing File or Web Page **in the Link to: pane**

   The Insert Hyperlink dialog box opens. The Existing File or Web Page button is selected in the Link to: pane, and the Current Folder button is selected in the Look in pane. The location where you store your Data Files should be the open folder.

QUICK TIP

Links can also be established between slides of the same presentation, a new presentation, an email address, or any webpage.

3. **Click the file** PPT 7-10.docx, **click OK, then click in a blank area of the slide**

   Now that you have made the text "Egypt Side Tour" a hyperlink to the file PPT 7-10.docx, the text is formatted in an orange color and is underlined, which is the color a hyperlink is formatted in this theme.

4. **Click the** Slide Show button 🖳 **on the status bar, point to** Egypt Side Tour, **notice the pointer change to** 🖑, **then click** Egypt Side Tour

   Microsoft Word opens, and the Word document containing a detailed description of the Pyramids & Tombs 5-day tour appears, as shown in **FIGURE 7-17**.

5. **Read the document, then close the** Word **window**

   The PowerPoint slide reappears in Slide Show view.

QUICK TIP

To edit, open, copy, or remove a hyperlink, right-click the hyperlink, then click the appropriate command on the shortcut menu.

6. **Press [Esc], click the** Slide 10 thumbnail **in the Slides tab, right-click the** Information action button, **click** Hyperlink, **click the** Hyperlink to option button, **click the** Hyperlink to list arrow, **then click** Other PowerPoint Presentation

   The Hyperlink to Other PowerPoint Presentation dialog box opens.

7. **Open the file** PPT 7-R2G.pptx **(that you worked on earlier in this module) from the location where you store your Data Files, then click** OK

   The Hyperlink to Slide dialog box opens. You can choose which slides you want to link to.

8. **Click** OK **to link to Slide 1, click** OK **to close the Action Settings dialog box, click** 🖳 **to start the slide show, click the** Information action button, **click the** action buttons **to view the slides in the presentation, press [Esc] to end the slide show, then press [Esc] again**

   The slide show ends. The hyperlinks and action buttons all work correctly.

9. **Add your name to the slides footer, save your changes, then click the** Slide Sorter button 🔳 **on the status bar**

   Compare your screen to **FIGURE 7-18**.

10. **Submit your presentation to your instructor, close the presentation, then exit PowerPoint**

FIGURE 7-17: Linked Word document

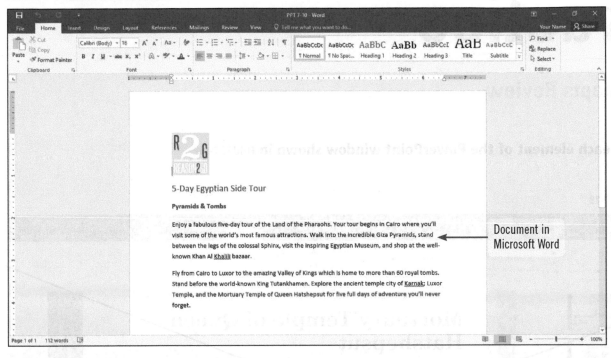

Document in
Microsoft Word

FIGURE 7-18: Final presentation in Slide Sorter view

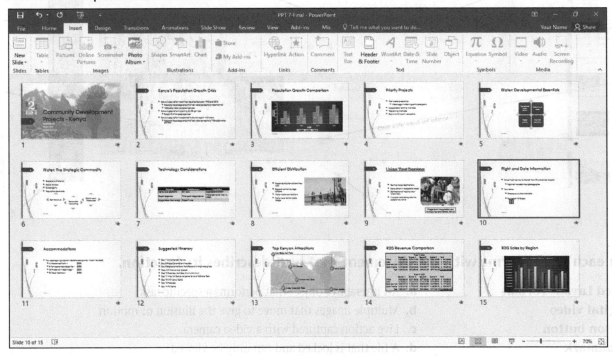

Inserting a screenshot

Using the Screenshot button in the Images group on the Insert tab, you can insert a picture, or screenshot, of an open program window or a specific part of the window. A screenshot is simply a picture of the window displayed on your screen. For example, you could use the screenshot feature to insert a picture of information you found on a webpage or found in other documents or programs that might not be easily transferable to PowerPoint. Screenshots are static and are not able to be updated if the source information changes. Only open nonminimized windows are available to be captured as a screenshot. When you click the Screenshot button all open program windows appear in the Available Windows gallery. To take a screenshot of part of a window, click the Screenshot button, then click Screen Clipping.

Practice

Concepts Review

Label each element of the PowerPoint window shown in FIGURE 7-19.

FIGURE 7-19

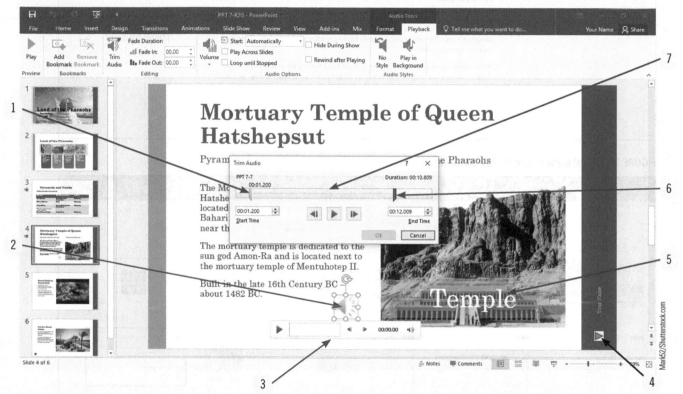

Match each of the terms with the statement that best describes its function.

8. **Fixed Layout Format**
9. **Digital video**
10. **Action button**
11. **Bookmark**
12. **Hyperlink**
13. **Animated video**

a. An interactive object that performs a specific task
b. Multiple images that move to give the illusion of motion
c. Live action captured with a video camera
d. A file that is locked and can only be viewed
e. A formatted word or graphic that you can click to open a document from another program
f. Can be used to jump to specific point in a video

Select the best answer from the list of choices.

14. Use a _____ to display content with an illustrative diagram.
- **a.** video
- **b.** SmartArt graphic
- **c.** table
- **d.** screen recording

15. You can use _____ to manually start or stop an audio clip.
- **a.** narrations
- **b.** action buttons
- **c.** bookmarks
- **d.** hyperlinks

16. Adjust the _____ to remove the background of a picture?
- **a.** picture border
- **b.** picture compression
- **c.** background transparency
- **d.** removal marquee box

17. To open a webpage during a slide show, you need to create a _____.
- **a.** hyperlink
- **b.** screenshot
- **c.** web file
- **d.** recording

18. _____ a picture changes the amount of color used in the picture.
- **a.** Embedding
- **b.** Sharpening
- **c.** Linking
- **d.** Compressing

Skills Review

1. Create a custom table.

  a. Start PowerPoint, open the presentation PPT 7-11.pptx from the location where you store your Data Files, then save it as **PPT 7-Dairy**.

  b. Go to Slide 3, select the table, click the Table Tools Design tab, click the More button in the Table Styles group, then click the Themed Style 1 - Accent 4 in the Best Match for Document section.

  c. Click the Pen Weight button in the Draw Borders group, select 3 pt, click the Pen Color button, then click White, Background 1.

  d. Apply the 3-pt line style to the vertical border lines between each of the cells in the first row, then click the Draw Table button.

  e. Select the whole table, click the Table Tools Layout tab, click the Cell Margins button in the Alignment group, then click Wide.

  f. Click anywhere in the bottom row, then click the Insert Below button in the Rows & Columns group.

  g. Click the left cell of the new row, type **Muenster**, press [Tab], type **52,982,000 lbs.**, press [Tab], type **32.5%**, press [Tab], type **1**, then save your changes.

2. Design a SmartArt graphic.

  a. Go to Slide 4, click the SmartArt graphic, then click the SmartArt Tools Design tab.

  b. Click the More button in the Layouts group, then click Vertical Picture List in the fourth row.

  c. Click the Add Shape list arrow in the Create Graphic group, then click Add Shape After.

  d. Open the Text pane, type **Cheese production**, press [Enter], click the Demote button in the Create Graphic group, type **American varieties 419,000 tons**, press [Enter], type **Italian varieties 711,100 tons**, press [Enter], type **Total 1.1 million tons**.

  e. Close the Text pane, click the Change Colors button in the SmartArt Styles group, then click Colorful Range - Accent Colors 5 to 6 in the Colorful section.

  f. Click the Right to Left button in the Create Graphic group, then save your changes.

3. Enhance a SmartArt graphic.

  a. Click the SmartArt Tools Format tab, click the top picture shape in the SmartArt graphic, click the Larger button in the Shapes group, then increase the size of the two other picture shapes.

PowerPoint 2016

Skills Review (continued)

    b. Click the Insert picture icon in the bottom picture shape, then locate and insert the file PPT 7-12.jpg from the location where you store your Data Files.

    c. Follow the above instructions, insert the file PPT 7-12.jpg to the other two picture shapes, then save your changes.

4. Insert and edit digital video.

    a. Go to Slide 2, click the Insert tab on the Ribbon, click the Video button in the Media group, then click Video on My PC.

    b. Locate the file PPT 7-13.mp4 from the location where you store your Data Files, click the Insert list arrow, then click Link to File.

    c. Click the number in the Height text box in the Size group, type **3.2**, press [Enter], then move the video clip to the center of the blank area of the slide.

    d. Move the pointer over the video control timeline, click at approximately 00:15.20 in the timeline, click the Poster Frame button in the Adjust group, then click Current Frame.

    e. On the Video Tools Playback tab, click the Rewind after Playing check box, then add a bookmark at about the 00:05.05 point on the video control timeline.

    f. Preview the video clip in Slide Show view, then save your presentation.

5. Insert and trim audio.

    a. Go to Slide 5, click the Insert tab, click the Audio button in the Media group, then click Audio on My PC.

    b. Locate and insert the sound file PPT 7-14.w4a from the location where you store your Data Files.

    c. Preview the sound, set the sound to start automatically during a slide show, then drag the sound icon above the text object.

    d. Use the Trim Audio dialog box to change the start point of the audio clip to 00:01.200 and the end point to 00:05.000.

    e. Click the Hide During Show check box in the Audio Options group, click the Slide Show button on the status bar, review the slide, press [Esc], then save your presentation.

6. Edit and adjust a picture.

    a. Go to Slide 5, click the Picture, then change the picture with PPT 7-15.jpg.

    b. Change the color of the picture to Temperature: 4700 K (Color Tone section), then correct the picture to Brightness: +20% Contrast: 0% (Normal).

    c. Change the picture to a Bending Picture Caption layout using the Picture Layout button, then type **Leslie Farms**.

7. Add action buttons.

    a. Go to Slide 1, click the More button in the Drawing group, then click Action Button: Forward or Next.

    b. Draw a small button, click OK in the Action Settings dialog box, then position the button in the lower-right corner of the slide.

    c. Click the Drawing Tools Format tab on the Ribbon, click the More button in the Shape Styles group, then click Intense Effect - Gold, Accent 1 in the sixth row.

    d. Copy and paste the action button on Slides 2, 3, and 4.

    e. Go to Slide 5, click the More button in the Drawing group, click Action Button: Beginning, draw a small button, click OK, then drag the button to the lower-right corner of the slide.

    f. Go to Slide 4, click the action button, click the Format Painter button in the Clipboard group, click Slide 5, then click the action button.

    g. Run the slide show from Slide 1, test the action buttons, exit the slide show, then save your work.

8. Insert hyperlinks.

    a. Go to Slide 5, then select the words "Jose Ferrar - U.S. Dairy News" in the text object.

    b. Click the Insert tab on the Ribbon, click the Hyperlink button, locate the file PPT 7-16.docx from the location where you store your Data Files, then click OK.

    c. Click in the Notes pane, then type **The hyperlink opens Jose's review of the cheddar**.

Skills Review (continued)

d. Open Slide Show view, click the hyperlink, read the review, then close the Word window.

e. Press [Esc], then add your name and the slide number as a footer to the slides.

f. Check the spelling in the presentation, then view the presentation in Slide Show view from Slide 1.

g. Make any necessary changes. The completed presentation is shown in **FIGURE 7-20**.

h. Submit your presentation to your instructor, then save and close the presentation.

FIGURE 7-20

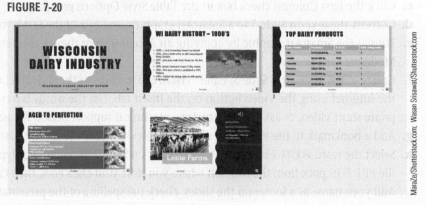

Independent Challenge 1

CP Industrial Engineering is a mechanical and industrial design company that specializes in designing manufacturing plants around the world. As a company financial analyst, you need to investigate and report on a possible contract to design and build a large manufacturing plant near Atlanta, Georgia.

a. Open the file PPT 7-17.pptx, then save it as **PPT 7-Atlanta**.

b. On Slide 4, apply a table style from the Best Match for Document section of the Table Styles gallery, then draw a 3-pt dashed line down the column divider of the table using the Pen Style button.

c. Select the top row of the table, insert a row above the top row, type **Line Item** in the left cell, then type **Budget** in the right cell.

d. Click the Overhead/Benefits cell, split the cell into two columns and one row, then move the word "Benefits" to the new cell and delete the slash.

e. Create a new SmartArt graphic on Slide 3 using the Vertical Box List layout, then add two new shapes to the graphic.

f. Starting with the top shape, type the following in the shapes: **Planning & Design**, **Site Acquisition**, **Site Development**, **Construction**, and **Building Final**.

g. Change the colors of the graphic to a colorful theme, then apply a 3D style.

h. Change the shape of the last shape in the SmartArt graphic using the Change Shape button, then use the Larger button in the Shapes group to make each shape larger.

i. Drag the sizing handles to make the SmartArt graphic larger, add your name as a footer on the slides, then save your changes.

j. Check the presentation spelling, view the presentation in Reading View, submit your presentation to your instructor, then close the presentation and exit PowerPoint.

Independent Challenge 2

You work for The Abbott Group, a large investment banking firm in Dumont, New Jersey. Abbott is considering buying RBB Financial Services, a smaller investment company. As part of the company financial operations team, you need to present some projections regarding the purchase to a special committee formed by Abbott to study the proposed deal. *Note: To complete the Independent Challenge, your computer must be connected to the Internet.*

a. Open the file PPT 7-18.pptx from the location where you store your Data Files, then save it as **PPT 7-RBB**.

b. On Slide 3, apply a table style from the Dark section of the Table Styles gallery, then format the three column divider lines in the first row of the table as 4½ pt dot line.

Independent Challenge 2 (continued)

c. Click the First Column check box in the Table Style Options group.

d. Convert the text on Slide 5 to a SmartArt graphic using one of the List layouts.

e. Format the SmartArt graphic by applying an Accent 4 color theme, then change the SmartArt style to Moderate Effect.

f. Create a new slide after Slide 3, enter **Abbott Profits** as the slide title, then link a digital or animated video from the Internet using the Video button on the Insert tab. Use the words **business** or **profits** to search for an appropriate short video, or ask your instructor or technical support person for assistance.

g. Add a bookmark to the video, then set a new preview image using the Poster Frame button.

h. Select the word **RBB Financial Services** on Slide 2, then use the Hyperlink button on the Insert tab, locate the file PPT 7-19.pptx from the location where you store your Data Files, then click OK.

i. Add your name as a footer on the slides, check the spelling of the presentation, then save your changes.

j. View the presentation in Slide Show view. Be sure to click the hyperlink on Slide 2 and watch the video on Slide 4.

k. Submit your presentation to your instructor, close the presentation, then exit PowerPoint.

Independent Challenge 3

You have been recently hired at JMS Services Inc., a U.S. company that imports and exports goods to all parts of Asia, including Japan, South Korea, China, and India. One of your new responsibilities is to prepare short presentations on different subjects for use on the company website using data provided to you by others in the company.
Note: To complete the Independent Challenge, your computer must be connected to the Internet.

a. Open the file PPT 7-20.pptx from the location where you store your Data Files, then save it as **PPT 7-JMS**.

b. Add a design theme, background shading, or other objects to make your presentation look professional.

c. Convert the text on Slide 2 to a SmartArt graphic, then format the graphic using any of the formatting commands available.

d. Insert a sound on Slide 2 using the Audio button on the Insert tab. Use the Record Audio feature to create your own audio narration, or ask your instructor or technical support person for assistance.

e. Set the audio clip to play automatically in Slide Show view, click the Rewind after Playing check box on the Audio Tools Playback tab, then move the sound icon to the bottom of the slide.

f. Change the layout, and format the charts on Slides 3, 4, and 5.

g. Create, format, and position Forward action buttons on Slides 1–5.

h. Create, format, and position Back action buttons on Slides 2–6, then create, format, and position a Home action button on Slide 6. Slides 2–6 will have two action buttons.

i. Add your name as a footer to the slides, check the spelling of the presentation, save your changes, then view the presentation in Slide Show view. See **FIGURE 7-21**.

j. Submit your presentation to your instructor, close the presentation, then exit PowerPoint.

FIGURE 7-21

Independent Challenge 4: Explore

One of the assignments in your business course at the university is to give a 10-minute presentation on any subject to the class. The goal of the assignment is for you to persuade the class (and your instructor) to make an informed decision about a product, marketing idea, or some other business concept.

To develop the content of this presentation:

- Choose your own subject matter, for example, new electronic toy, or personal computer device.
- Use your own media clips (pictures, sounds, or video) or use the Internet to search for appropriate clips.

a. Create a new presentation, then save it as **PPT 7-Presentation**.

b. Add your name and the slide number as the footer on all slides.

c. Decide on a presentation subject, then think about what results you want to see and what information you will need to create the slide presentation.

d. Give each slide a title, add text where appropriate, then apply an appropriate theme.

e. Insert an appropriate audio clip from your computer. If you have a microphone, you can record your own sound to insert into the presentation.

f. Insert an appropriate video clip from your computer or the Internet. If you have a video camera, you can record your own video to insert into the presentation.

g. Use the formatting and playback tools to trim the audio and video clips, and then format the clips as necessary.

h. Create a table and a SmartArt graphic with appropriate information, then format the objects. An example of a presentation slide might look like **FIGURE 7-22**.

i. Check the spelling of the presentation, view the final presentation in Slide Show view, save the final version, then submit the presentation to your instructor.

j. Close the presentation, then exit PowerPoint.

FIGURE 7-22

Visual Workshop

Create a new presentation, then save it as **PPT 7-Rose**. Locate the file PPT 7-21.jpg from the location where you store your Data Files, then insert the picture. Change the width of the picture to 6", then remove the background from the picture. On the Background Removal tab, click the Mark Areas to Remove button, then click the rose stem as shown in **FIGURE 7-23**. Click the Keep Changes button in the Close group to save the changes to the picture and create a finished slide that looks like the example in **FIGURE 7-24**. Add your name as a footer on the slide, save the presentation, then submit the presentation to your instructor.

FIGURE 7-23

FIGURE 7-24

Using Advanced Features

CASE ▶ Before you distribute the R2G Kenyan tour presentation, you need to have other people in the company review it. Once others have reviewed your presentation, you can incorporate their changes and comments. You will then create a custom slide show, change slide show options, and prepare the presentation for distribution. You end your day by creating a photo album of your last trip to the Caribbean and make it possible for others to view the photo album on the Internet.

Module Objectives

After completing this module, you will be able to:

- Customize handout and notes masters
- Send a presentation for review
- Combine reviewed presentations
- Set up a slide show

- Create a custom show
- Prepare a presentation for distribution
- Create a photo album
- Deliver a presentation online

Files You Will Need

PPT 8-1.pptx	PPT 8-9.jpg
PPT 8-2.pptx	PPT 8-10.jpg
PPT 8-3.jpg	PPT 8-11.jpg
PPT 8-4.jpg	PPT 8-12.jpg
PPT 8-5.jpg	PPT 8-13.pptx
PPT 8-6.jpg	PPT 8-14.pptx
PPT 8-7.pptx	PPT 8-15.pptx
PPT 8-8.pptx	PPT 8-16.jpg

Customize Handout and Notes Masters

Learning Outcomes
- Modify the handout master
- Change page orientation

It is often helpful to provide your audience with supplemental materials of the presentation. Creating handouts for your audience provides them a way to follow along and take notes during your presentation. As the presenter, creating notes pages that you can refer to while giving the presentation can be useful, especially when your presentation is complex or detailed. Before you create handouts or notes pages you might want to customize them to fit your specific needs. **CASE** ▶ *You plan to create supplemental materials to hand out when you give the presentation. You customize the handout master by changing the slides per page and the background style. Then you modify the notes master by changing the page setup and the notes page orientation.*

STEPS

1. **Start PowerPoint, open the presentation** PPT 8-1.pptx **from the location where you store your Data Files, then save the presentation as** PPT 8-R2G

2. **Click the** View tab **on the Ribbon, then click the** Handout Master button **in the Master Views group**

   The Handout Master view opens. The master has six large empty placeholders that represent where the slides will appear on the printed handouts. The four smaller placeholders in each corner of the page are the header, footer, date, and page number placeholders. The date placeholder displays today's date.

   QUICK TIP
   To change the orientation of the slides on the handout, click the Handout Orientation button in the Page Setup group.

3. **Click the** Background Styles button **in the Background group, then click** Style 11

   When you print handouts on a color printer, they will have a blue fill background.

4. **Click the** Slides Per Page button **in the Page Setup group, then click** 2 Slides **on the menu**

   Two slide placeholders appear on the handout as shown in **FIGURE 8-1**.

5. **Click the** Header placeholder, **drag the** Zoom Slider **on the status bar to** 100%, **type** Kenyan Water Wells, **press [Pg Dn], click the** Footer placeholder, **then type your name**

   Now your handouts are ready to print when you need them.

6. **Click the** Fit slide to current window button ⊞ **on the status bar, then click the** Close Master View button **in the Close group**

   Your presentation is in Normal view so you don't see the changes you made to the handout master.

   QUICK TIP
   To create custom theme fonts, click the View tab, click the Slide Master button, click the Fonts button, then click Customize Fonts.

7. **Click the** View tab **on the Ribbon, then click the** Notes Master button **in the Master Views group**

   Notes Master view opens. It has four corner placeholders—one each for the header, footer, date, and page number—a large notes text box placeholder, and a large slide master image placeholder.

8. **Click the** Notes Page Orientation button **in the Page Setup group, then click** Landscape

   The page orientation changes to landscape. Notice that all of the text placeholders are now resized to fill the width of the page. Compare your screen to **FIGURE 8-2**.

9. **Click the** Close Master View button **in the Close group, submit the presentation to your instructor, then save your work**

   If required by your instructor, print the presentation with a handout or notes page setting.

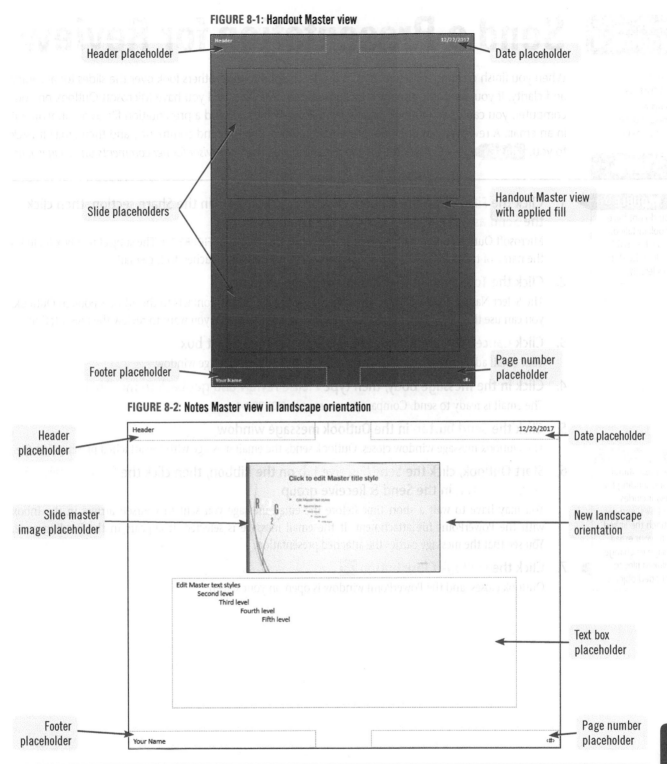

FIGURE 8-1: Handout Master view

Header placeholder

Date placeholder

Slide placeholders

Handout Master view with applied fill

Footer placeholder

Page number placeholder

FIGURE 8-2: Notes Master view in landscape orientation

Header placeholder

Date placeholder

Slide master image placeholder

New landscape orientation

Click to edit Master title style

Edit Master text styles
Second level
Third level
Fourth level
Fifth level

Text box placeholder

Footer placeholder

Page number placeholder

Your Name

Creating handouts in Microsoft Word

Sometimes it's helpful to use a word processing program like Microsoft Word to create detailed handouts or notes pages. You might also want to create a Word document based on the outline of your presentation. To send your presentation to Word, click the File tab on the Ribbon, click Export, click Create Handouts, then click the Create Handouts button. The Send to Microsoft Word dialog box opens and provides you with five document layout

options. There are two layouts that include notes entered in the Notes pane. Select a layout, then click OK. Word opens and a new document opens with your inserted presentation, using the layout you selected. To send just the text of your presentation to Word, click the Outline only page layout. To link the slides to your Word document, which will reduce the file size of the handout, click the Paste link option button.

Send a Presentation for Review

When you finish creating a presentation, it is often helpful to have others look over the slides for accuracy and clarity. If you are not in the same location as the reviewers, and you have Microsoft Outlook on your computer, you can open Outlook directly from PowerPoint and send a presentation file as an attachment in an email. A reviewer can open the presentation, make changes and comments, and then email it back to you. **CASE** *Use Outlook to send the presentation to your supervisor for her comments and suggestions.*

STEPS

1. **Click the File tab on the Ribbon, click Share, click Email in the Share section, then click the Send as Attachment button in the Email section**

   Microsoft Outlook opens with a new message window as shown in **FIGURE 8-3**. The subject text box includes the name of the presentation. The presentation is automatically attached to the email.

2. **Click the To button in the Outlook message window**

   The Select Names: Contacts dialog box opens. If you have added Contacts to the address book in Outlook, you can use this dialog box to select email addresses for the people you want to review the presentation.

3. **Click Cancel, then type your email address in the To text box**

   Your email address appears in the To text box in the Outlook message window.

4. **Click in the message body, then type Please review and get back to me. Thanks**

   The email is ready to send. Compare your screen to **FIGURE 8-4**.

5. **Click the Send button in the Outlook message window**

   The Outlook message window closes. Outlook sends the email message with the attached presentation file.

6. **Start Outlook, click the Send/Receive tab on the Ribbon, then click the Send/Receive All Folders button in the Send & Receive group**

   You may have to wait a short time before the email message you sent to yourself arrives in the Inbox with the PowerPoint file attachment. If the email message is selected, it appears in the Reading pane. You see that the message carries the attached presentation.

7. **Click the Outlook Close button ☒**

   Outlook closes, and the PowerPoint window is open on your screen.

FIGURE 8-3: Outlook message window

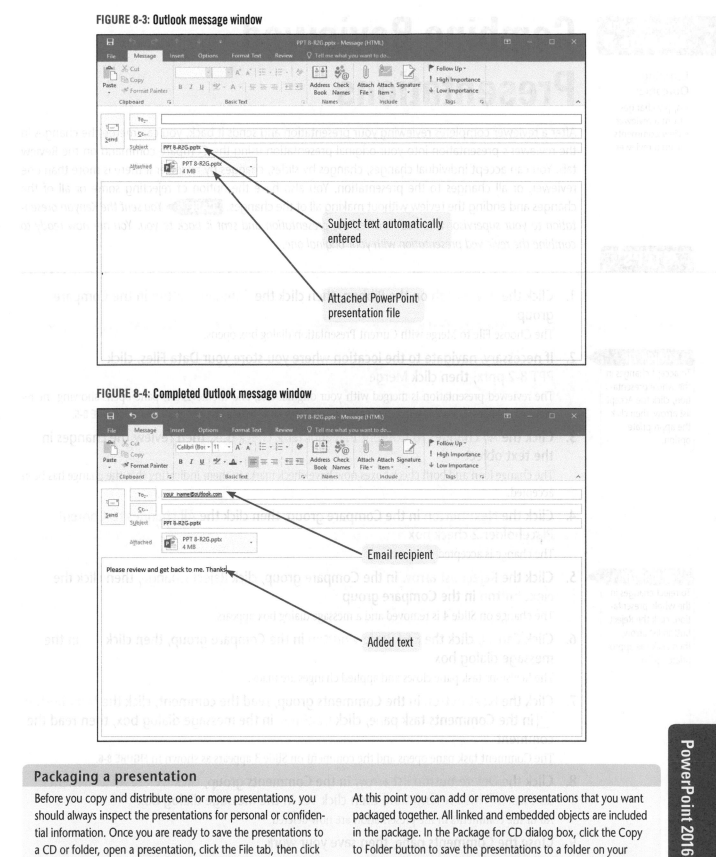

Subject text automatically entered

Attached PowerPoint presentation file

FIGURE 8-4: Completed Outlook message window

Email recipient

Please review and get back to me. Thanks

Added text

Packaging a presentation

Before you copy and distribute one or more presentations, you should always inspect the presentations for personal or confidential information. Once you are ready to save the presentations to a CD or folder, open a presentation, click the File tab, then click Export. Click Package Presentation for CD, then click the Package for CD button. The Package for CD dialog box opens with the current open presentation shown in the list of files to be copied.

At this point you can add or remove presentations that you want packaged together. All linked and embedded objects are included in the package. In the Package for CD dialog box, click the Copy to Folder button to save the presentations to a folder on your computer or network, or insert a CD into your computer and click the Copy to CD button. Follow the instructions, then click Close when the saving process is completed.

Learning
Outcomes
• Apply changes
  from a reviewer
• View comments
  from a reviewer

Combine Reviewed Presentations

After a reviewer completes reviewing your presentation and sends it back, you can merge the changes in the reviewer's presentation into your original presentation using the Compare command on the Review tab. You can accept individual changes, changes by slides, changes by reviewer if there is more than one reviewer, or all changes to the presentation. You also have the option of rejecting some or all of the changes and ending the review without making all of the changes. **CASE** *You sent the Kenyan presentation to your supervisor who has reviewed the presentation and sent it back to you. You are now ready to combine the reviewed presentation with your original one.*

STEPS

1. **Click the** Review tab **on the Ribbon, then click the** Compare button **in the Compare group**

   The Choose File to Merge with Current Presentation dialog box opens.

QUICK TIP

To accept changes in the whole presentation, click the Accept list arrow, then click the appropriate option.

2. **If necessary, navigate to the location where you store your Data Files, click** PPT 8-2.pptx, **then click** Merge

   The reviewed presentation is merged with your original one, and the Revisions pane opens showing the reviewer's changes. Slide 2 is selected because it is the first slide with a change as shown in **FIGURE 8-5**.

3. **Click the** All changes to Content Placeholder 2 check box, **then review the changes in the text object**

   The change icon and both check boxes now have check marks in them indicating that the change has been accepted.

4. **Click the** Next button **in the Compare group, then click the** All changes to Content Placeholder 2 check box

   The change is accepted.

QUICK TIP

To reject changes in the whole presentation, click the Reject button list arrow, then click the appropriate option.

5. **Click the** Reject list arrow **in the Compare group, click** Reject Change, **then click the** Next button **in the Compare group**

   The change on Slide 4 is removed and a message dialog box appears.

6. **Click** Cancel, **click the** End Review button **in the Compare group, then click** Yes **in the message dialog box**

   The Revisions task pane closes and applied changes are made.

7. **Click the** Next button **in the Comments group, read the comment, click the** Next button **in the Comments task pane, click** Continue **in the message dialog box, then read the comment**

   The Comment task pane opens and the comment on Slide 3 appears as shown in **FIGURE 8-6**.

8. **Click the** Delete button list arrow **in the Comments group, click** Delete All Comments and Ink in This Presentation, **then click** Yes **in the message dialog box**

   All of the comments in the presentation are now deleted.

9. **Close the Comments pane, then save your work**

FIGURE 8-5: Open Revisions pane showing reviewer's changes

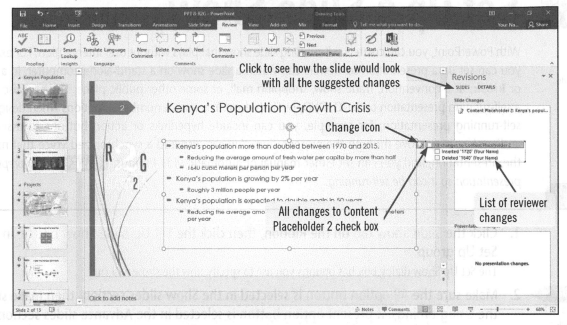

FIGURE 8-6: Open Comments pane showing reviewer's comment

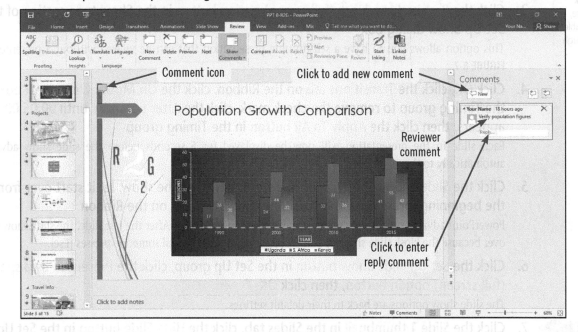

Coauthoring a presentation

By using collaboration software, such as SharePoint Online, or saving a presentation to a OneDrive location, you have the ability to work with others on a presentation over the Internet at the same time. To set up a presentation to be coauthored with you as the original author, click the File tab, click Share, click Share with People, click Save To Cloud, then click your OneDrive location. Choose a shared location or server to store a primary copy of your presentation, then click the Save button. Open the

presentation and begin working, and if someone else is working on the presentation, you will see a Co-authoring icon in the status bar. All changes made to the presentation are recorded, including who is working on the presentation and where in the presentation they are working. When updates to a presentation are available, an Updates Available button appears in the status bar. To use this feature, all authors must have PowerPoint 2010 or later installed on their computers.

Set Up a Slide Show

Learning
Outcomes
• Automate a slide
  show
• Hide a slide

With PowerPoint, you can create a self-running slide show that plays without user intervention. For example, you can set up a presentation so viewers can watch a slide show on a stand-alone computer, in a booth or **kiosk**, at a convention, trade show, shopping mall, or some other public place. You can also create a self-running presentation on a CD, DVD, or Flash drive. You have a number of options when designing a self-running presentation; for example, you can include hyperlinks or action buttons to assist your audience as they move through the presentation. You can also add a synchronized voice that narrates the presentation, and you can set either manual or automatic slide timings. **CASE** ▶ *You prepare the presentation so it can be self-running.*

STEPS

1. **Click the** Slide Show tab **on the Ribbon, then click the** Set Up Slide Show button **in the Set Up group**

   The Set Up Show dialog box has options you use to specify how the show will run.

QUICK TIP
You must use auto-
matic timings, navi-
gation hyperlinks, or
action buttons when
you use the kiosk
option; otherwise,
you will not be able
to progress through
the slides.

2. **Make sure the** All option button **is selected in the Show slides section, then make sure the** Using timings, if present option button **is selected in the Advance slides section**

   All the slides in the presentation are included in the slide show, and PowerPoint will advance the slides at time intervals you set.

3. **Click the** Browsed at a kiosk (full screen) option button **in the Show type section of the Set Up Show dialog box**

   This option allows you to have a self-running presentation that can be viewed without a presenter. See **FIGURE 8-7**.

4. **Click** OK, **click the** Transitions tab **on the Ribbon, click the** On Mouse Click check box **in the Timing group to remove the check mark, click the** After up arrow **until** 00:05.00 **appears, then click the** Apply To All button **in the Timing group**

   Each slide in the presentation will now be displayed for 5 seconds before the slide show advances automatically to the next slide.

5. **Click the** Slide Show button 🖵 **on the status bar, view the show, let it start over from the beginning, press** [Esc], **then click the** Slide Show tab **on the Ribbon**

   PowerPoint advances the slides automatically at 5-second intervals. After the last slide, the slide show starts over because the kiosk slide show option loops the presentation until someone presses [Esc].

6. **Click the** Set Up Slide Show button **in the Set Up group, click the** Presented by a speaker (full screen) option button, **then click** OK

   The slide show options are back to their default settings.

QUICK TIP
To view a hidden
slide while in Slide
Show view, click the
See all slides button
on the Slide Show
toolbar, then click
the hidden slide.

7. **Click the** Slide 1 thumbnail **in the Slides tab, click the** Hide Slide button **in the Set Up group, click the** From Beginning button **in the Start Slide Show group, watch the slide appear then press** [Esc]

   The slide show begins with Slide 2. Notice the Slide 1 thumbnail in the Slides tab is dimmed and has a back-slash through its number indicating it is hidden, as shown in **FIGURE 8-8**.

8. **Right-click the** Slide 1 thumbnail **in the Slides tab, click** Hide Slide **in the shortcut menu, then save your changes**

   Slide 1 is no longer hidden, the slide thumbnail is not dimmed, and the backslash over the slide number is removed.

FIGURE 8-7: Set Up Show dialog box

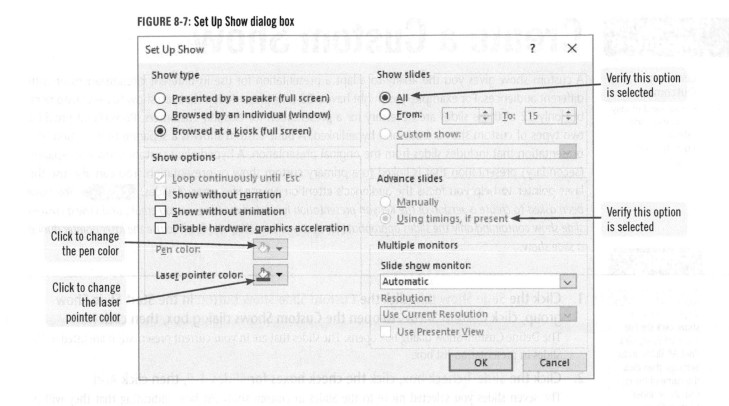

Verify this option is selected

Verify this option is selected

Click to change the pen color

Click to change the laser pointer color

FIGURE 8-8: Slide 1 is a hidden slide

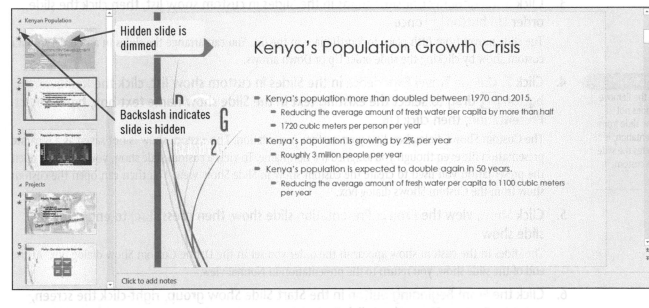

Hidden slide is dimmed

Backslash indicates slide is hidden

Installing and using Office Add-ins

Office add-ins are applications you can download to PowerPoint and your other Office programs for free (or for a small fee) from the Microsoft Office Store on the Internet. Add-ins can help you speed up and locate information on the Internet and help you be more productive when creating content for your presentation. Typical add-ins available to download to PowerPoint include navigation and mapping add-ins, dictionary and word usage add-ins, as well as news and social media add-ins. To install an add-in for the first time, click the Store button on the Insert tab, then search through the add-in categories. After you locate the add-in you want, add it to PowerPoint. To use an app already installed, click the Insert tab, click the My Add-ins button, then click the add-in.

Create a Custom Show

Learning Outcomes
- Create and modify a custom slide show
- Use the laser pointer

A custom show gives you the ability to adapt a presentation for use in different circumstances or with different audiences. For example, you might have a 25-slide presentation that you show to new customers, but only 12 of those slides are necessary for a presentation for existing customers. PowerPoint provides two types of custom shows: basic and hyperlinked. A basic custom show is a separate presentation or a presentation that includes slides from the original presentation. A hyperlinked custom show is a separate (secondary) presentation that is linked to a primary custom show or presentation. You can also use the laser pointer to help you focus the audience's attention on specific areas of slides. **CASE** *You have been asked to create a version of the Kenyan presentation for a staff meeting, so you create and view a custom slide show containing only the slides appropriate for that audience. You also learn to use the laser pointer during a slide show.*

STEPS

QUICK TIP

To print a custom show, click the File tab, click Print, click Print All Slides under Settings, then click the name of the custom show under Custom Shows.

1. **Click the** Slide Show tab, **click the** Custom Slide Show button **in the Start Slide Show group, click** Custom Shows **to open the Custom Shows dialog box, then click** New
   The Define Custom Show dialog box opens. The slides that are in your current presentation are listed in the Slides in presentation list box.

2. **Click the** Slide 1 check box, **click the check boxes for** Slides 4–9, **then click** Add
   The seven slides you selected move to the Slides in custom show list box, indicating that they will be included in the custom show. See **FIGURE 8-9**.

3. **Click** 5. Technology Considerations **in the Slides in custom show list, then click the slide order** Up button ↑ **once**
   The slide moves from fifth place to fourth place in the list. You can arrange the slides in any order in your custom show by clicking the slide order Up or Down arrows.

QUICK TIP

Clicking the Remove button does not delete the slide from the presentation; it only deletes the slide from the custom show.

4. **Click** 7. Unique Travel Experience **in the Slides in custom show list, click the** Remove button ✕, **drag to select the existing text in the Slide show name text box, type** Project Presentation, **then click** OK
   The Custom Shows dialog box lists your custom presentation. The custom show is not saved as a separate presentation file even though you assigned it a new name. To view a custom slide show, you must first open the presentation you used to create the custom show in Slide Show view. You then can open the custom show from the Custom Shows dialog box.

5. **Click** Show, **view the** Project Presentation **slide show, then press** [Esc] **to end the slide show**
   The slides in the custom show appear in the order you set in the Define Custom Show dialog box. At the end of the slide show, you return to the presentation in Normal view.

6. **Click the** From Beginning button **in the Start Slide Show group, right-click the screen, point to** Custom Show, **then click** Project Presentation
   The Project Presentation custom show appears in Slide Show view.

QUICK TIP

To change the color of the laser pointer, click the Slide Show tab, click the Set Up Slide Show button, then click the Laser pointer color button.

7. **When Slide 1 appears, press and hold** [Ctrl], **press and hold the** left mouse button, **move the laser pointer around the slide as shown in** FIGURE 8-10, **release** [Ctrl], **then release the** left mouse button
   Automatic slide timings are set so your slide show can advance to the next slide even though you use the laser pointer. You can use the laser pointer in any presentation on any slide during a slide show.

8. **Press** [Esc] **at any point to end the slide show, then save your changes**

FIGURE 8-9: Define Custom Show dialog box

Slides in the custom show

Up button

Remove button

Down button

FIGURE 8-10: First slide of custom slide show with laser pointer

Laser pointer

Africanmoose/Shutterstock.com

Linking to a custom slide show

You can use action buttons to switch from the "parent" show to the custom show. Click the Shapes button in the Drawing group on the Home tab, then click an action button. Draw an action button on the slide. Click the Hyperlink to list arrow, click Custom Show, click the custom show you want to link, then click OK.

Now when you run a slide show you can click the action button you created to run the custom show. You can also create an interactive table of contents using custom shows. Create your table of contents entries on a slide, then hyperlink each entry to the section it refers to using a custom show for each section.

Learning Outcomes
- Protect a presentation with a password
- Check presentation compatibility

Prepare a Presentation for Distribution

Reviewing and preparing your presentation before you share it with others is an essential step, especially with so many security and privacy issues on the Internet. One way to help secure your PowerPoint presentation is to set a security password, so only authorized people can view or modify its content. If you plan to open a presentation in an earlier version of PowerPoint, it is a good idea to determine if the presentation is compatible. Some features in PowerPoint 2016, such as sections and SmartArt graphics, are not compatible in earlier versions of PowerPoint. **CASE** ▸ *You want to learn about PowerPoint security and compatibility features so you can use them on presentations and other documents.*

STEPS

1. **Click the** Slide 1 thumbnail **in the Slides tab, click the** File tab **on the Ribbon, click the** Protect Presentation button, **then click** Encrypt with Password **on the menu**
   The Encrypt Document dialog box opens.

2. **Type** 123abc
   As you type, solid black symbols appear in the text box, as shown in **FIGURE 8-11**, which hides the password and makes it unreadable. This protects the confidentiality of your password if anyone happens to be looking at your screen while you type.

3. **Click** OK **to open the Confirm Password dialog box, type** 123abc, **then click** OK
   A password is now required to open this presentation. Once the presentation is closed, this password must be entered in the Password dialog box to open the presentation. The presentation is now password protected from unauthorized users.

4. **Click** Close, **click** Save **to save changes, click the** File tab, **then click** PPT 8-R2G.pptx **in the Recent Presentations list**
   The Password dialog box opens.

5. **Type** 123abc, **then click** OK **to open the presentation**
   The presentation opens. Be aware that if you don't remember your password, there is no way to open or view the presentation.

6. **Click the** File tab **on the Ribbon, click the** Protect Presentation button, **click** Encrypt with Password, **select the** password, **press** [Delete], **click** OK, **then click** Save
   The password is removed and is no longer needed to open the presentation.

7. **Click the** File tab **on the Ribbon, click the** Check for Issues button, **then click** Check Compatibility
   The Compatibility Checker analyzes the presentation, and the Microsoft PowerPoint Compatibility Checker dialog box opens, as shown in **FIGURE 8-12**. Each item in the dialog box represents a feature that is not supported in earlier versions of PowerPoint. This means that if you try to run this presentation using an earlier version of PowerPoint, the items listed will function in a limited capacity or not at all.

8. **Click the** down scroll arrow, **read all of the items in the dialog box, click** OK, **add your name to the slide footer, then click the** Slide Sorter button 🔠 **on the status bar**
   The dialog box closes. Compare your screen to **FIGURE 8-13**.

9. **Save your work, submit your presentation to your instructor, then close the presentation but do not exit PowerPoint**

FIGURE 8-11: Encrypt Document dialog box

Encrypt Document   ?   ✕

Encrypt the contents of this file

Password:

Hidden → ••••••
password

Caution: If you lose or forget the password, it
cannot be recovered. It is advisable to keep a list of
passwords and their corresponding document
names in a safe place.
(Remember that passwords are case-sensitive.)

              OK   Cancel

FIGURE 8-12: Compatibility Checker dialog box

Microsoft PowerPoint Compatibility Checker   ?   ✕

ⓘ The following features in this presentation are not supported by
    earlier versions of PowerPoint. These features may be lost or
    degraded when you save this presentation in an earlier file format.

Summary   Occurrences

A chart in this document may contain data in cells outside of the row and column limit of the selected file format. Data beyond 256 (IV) columns by 65,536 rows cannot be saved. (Slide 3)	1
Help	
The shape and any text in it cannot be edited when using earlier versions of PowerPoint. (Slide 4)	1
Help	
The table and any text in it cannot be edited when using earlier versions of PowerPoint. (Slide 7)	1
Help	
The SmartArt graphic and any text in it cannot be edited	1

☑ Check compatibility when saving in PowerPoint 97-2003 formats.

                                            OK

FIGURE 8-13: Final presentation in Slide Sorter view

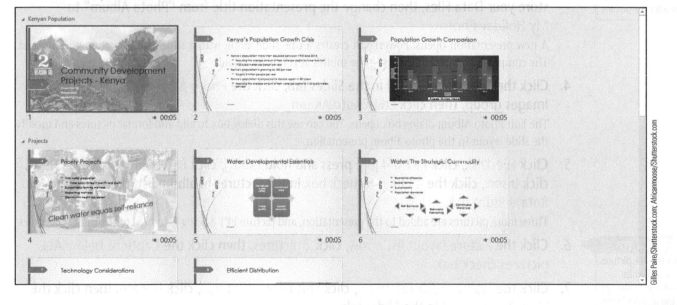

▸ Kenyan Population

1	Community Development Projects - Kenya	⁂ 00:05
2	Kenya's Population Growth Crisis	⁂ 00:05
3	Population Growth Comparison	⁂ 00:05

▸ Projects

4	Priority Projects / Clean water equals self-reliance	⁂ 00:05
5	Water: Developmental Essentials	⁂ 00:05
6	Water: The Strategic Commodity	⁂ 00:05

| 7 | Technology Considerations |
| 8 | Efficient Distribution |

Recording a slide show

With the Record Slide Show feature you have the ability to record
and save audio narrations, slide and animation timings, and laser
pointer gestures for each slide during a slide show. This feature is
great to use if you want to record audience comments so that
people who were unable to attend the presentation live can view
and listen to it later. To record a slide show, click the Slide Show
tab, click the Record Slide Show button list arrow in the Set Up
group, then start recording from the beginning or the current
slide. You then have to choose which elements you want to
record during the slide show. If you choose to record audio narrations, you must have a microphone, a sound card, and speakers.
A sound icon appears on every narrated slide.

Create a Photo Album

Learning Outcomes
• Create a photo album
• Customize a photo album

A PowerPoint photo album is a presentation designed specifically to display photographs. You can add pictures to a photo album from any storage device such as a hard drive, flash drive, digital camera, scanner, or web camera. As with any presentation, you can customize the layout of a photo album presentation by adding title text to slides, applying frames around the pictures, and applying a theme. You can also format the pictures of the photo album by adding a caption, converting the pictures to black and white, rotating them, applying artistic effects, and changing their brightness and contrast. **CASE** ▶ *On a break from work, you decide to create a personal photo album showing some of the pictures you took on a trip to the Caribbean.*

STEPS

1. **Click the** Insert tab **on the Ribbon, click the** Photo Album list arrow **in the Images group, then click** New Photo Album
   The Photo Album dialog box opens.

> **QUICK TIP**
> In the Photo Album dialog box click a picture check box, then click New Text Box to create a text box after the picture.

2. **Click** File/Disk, **select the file** PPT 8-3.jpg **from the location where you store your Data Files, then click** Insert
   The picture appears in the Preview box and is listed in the Pictures in album list, as shown in **FIGURE 8-14**.

3. **Click** Create, **save the presentation as** PPT 8-Photo Album **to the location where you store your Data Files, then change the presentation title from "Photo Album" to** My Holiday Photos
   A new presentation opens. PowerPoint creates a title slide along with a slide for the picture you inserted. The computer user name appears in the subtitle text box by default.

4. **Click the** Slide 2 thumbnail **in the Slides tab, click the** Photo Album list arrow **in the Images group, then click** Edit Photo Album
   The Edit Photo Album dialog box opens. You can use this dialog box to add and format pictures and modify the slide layout in the photo album presentation.

5. **Click** File/Disk, **click** PPT 8-4.jpg, **press and hold** [Shift], **click** PPT 8-6.jpg, **release** [Shift], **click** Insert, **click the** 4 PPT 8-6 check box **in the Pictures in album list, then click the** Rotate Right button 🔲
   Three more pictures are added to the presentation, and picture PPT 8-6.jpg is rotated to the right 90 degrees.

> **QUICK TIP**
> Click the ALL pictures black and white check box to change all the pictures in the photo album to black and white.

6. **Click the** Picture layout list arrow, **click** 2 pictures, **then click the** Captions below ALL pictures check box

7. **Click the** Frame shape list arrow, **click** Soft Edge Rectangle, **click** Update, **then click the** Slide 2 thumbnail **in the Slides tab**
   Two pictures with a caption below each picture (currently the picture filename) appear on each slide, and each picture is formatted with a soft edge.

8. **Click the** Slide Sorter view button 🔲, **then drag the** Zoom Slider 🔲 **on the status bar until your screen looks similar to FIGURE 8-15**

9. **Add your name to the slides footer, save your changes, then submit your presentation to your instructor**

FIGURE 8-14: Photo Album dialog box

Brightness buttons

Click to move a picture up or down in the list

Contrast buttons

Click to apply a design theme to the photo album

Shows current picture layout

Mihai-Bogdan Lazar/Shutterstock

FIGURE 8-15: Completed photo album

Picture captions

Mihai-Bogdan Lazar/Shutterstock; Tami Freed/Shutterstock; Ruth Choi/Shutterstock;
Andrzej Kubik/Shutterstock.com

Publishing slides to a Slide Library

If your computer is connected to a network server running Office SharePoint Server software, you can store slides in a folder called a **Slide Library** for others to access, modify, and use. Using a Slide Library, others can make changes to your slides, and you in turn can track and review all changes and have access to the latest version of your slides. To publish slides from PowerPoint to a Slide Library (after a Slide Library is created on a server), click the File tab, click Share, click Publish Slides, then click the Publish Slides button. The Publish Slides dialog box opens. Use Browse in the dialog box to select the Slide Library location you are going to use. To add slides to a Slide Library, click the check box next to each slide, then click Publish.

Deliver a Presentation Online

Being able to assemble everyone in the same room for a presentation can be difficult, which is why PowerPoint provides a way to share your presentation with remote viewers. Using PowerPoint, you can host an online presentation in real time over the Internet to viewers using Microsoft's free Office Presentation Service. Viewers of an online presentation need to have a computer connected to the Internet, a web browser, and a link to an Internet address, called a **URL**, which is automatically supplied by PowerPoint. The URL link for your online broadcast can be emailed to viewers directly from PowerPoint. **CASE** ▶ *In preparation for hosting an online presentation to others in your company, you test the online broadcasting features in PowerPoint. NOTE: To complete this lesson as a host, you need to be logged into PowerPoint 2016 with a Microsoft account and have Internet access. As a viewer, you need Internet access and the URL link entered into a web browser.*

STEPS

1. **Click the** Normal button 🖵 **on the status bar, click the** Slide 1 thumbnail **in the Slides tab, click the** File tab **on the Ribbon, click** Share, **then click** Present Online

    Read the information on the screen. If you don't have a Microsoft account, you need to acquire one from the Microsoft website before you proceed.

2. **Click the** Present Online button

    The Present Online dialog box opens, and PowerPoint connects to the Office Presentation Service online. Once connected, PowerPoint prepares your presentation to be viewed online, which may take a couple of minutes. The Present Online dialog box eventually displays a URL link, as shown in **FIGURE 8-16**.

3. **If approved by your instructor, click the** Send in Email link **to open an Outlook new message window, type an** email address **in the To text box, then click** Send

    The Microsoft Outlook window opens with the URL link in the message box and is then sent to the person you want to view the online presentation. Anyone you provide the URL link to can enter the link into their web browser and watch the broadcast.

4. **Click the** START PRESENTATION button

    The first slide of the presentation opens in Slide Show view. Make sure viewers can see the presentation in their web browser.

5. **Press [Spacebar], wait for your viewers to see the slide, press [Spacebar], wait for your viewers to see the slide, end the slide show, then click the** Present Online tab **on the Ribbon**

    Each slide in the presentation is viewed by you and your online viewers. The Present Online tab opens, as shown in **FIGURE 8-17**. Use this tab to start the slide show from different slides, share meeting notes using OneNote, invite others to view the broadcast, and end the broadcast.

6. **When you are finished broadcasting click the** End Online Presentation button **in the Present Online group**

    A message box opens asking if you want to end the online presentation.

7. **Click** End Online Presentation, **close the presentation, then exit PowerPoint**

    The online presentation stops, and the presentation closes.

FIGURE 8-16: Present Online dialog box

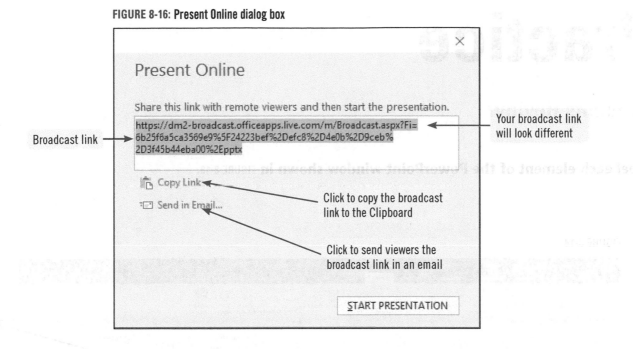

Broadcast link

Your broadcast link will look different

Click to copy the broadcast link to the Clipboard

Click to send viewers the broadcast link in an email

FIGURE 8-17: Online presentation broadcast

New tab

Presentation being broadcast

Tami Freed/Shutterstock; Ruth Choi/Shutterstock

Mastering PowerPoint features and online presentations

Not all PowerPoint features are supported for broadcasting, and some features are altered altogether. For example, you cannot annotate or markup slides during an online presentation, and hyperlinks are not shown to your audience. Keep in mind too that if you have a large presentation you might have file size limitations imposed on your presentation file when trying to broadcast.

Practice

Concepts Review

Label each element of the PowerPoint window shown in FIGURE 8-18.

FIGURE 8-18

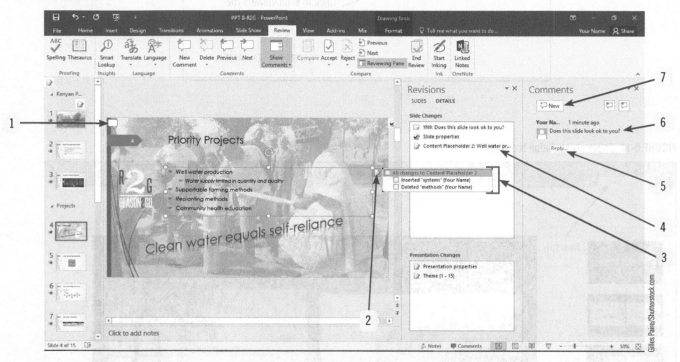

Gilles Paire/Shutterstock.com

Match each term with the statement that best describes its function.

8. Basic custom show
9. URL
10. Kiosk
11. Photo album
12. Office add-in

a. A presentation specifically designed to display photographs
b. An Internet web address
c. A slide show created from selected slides in a presentation
d. A small booth for a stand-alone computer that can run a slide show without user intervention
e. A mini application you can download to PowerPoint

Select the best answer from the list of choices.

13. You must use automatic _____ or action buttons when you create a self-running slide show.
    a. transitions
    b. timings
    c. animations
    d. bullets

14. How can you collaborate on a presentation at the same time with another person?
    a. Email the presentation.
    b. Present the presentation online.
    c. Package the presentation
    d. Save the presentation to a OneDrive location

15. What is a hyperlinked custom show?
    a. A secondary presentation linked to a primary presentation.
    b. A presentation that is packaged.
    c. A presentation you present online.
    d. A presentation sent as an Internet fax.

16. What does the Compatibility Checker do to a presentation?
    a. Inspects for unsupported features.
    b. Inspects for hidden properties.
    c. Checks for reading disability content.
    d. Restricts access to editing and printing.

17. What is the easiest way to present a presentation to multiple viewers in different locations at the same time?
    a. Publish to a Slide Library.
    b. Create handouts.
    c. Broadcast over the Internet.
    d. Create a PDF document.

18. What is a photo album specifically designed to do?
    a. Create a video using photographs.
    b. Display photographs.
    c. Organize photographs in a database.
    d. Broadcast photographs on the Internet.

19. Use _____ view to display a custom slide show.
    a. Slide
    b. Custom Show
    c. Presenter
    d. Slide Show

Skills Review

1. **Customize handout and notes masters.**
   a. Start PowerPoint, open the file PPT 8-7.pptx from the drive and folder where you store your Data Files, then save it as **PPT 8-Java Stop**. *Note: You need to have access to Outlook and the Internet to complete all the steps in this Skills Review*.
   b. Switch to Handout Master view, then change the slides per page to 4 slides.
   c. Change the handout orientation to Landscape, then type **The Java Stop** in the header text placeholder.
   d. Type your name in the footer text placeholder, then switch to Notes Master view.
   e. Change the background style to Style 9, type **Proposal** in the header text placeholder, then type your name in the footer text placeholder.
   f. Close Notes Master view, then save your work.

2. **Send a presentation for review.**
   a. Click the File tab, click Share, click Email, then click the Send as Attachment button.
   b. Type a brief message in the email message, then send the presentation to yourself.
   c. Open Microsoft Outlook, open the message you sent to yourself, then close Outlook.

Skills Review (continued)

3. Combine reviewed presentations.

a. Click the Review tab, then click the Compare button in the Compare group.

b. Navigate to the location where you store your Data Files, click PPT 8-8.pptx, then click Merge.

c. Accept the changes to the text box and the action button on Slide 1, then click the Next button in the Compare group.

d. Accept the changes to the text object, accept the rest of the changes in the presentation, then end the review.

e. Open the Comments pane, then use the Next button in the Comments task pane to read all the comments in the presentation.

f. Delete all comments in the presentation, close the Comments pane, then save your work.

4. Set up a slide show.

a. Click the Slide Show tab, click the Set Up Slide Show button, use automatic slide timings, set up a slide show so it will be browsed at a kiosk, then click the Transitions tab.

b. Remove the check mark from the On Mouse Click check box, set a slide timing of 3 seconds to all the slides, run the slide show all the way through to Slide 1, then end the slide show.

c. Change the slide show options to be presented by a speaker, then change the slide timings to manual in the Set Up Show dialog box.

d. Run through the slide show from Slide 1 using the action buttons at the bottom of the slides. Move forward and backward through the presentation, then press [Esc] when you are finished.

e. Hide Slide 5, then run through the slide show.

f. When you have finished viewing the slide show, reset the slide timings to automatic, then save your work.

5. Create a custom show.

a. Create a custom show called **Issues** that includes Slides 2, 3, and 4.

b. Move Slide 3 Publicity above Slide 2 Considerations.

c. View the show from within the Custom Shows dialog box, then press [Esc] to end the slide show.

d. Go to Slide 1, begin the slide show, then, when Slide 1 appears, go to the Issues custom show.

e. View the custom slide show, return to Normal view, then save your work.

6. Prepare a presentation for distribution.

a. Click the File tab, click Protect Presentation, then click Encrypt with Password.

b. Type **123abc**, then type the same password in the Confirm Password dialog box.

c. Close the presentation, save your changes, open the presentation, then type **123abc** in the Password dialog box.

d. Open the Encrypt Document dialog box again, then delete the password.

e. Click the File tab, click Check for Issues, click Check Compatibility, read the information, then close the dialog box.

f. Save your work, add your name to the slides footer, then check the spelling in the presentation. The completed presentation is shown in **FIGURE 8-19**.

g. Submit your presentation to your instructor, then close the presentation.

7. Create a photo album.

a. Create a new photo album presentation, navigate to the location where you store your Data Files, then insert the files PPT 8-9.jpg, PPT 8-10.jpg, PPT 8-11.jpg, and PPT 8-12.jpg.

FIGURE 8-19

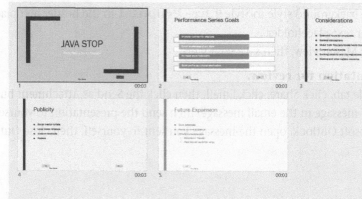

Skills Review (continued)

b. Rotate picture PPT 8-12.jpg to the right, move the picture so it is first in the list, create the photo album, then save it as **PPT 8-Hackensack** to the location where you store your Data Files.

c. Change the title on the title slide to **Up the Hackensack**, then type your name in the subtitle text box.

d. Open the Edit Photo Album dialog box, change the picture layout to 1 picture, then change the frame shape to Simple Frame, White.

FIGURE 8-20

e. Make all pictures black and white, add captions to all pictures, update the presentation, then save your changes.

f. Submit your presentation to your instructor. The completed photo album is shown in **FIGURE 8-20**.

8. Deliver a presentation online.

a. Click the File tab, click Share, click Present Online, then click the Present Online button.

b. Send invitations to people you want to view the broadcast using the Send in Email link in the Present Online dialog box.

c. Start the online presentation, then move through each slide in the presentation.

d. When you are finished broadcasting, end the online presentation, save your work, close the presentation, then exit PowerPoint.

Independent Challenge 1

You work for The Cruise Guide, online company that reviews cruises throughout the world. You have to develop a presentation on a new river cruise on the Mekong River in Vietnam. To complete the presentation, you need to compare two presentations and then add media and slide effects. Note: *To complete all the steps of this Independent Challenge, you must be connected to the Internet.*

a. Start PowerPoint, open the presentation PPT 8-13.pptx, then save it as **PPT 8-Vietnam** to the location where you store your Data Files.

b. Open the Review tab on the Ribbon, merge the file PPT 8-14.pptx, then apply all changes to the presentation, which includes a new slide.

c. Read all comments in the presentation, then delete the comment on the Cruise Lines slide.

d. Use the Previous button in the Comments group to move back to slides that have comments, then write a reply comment to each of the original comments.

e. Use the Compatibility Checker on the presentation.

f. Use the Internet to research information on the city of Hanoi Vietnam, then add content to Slide 6 of the presentation.

g. Insert and format at least two different media clips (pictures, videos, or sounds). Use approved media clips from legal sources.

h. Apply slide transitions, timings, and animations to all the slides in the presentation.

i. Convert the text on Slide 4 to a SmartArt diagram, then format the diagram using the techniques you learned in this book.

PowerPoint 2016

Independent Challenge 1 (continued)

j. Use the Compatibility Checker again on the presentation. Note any differences, then view the presentation in Slide Show view and use the laser pointer.

k. Add your name as a footer on all slides, then check the spelling in the presentation.

l. Submit your presentation to your instructor, close the presentation, then exit PowerPoint.

Independent Challenge 2

You work at the Oregon Department of Agriculture. Part of your job is to compile agricultural information gathered from all the state counties and create presentations that display the data for public viewing. You are currently working on a summary presentation that will be made public on the agency website.

a. Start PowerPoint, open the presentation PPT 8-15.pptx, then save it as **PPT 8-Oregon** to the location where you store your Data Files.

b. Insert the file PPT 8-16.jpg from the location where you store your Data Files on Slide 2.

c. Format the picture using the commands on the Picture Tools Format tab.

d. Change the table layout on Slide 4 by splitting each of the four cells that contain more than one piece of data, such as the Fruits and Berries cell.

e. Separate the data in the split cells, then format the table.

f. Create a custom slide show that displays any two slides from the presentation, then save it as **Custom**.

g. Insert and format at least two media clips (pictures, videos, or sounds). Use approved media clips from legal sources.

h. Change the handout master to two slides per page, then apply the Style 9 background style.

i. Save the presentation, add your name as the footer on all notes and handouts, check the spelling of the presentation, then view the presentation in Slide Show view.

j. Use the Present Online feature to invite others in your class to watch an online presentation.

k. Submit your presentation to your instructor, close the presentation, then exit PowerPoint.

Independent Challenge 3

You are the assistant director of operations at AsiaWest, an international marine shipping company based in Seattle, Washington. AsiaWest handles 55 percent of all the trade between Asia, the Middle East, and the West Coast of the United States. You need to give a quarterly presentation to the company's operations committee outlining the type and amount of trade AsiaWest handled during the previous quarter.

Plan a presentation with at least five slides that details the type of goods AsiaWest carries. Create your own content, but assume the following:

- AsiaWest transports automobiles from South Korea to Seattle. AsiaWest usually carries between 60,000 and 70,000 automobiles in a quarter.
- AsiaWest transports large equipment from the United States.
- AsiaWest transports container cargo that includes all types of household goods.
- AsiaWest also transports grain, gypsum board, logs, petroleum, and molasses.

Note: To complete the Independent Challenge, your computer must be connected to the Internet.

a. Start PowerPoint, create a new presentation, save it as **PPT 8-AsiaWest**, then apply a design theme to the presentation.

b. Use the information provided to help develop the content for your presentation. If you have Internet access, use the Internet to research the shipping business.

Independent Challenge 3 (continued)

c. Insert and format at least two media clips (pictures, videos, or sounds). Use approved media clips from legal sources.

d. Set transitions and animations, rehearse slide timings, then view the presentation in Slide Show view.

e. Change the handout master to 6 slides per page, change the background style to Style 8, then change the orientation to Landscape.

f. Send the presentation to a friend as an email attachment.

g. Check the spelling of the presentation, add your name as a footer on all notes and handouts, then save your work.

h. Submit your presentation to your instructor, close the presentation, then exit PowerPoint.

Independent Challenge 4: Explore

You have just been given an assignment in your Cultural Anthropology class to create a photo album that shows your personal family history. You must use your own pictures of past family members, homes, businesses, vacations, and other pictures that help tell your personal family life story and history.

a. Start PowerPoint, create a photo album presentation, insert your pictures, then save the presentation as **PPT 8-Family History** to the location where you store your Data Files.

b. Enter a title in the title text placeholder, add your name to the subtitle text placeholder and as the footer on the slides, then apply a design.

c. Use the Edit Photo Album dialog box to format the pictures as needed. An example of a family photo album is shown in **FIGURE 8-21**.

d. Send the presentation for review to at least one friend, and ask them to provide changes and comments. Use the Compare feature to merge your original presentation with the reviewed presentation.

e. Accept or reject reviewer changes, then leave any comments made by the reviewer in your presentation.

f. Check the spelling of the presentation, save your changes, then broadcast this presentation to two friends using the Present Online feature.

g. Click the File tab, click Export, click Create Handouts, then click the Create Handouts button.

h. Click the Blank lines next to slides option button, click OK, then save the Word document as **PPT 8-Handout** to the location where you store your Data Files.

i. Submit your presentation and your handout to your instructor. Close the Word document, exit Word, close the presentation, then exit PowerPoint.

FIGURE 8-21

Visual Workshop

Create a presentation and save it as **PPT 8-Project Final**. Use an instructor-approved topic and the following task list to help you complete this Visual Workshop:

- Create and save a new presentation, then enter and format slide text.
- Create and format new slides, then create slide sections.
- Apply a design theme and variation or template, then modify the master by inserting a picture.
- Insert and format at least one picture, video, and audio.
- Insert, format, and merge shapes, then insert and format a SmartArt graphic.
- Insert, format, and animate a chart, then apply animations, transitions, and timings to objects and slides.
- Modify slide, handout and notes masters, then create a custom show.
- Insert action buttons or hyperlinks, then send to a class member for revision changes and comments.
- Merge the reviewed presentation with your original presentation; make necessary changes and keep comments.
- Deliver the presentation online to members of your class.

Add your name as a footer on the slide, save the presentation, then submit the presentation to your instructor. **FIGURE 8-22** shows an example of a presentation you can create.

FIGURE 8-22

Glossary

Action button An interactive button created from the Shapes gallery that you click in Slide Show view to perform an activity, such as advancing to the next slide or play a video or sound file.

Active cell The selected cell in a worksheet.

Adjustment handle A small yellow handle that changes the appearance of an object's most prominent feature.

Align To place objects' edges or centers on the same plane.

Animation tag Identifies the order an object is animated on a slide during a slide show.

Animated video A video that contains multiple images that stream together to give the illusion of motion.

Axis label Text on the horizontal or vertical axis that identifies data in a chart.

Background The area behind the text and graphics on a slide.

Background graphic An object placed on the slide master.

Bookmark A point in a video that can be used to jump to a specific point in the video; identified with a yellow circle in the video control timeline.

Bullet A small graphic symbol, usually a round or square dot, that is placed at the left of a new line; used to identify the beginning of a new item in a list.

Category axis The axis in a chart that contains the categories or labels defining the data series.

Category axis title A title entered on the category axis of a chart that contains the categories or labels defining the data series.

Cell The intersection of a column and row in a worksheet, or table.

Chart A graphical representation of numerical data from a worksheet. Chart types include 2-D and 3-D column, bar, pie, area, and line charts.

Cloud computing When data, applications, and resources are stored on servers accessed over the Internet or a private internal network rather than on a local computer.

Column heading The box containing the column letter on top of the columns in the worksheet.

Comments button A button on the PowerPoint status bar in Normal view allows you to open the Comments pane where you can create, edit, select, and delete comments.

Compatibility Checker Finds potential compatibility issues between a PowerPoint 2016 presentation and earlier versions of PowerPoint.

Connection site An anchor point to attach a line or an arrow on a shape.

Content placeholder A placeholder that is used to enter text or objects such as clip art, charts, or pictures.

Crop To hide part of an object by using the Cropping tool or to delete a part of a picture.

Custom show Feature used to adapt the order or slides used in a presentation for use in different circumstances or with different audiences.

Data series A column or row in a worksheet.

Data series label Text in the first row and column of a worksheet that identifies data in a chart.

Data series marker A graphical representation of a data series, such as a bar or column.

Destination file The file an object is embedded into, such as a presentation.

Destination presentation The presentation you insert slides to when you reuse slides from another presentation.

Digital signature A way to authenticate a presentation files using computer cryptography. A digital signature is not visible in a presentation.

Digital video Live action captured in digital format by a video camera.

Distribute To evenly divide the space horizontally or vertically between objects relative to each other or the slide edges.

Document Inspector A PowerPoint feature that examines a presentation for hidden data or personal information.

Embedded object An object that is created in one application and inserted to another; can be edited using the original program file in which they were created.

Error bars Used in a chart to identify potential error amounts relative to each data marker in a data series.

Fixed layout format A specific file format, such as .pdf or .xps, that locks the file so no changes can be made but allows viewing and printing of the file.

Gallery A visual collection of choices you can browse through to make a selection. Often available with Live Preview.

Gridlines Evenly spaced horizontal and vertical lines on the slide that help you align objects.

Group A PowerPoint feature in which you combine multiple objects into one object.

Groups Areas of the Ribbon that arrange commands based on their function, for example, text formatting commands such as Bold, Underline, and Italic are located on the Home tab, in the Font group.

Handout Master view The master view used to specify the header and footer placeholders, the page orientation, and specify the number of slides to print for printed handouts.

Hanging indent The first line of a paragraph begins to the left of all subsequent lines of text.

Hyperlink An specially formatted object (a filename, word, phrase, or graphic) that, when clicked, "jumps to" another location specified in the current file or opens another PowerPoint presentation, a Word, Excel, or Access file, or an address on the web. *Also called* link.

Indent levels Text levels in the master text placeholder. Each level is indented a specified amount from the left margin; control their placement by dragging indent markers on the ruler.

Indent markers Small markers (two triangles and one square) on the horizontal ruler that indicate the indent settings for the selected text.

Ink annotations A freehand drawing on the screen in Slide Show view made by using the pen or highlighter tool.

Inking Freehand pen and highlighter marks you can draw on a slide in Normal view to emphasize information.

Insertion point A blinking vertical line that indicates where the next character will appear when text is entered in a text placeholder in PowerPoint.

Kiosk A freestanding booth usually placed in a public area that can contain a display device used to show information.

Landscape A slide orientation that displays slides horizontally (wider than taller).

Laser pointer A virtual pointer that moves as you move the mouse used in Slide Show view to highlight parts of the slide.

Leading The spacing between lines of text in a text object within the same paragraph.

Legend Text box feature in a chart that provides an explanation about the data presented in a chart.

Link A connection between a source file and a destination file, which when the source file is updated, the destination file can also be updated. Also formatted text that has a URL which is used to jump to a webpage on the Internet. *See also* Hyperlink.

Live Preview A feature that shows you the result of an action such as a theme change before you apply the change.

Macro A set actions that are used to automate tasks.

Major gridlines Identify major units on a chart axis.

Margins The distance between the edge of the text and all four edges of the text box, text object, or slide.

Master Thumbnails pane On the left side of Slide Master view, used to navigate through the master slide layouts.

Master view A specific view in a presentation that stores information about font styles, text placeholders, and color themes. There are three master views: Slide Master view, Handout Master view, and Notes Master view.

Masters One of three views (Slide Master view, Handout Master view, and Notes Master view) that stores information about the presentation theme, fonts, placeholders, and other background objects.

Merge A feature in PowerPoint used to combine multiple shapes together; provides you a way to create a variety of unique geometric shapes that are not available in the Shapes gallery.

Metadata Another name for document properties that includes the author name, the document subject, the document title, and other personal information.

Mini toolbar A small toolbar that appears next to selected text that contains basic text-formatting commands.

Minor gridlines Identify minor units on a chart axis.

Narration A voice recording you make using a microphone on one or more slides. Narrations can be heard through speakers or a headset during a slide show.

Normal view The primary view that you use to write, edit, and design a presentation. Normal view is divided into three areas: Slides tab, Slide pane, and Notes pane.

Notes button A button on the status bar in PowerPoint that opens the Notes pane.

Notes Master view The master view for Notes Pages view.

Notes Page view A presentation view that displays a reduced image of the current slide above a large text box where you can type notes.

Notes pane The area in Normal view that shows speaker notes for the current slide; also in Notes Page view, the area below the slide image that contains speaker notes.

Object An item you place or draw on a slide that can be modified. Examples of objects include drawn lines and shapes, text, and imported pictures.

Office Add-ins Applications available for download to PowerPoint from the Microsoft Office Store on the Internet. Add-ins can be used for mapping, word usage, and other productivity applications.

Office Mix A free add-in application integrated to the PowerPoint Ribbon that allows you to create interactive content.

Office Online Apps Versions of the Microsoft Office applications with limited functionality that are available online from Microsoft OneDrive. Users can view documents online and then edit them in the browser using a selection of functions.

OneDrive An online storage and file sharing service. Access to OneDrive is through a Windows Live account.

Online collaboration The ability to incorporate feedback or share information across the Internet or a company network.

Outline view A view in PowerPoint where you can enter text on slides in outline form. Includes three areas. The Outline pane where you enter text, the Slide pane for the main slide, and the Notes pane where you enter notes.

Pane A section of the PowerPoint window, such as the Slide or Notes pane.

Paragraph spacing The space before and after paragraph text.

Paste Special A method that is used to paste text or objects using special formats, such as plain text without formatting or an object as a picture.

Photo album A type of presentation designed specifically to display photographs.

Picture A digital photograph, piece of line art, or other graphic that is created in another program and is inserted into PowerPoint.

Portrait A slide orientation that displays slides vertically (taller than wider).

Poster frame The image that appears on an inserted digital video, also known as the preview image.

PowerPoint window A window that contains the running PowerPoint application including the Ribbon, panes, and tabs.

Presentation software A software program used to organize and present information typically as part of an electronic slide show.

Presenter view A PowerPoint view you access while in Slide Show view. Typically you use this view when showing a presentation through two monitors, one that you see as the presenter and one that the audience sees.

Preview image *See* Poster frame.

Previewing Prior to printing, seeing onscreen exactly how the printed document will look.

Quick Access toolbar A small toolbar on the left side of a Microsoft application program window's title bar, containing buttons that you click to quickly perform common actions, such as saving a file.

Quick Style Determines how fonts, colors, and effects of the theme are combined and which color, font, and effect is dominant. A Quick Style can be applied to shapes or text.

Reading view A view you use to review a presentation or present a slide show to someone on a computer monitor.

Read-only A file that can't be edited or modified.

Removal marquee box The box that surrounds the part of a picture that you want to retain when the background or other areas of the picture are being deleted.

Removal marquee sizing handle The sizing handles around a removal marquee box that are dragged to change how much of the background or sections of a picture are to be deleted.

Ribbon A wide band of buttons spanning the top of the PowerPoint window that organizes all of PowerPoint's primary commands.

Rotate handle A small round arrow at the top of a selected object that you can drag to turn the selected object.

Row heading The box containing the row number to the left of the row in a worksheet.

Screen capture An electronic snapshot or picture of your screen, placed in the clipboard which you can then paste into a document.

Screenshot A static picture you take of an open program window; can be inserted on a slide.

Selection box A dashed border that appears around a text object or placeholder, indicating that it is ready to accept text.

Sizing handles The small squares that appear around a selected object. Dragging a sizing handle resizes the object.

Slide layout This determines how all of the elements on a slide are arranged, including text and content placeholders.

Slide Library A folder that you and others can access to open, modify, and review presentation slides.

Slide pane The main section of Normal view that displays the current slide.

Slide Show view A view that shows a presentation as an electronic slide show; each slide fills the screen.

Slide Sorter view A view that displays a thumbnail of all slides in the order in which they appear in a presentation; used to rearrange slides and slide transitions.

Slide thumbnail *See* Thumbnail.

Slide timing The amount of time each slide is visible on the screen during a slide show.

Slide transition The special effect that moves one slide off the screen and the next slide on the screen during a slide show. Each slide can have its own transition effect.

Slides tab On the left side of the Normal view, displays the slides in the presentation as thumbnails.

Smart Guides A feature in PowerPoint used to help position objects relative to each other and determine equal distances between objects.

SmartArt A professional quality graphic diagram that visually illustrates text.

SmartArt Style A pre-set combination of formatting options that follows the design theme that you can apply to a SmartArt graphic.

Source file Where an object you create with the source program is saved on a storage device.

Source presentation The presentation you insert slides from when you reuse slides from another presentation.

Source program The program in which a file was created.

Status bar The bar at the bottom of the PowerPoint window that contains messages about what you are doing and seeing in PowerPoint, such as the current slide number or the current theme.

Subtitle text placeholder A box on the title slide reserved for subpoint text.

Tab A section of the Ribbon that identifies groups of commands like the Home tab.

Tab selector Tab icon on the horizontal ruler that, when clicked, cycles through four tab alignment options.

Template A type of presentation that contains custom design information such as a set of theme colors, fonts, background styles, and effects on the slide master. Can also include custom slide layouts, sample text, and graphics.

Text placeholder A box with a dotted border and text that you replace with your own text.

Theme A set of colors, fonts, and effects that you apply to a presentation from the Themes Gallery.

Theme colors The set of 12 coordinated colors that make up a PowerPoint presentation; a theme assigns colors for text, lines, fills, accents, hyperlinks, and background.

Theme effects The set of effects for lines and fills.

Theme fonts The set of fonts for titles and other text.

Thumbnail A small image of a slide on the Slides tab and in Slide Sorter view.

Tick mark A small line of measurement that intersects an axis and identifies the categories, values, or series of a chart.

Title placeholder A box on a slide reserved for the title of a presentation or slide.

Title slide The first slide in a presentation.

Trendline A graphical representation of an upward or downward movement in a data series, used to predict future tendencies.

URL Abbreviation for uniform resource locator, which is an address of a webpage on the Internet.

Value axis The axis in a chart that contains the values or numbers defining the data series.

Value axis title A title entered on the value axis of a chart that contains values or numbers defining the data series.

Variant A custom variation of the applied theme that uses different colors, fonts, and effects.

Video frame A single photographic image, or picture, in a video.

View A way of displaying a presentation, such as Normal view, Reading view, Notes Page view, Outline view, Slide Sorter view, and Slide Show view.

View Shortcuts The buttons at the bottom of the PowerPoint window on the status bar that you click to switch among views.

WordArt A set of decorative styles or text effects that is applied to text.

Worksheet The grid of rows and columns that stores the numerical data for a chart.

Zoom slider A feature on the status bar that allows you to change the size of the slide visible in the Slide pane.

Index